Once upon a Time at the Opera House

Once upon a Time at the Opera House

DRAMA AT THREE HISTORIC MICHIGAN THEATERS, 1882–1928

James Berton Harris

Michigan State University Press | East Lansing

⊜ The paper used in this publication meets the minimum requirements
of ANSI/NISO Z39.48-1992 (R 1997) (Permanence of Paper).

Michigan State University Press
East Lansing, Michigan 48823-5245

Printed and bound in the United States of America.

28 27 26 25 24 23 22 21 20 19 1 2 3 4 5 6 7 8 9 10

LIBRARY OF CONGRESS CATALOGING-IN-PUBLICATION DATA
Names: Harris, James Berton author.
Title: Once upon a time at the opera house : drama at three historic Michigan theaters, 1882–1928 / James Berton Harris.
Description: East Lansing : Michigan State University Press, 2018. | Includes bibliographical references and index.
Identifiers: LCCN 2017061027 | ISBN 9781611863017 (cloth : alk. paper)
Subjects: LCSH: Theaters—Michigan—History—19th century. | Theaters—Michigan—History—20th century. | Historic buildings—Michigan.
Classification: LCC PN2275.M43 H38 2018 | DDC 792.09774—dc23
LC record available at https://lccn.loc.gov/2017061027

Book design by Charlie Sharp, Sharp DesIgns, East Lansing, MI
Cover design by Erin Kirk New
Cover photograph of the Interior of the Calumet Theatre (2017) by Laura Miller, used courtesy of the Calumet Theatre.

green press INITIATIVE Michigan State University Press is a member of the Green Press Initiative and is committed to developing and encouraging ecologically responsible publishing practices. For more information about the Green Press Initiative and the use of recycled paper in book publishing, please visit *www.greenpressinitiative.org.*

Visit Michigan State University Press at *www.msupress.org*

They "lit the lamp and led the way."

Sir Arthur Conan Doyle, *The Adventure of the Speckled Band*, 1892

Kristine Antcliff

Audrey Frair

Nancy Lyon

Joan Woodward

Contents

PROGRAM NOTES ix

OVERTURE: An Introduction xiii

PROLOGUE: An Overview xvii

ACT I: TIBBITS OPERA HOUSE, Coldwater (1882)

Scene i: Building Going Up! 3

Scene ii: Curtain Going Up! 25

ACT II: CALUMET THEATRE, Red Jacket (1900)

Scene i: Building Going Up! 55

Scene ii: Curtain Going Up! 81

ACT III: RAMSDELL THEATRE, Manistee (1903)

Scene i: Building Going Up! 99

Scene ii: Curtain Going Up! 119

EXTRA-ADDED ATTRACTIONS!

Minstrel Shows, Vaudeville, and Moving Pictures 139

EPILOGUE: The Denouement 151

APPENDIX I: Now Playing!

Particularly Popular Plays 155

Ethnic Plays and Personalities 169

New Plays for a New Century 177

The Musicals 189

APPENDIX II: Now Appearing at a Theater Near You!

Stars of the Stage 211

CURTAIN CALL: Acknowledgments 231

FINAL CREDITS: Books and Sources 233

INDEX 237

Program Notes

"What's Goin' On Here?"

Paint Your Wagon, lyrics by Alan Jay Lerner, music by Frederick Loewe, 1951

According to the Grammarist.com website, "there is no difference in meaning between *theater* and *theatre*. . . . *Theater* is the preferred spelling in American English, and *theatre* is preferred virtually everywhere else." Continuing on it states that some Americans do make a distinction between the two, that theater is a venue while theatre is an art form. Apparently these distinctions are preferences, not rules, and they are not employed consistently in real-world usage.

As an American writer who does make a distinction, I have used "theater" when identifying a real structure and "theatre" when referring to the art form. Although I have tried to be consistent throughout this work, history and the people who name buildings have not always shared my preference. Over the years, many theaters have been named "theatres" (the Calumet Theatre, the Ramsdell Theatre), and even that was not always consistent. In a 1916 issue of the Calumet newspaper, there were two separate advertisements announcing two different coming attractions at the playhouse. At the top of one ad was printed "Calumet Theatre," and on the same page in close proximity to it was the second ad at the top of which was printed "Calumet Theater." No wonder folks are confused.

To further complicate matters, because of the lack of rules, often the two spelling options have been and are still used interchangeably. Consequently, when presenting a direct quote from a newspaper article or other source, that writer's choice may be in conflict with what I am doing here. This is the point: the seemingly inconsistent spelling and usage of theater/theatre in this work is not due to author oversight; it is due to a history of grammatical anarchy.

The subheadings sprinkled throughout many of the chapters in this text are signposts to indicate that the author has changed the subject or is off on a tangent. They consist of an eclectic mix of song titles, lines of dialogue from plays, quotes, expressions, idioms, and some phrases that, like Athena, sprang fully developed from the head of the author. An asterisk next to a play's title or actor's name indicates that there is a synopsis and production history of that play or biography of the actor that may be referenced in one of the two appendixes to the text.

Never Let the Truth Stand in the Way of a Good Story

erroneously attributed to Mark Twain

If you're looking for footnotes or endnotes, you won't find them here. This is not a textbook, reference book, or dissertation. It is a storybook. The stories in *Once upon a Time at the Opera House* are based on historical facts, anecdotes, urban legends, and tall tales associated with three of the over one hundred opera houses that existed in Michigan in the early 1900s. As there are similar stories about similar structures throughout Michigan as well as in other Midwestern and Western states, this could be considered a storybook about the Golden Age of Opera Houses in many of America's rural regions.

Once upon a Time at the Opera House

FIGURE 1. The Calumet Theatre, ca. 1900. (Photograph courtesy of the Calumet Theatre.)

OVERTURE

An Introduction

"I Could Write a Book"

Pal Joey, lyrics by Lorenz Hart, music by Richard Rodgers, 1940

Some time ago, I had occasion to stop by a local frame shop to pick up a completed order. The newly framed item was a poster celebrating the centennial of the Calumet Theatre in Michigan's Keweenaw Peninsula. The image on the poster was a sepia-toned reproduction of a photograph of the theater taken at about the time of its opening.

The manager of the frame shop removed the brown paper wrapping to reveal the large, oak-framed picture. He said, "I know from other items you've brought in to be framed that you have an interest in the theatre, but why this particular playhouse?"

"Well," I explained, "I have a strong interest in the Calumet Theatre for two reasons. First of all, I worked there during the three summers I was in graduate school, and, second, it's one of the theaters I am currently researching for what I hope will be a book about Michigan opera houses."

He looked incredulous. "Opera houses!" he said, "I don't mean to diminish your efforts, but won't that be a rather slim volume?"

I looked incredulous. I thought, "Why would he think that?" Then it hit me! This fellow probably suffers under the misconception that in 1900 America an opera house was a place where opera was actually produced and performed.

What an extraordinary notion!

To be fair, however, there is some basis for his misconception. There are those facilities in this country called opera houses that did and still do produce and present operas (the Metropolitan Opera House in New York City being an obvious example). On the other hand, to my knowledge, *La Traviata* has never been performed at the Grand Ole Opry House in Nashville, Tennessee, and probably won't be anytime soon.

If presenting the art form that the name implies was the sole prerequisite for being called an opera house, then the frame shop manager would be right—this would be a rather slim volume. But from 1787 until the early part of the twentieth century, the vast majority of theaters in this country that were referred to as "opera houses" seldom presented that particular form of musical entertainment.

The official name of the theater in Coldwater is, and for much of its existence has been, the Tibbits Opera House. However, operas were infrequently performed there; pantomime and minstrel shows, melodramas and vaudeville, plays by Shakespeare, political rallies, community meetings, lectures, commencement exercises, and then movies were the main attractions that filled the house with local citizens.

Non–operatic music performances often took place in Michigan's opera houses. There were concerts by vocalists, instrumentalists, bands, and orchestras as well as operettas, but "grand opera" was hardly ever presented.

"Put It in the Book"

The Roar of the Greasepaint–The Smell of the Crowd, lyrics and music by Leslie Bricusse and Anthony Newly, 1965

The catalog titled *Julius Cahn's Official Theatrical Guide*, published annually from 1896 to 1920, was accepted by booking agents and company managers as the definitive source of information necessary in order to take shows on tour. The *Guide* listed playhouses that were appropriate venues for touring productions in every state. It provided detailed information about the facility: the seating capacity, the depth and width of the stage, and the height of the rigging loft.

According to the 1904–5 edition of the *Official Theatrical Guide* there were 107 theaters or opera houses in ninety-six Michigan towns; larger cities such as Detroit and Grand Rapids had more than one facility. However, not every opera house that existed in Michigan at that time made it into the publication. There were opera houses in Albion, Howell, and Vermontville, among other towns, that, for whatever reasons, were not included in the *Guide*. Therefore, 107 operating opera houses in Michigan at the beginning of the twentieth century is a somewhat conservative estimate.

Of those 107 facilities listed, seventy-two used "opera house" as part of their official name whereas only twenty-one were named "theatres." Fourteen used some other designation such as "music hall" or "academy of music."

"Money Makes the World Go 'Round"

Two Lots in the Bronx, lyrics by Edward Paulton and Adolf Philipp, music by Adolf Philipp, 1913

Although there are many similarities shared by Michigan's historic opera houses, originally they were financed in several different ways: the Adrian Union Hall (aka the Croswell Opera House) was paid for by local businessmen who bought shares of stock in the venture; the Calumet Theatre and Cheboygan Opera House were two of the first municipally financed theaters in the country; the Tibbits Opera House and the Ramsdell Theatre were each underwritten primarily by a single benefactor. Today, they are all funded from various sources including, but not limited to, grants, donations, individual and corporate memberships, ticket sales, special fund-raising events, and rental of the facility.

Here Today, Gone Tomorrow

Unfortunately, many of Michigan's wonderful old jewel boxes have been razed or burned down. Some, still standing, have been neglected for years. While almost every town in the state once had a facility referred to as an opera house, there are no longer 107 of them. How many are still standing, and of those, how many are still in operation? That's a good question. Several sources exist that catalog Michigan's historic opera houses and theaters; since each source has its own criteria, no two lists are the same. The League of Historic American Theatres' inventory, posted in 2015, presents a comprehensive slate of over sixty facilities that includes conventional theaters along with others that are less traditional: the Detroit Institute of Arts Auditorium; the Red Barn Playhouse in Saugatuck, which was literally a red barn that was converted into a performance space; and the Grand Ledge Opera House that opened as a roller skating rink.

In 2014 on Kevin Pistick's website *Michigan's Historic Theatres and Opera Houses* the tally was thirty-one facilities. All of the structures in this lineup were at one time used as a theater; the criterion for their inclusion is that the building must still be standing regardless of its original or subsequent use. Gene Chesley's *National List of Historic Theatre Buildings* from 1979 lists twenty-four opera houses. In 2017 the Water Winter Wonderland website listed fifty-one Michigan opera houses, and of those, it indicated that six have been demolished, thirty-seven are closed, and eight are currently open for business.

The stories in this book are about three still-operating facilities: the Tibbits Opera House in Coldwater, the Ramsdell Theatre in Manistee, and the Calumet Theatre. They cover a forty-six-year period from 1882, when the Tibbits Opera House opened, through 1928, after which time no professional touring productions played the Calumet Theatre for over a decade—movies and local events only.

Although there are other historically interesting opera houses in the state, these three were selected for scrutiny because of a certain similitude between their geneses, histories, and the towns in which they are located. The selection was based on the following criteria: they are all stand-alone structures with impressive street-level entrances located in towns with a population of twelve thousand or less; they have retained or restored their original architecture and decor; they have particularly similar production histories; and at the time of their opening, their mission and stated intent was to be a venue for live professional theatre productions, and all three are still venues for live entertainment today. An added attraction is that each of these three playhouses is a representative from a different region of the state: southern Michigan, northern Michigan, and the Upper Peninsula.

FIGURE 2. "Calumet Opera House and City Hall." Architectural Drawing, 1899. (Photograph courtesy of the National Park Service, Keweenaw National Historic Park, Keweenaw Historic Publications Collection, "Our Boys in the Spanish American War.")

PROLOGUE

An Overview

> I love the opera houses. . . . They're a special part of Americana that I'm happy to, in my small way, kind of support. —Michigan resident and actor, Jeff Daniels discussing the venues in which he performs when on tour as a musician, singer-songwriter, *Ann Arbor News*, August 17, 2014

From the late eighteenth century through the first decades of the twentieth century the term "opera house" was liberally employed both as a common and as a proper noun. As a common noun it identified a traditional theater space as well as an assembly hall that was suitable for theatrical performances. As a proper noun it was incorporated into the official names of theaters. However, by the early twentieth century, when it came to naming theaters, the use of the term "opera house" went out of style. This probably had more to do with the fact that it sounded old-fashioned rather than any concern that the term was misleading. At that time, the use of the term "opera house" was still prevalent in documents and newspapers and was used to identify many facilities that were officially named "theatres." For example, the minutes of the Red Jacket (now Calumet) Common Council meetings from 1898 recorded that body's deliberation concerning the construction of a new "opera house." Even the architect's original drawing for the building was labeled "opera house." However, it opened in 1900 as the Calumet Theatre.

Over three-quarters of a century later, when the theater manager submitted information to the National List of Historic Theatre Buildings, he responded to the question regarding the name of the facility with, "Calumet Theatre, commonly called The Opera House."

The architect's blueprints for the playhouse in Manistee were labeled "Opera House for T. J. Ramsdell, Esq., April 1902." But when the building opened in 1903, the newspapers, posters, and programs announced the attractions that were coming to or playing at the Ramsdell Theatre. However, as late as 1927, *Polk's Michigan State Gazetteer and Business Directory* listed sixty-eight facilities in towns across the state that used "opera house" as part of their official name.

Opera house, playhouse, theater—what's the difference between them? Back in the day, the three terms were used interchangeably. Today, for many people "opera house" has a more precise connotation. But this book is about back in the day when "opera house" was just another name for a theater.

There are at least two reasons and one historic precedent for referring to a theater as an opera house. F. Clever Bald explains the two reasons for the use of the euphemism in his history, *Michigan in Four Centuries*: "It was adopted because it sounded cultural and because the term theater was distasteful to many persons."

"Life upon the Wicked Stage"

Show Boat, lyrics by Oscar Hammerstein II, music by Jerome Kern, 1927

Because of the strong Puritanical influence that pervaded social and political points of view at the time this country was founded, many upstanding, churchgoing Americans were under the impression that theatre, more than "distasteful," was actually sinful and a corrupting element in society. A resolution from the Continental Congress in 1774 encouraged the states to pass laws "to prevent theatrical entertainment, horse racing, and other diversions as are productive of idleness."

In addition to encouraging idleness, theatre represented, for many people, immorality, depravity, and a decadent lifestyle. Those who engaged in theatrical endeavors as a means of livelihood were assumed to be rascals, thieves, and prostitutes. Those who purchased tickets to attend the theatre not only supported it financially but also, by extension, condoned that lifestyle.

Some attitudes die hard; the bias against the theatre did not end with the eighteenth century. In 1913 the *Coldwater Daily Reporter* printed a series of letters to the editor, a four-part diatribe denouncing theatre, submitted by a local Methodist Episcopal minister, the Reverend R. E. Meader. In his first letter he claimed,

> The theatre is the devil's trap. It is baited with things people like very much but it crushes the spiritual life out of those who bite. . . . Cheese is good for a rat if it is not on the trigger that releases a death-dealing spring.

In his second letter, Meader reported the results of a script study of sixty plays that had been produced in New York City between 1910 and 1913: fifty of them were deemed to be objectionable. About Shakespeare's plays, he stated that "they should not be read, much less seen and heard, without first being expurgated."

He expressed his particular concern about the spiritual well-being of women and young men who attended the theatre. He believed that all females were as impressionable as postadolescent males and that both groups were especially vulnerable to theatre's immoral trap. To support his thesis, he quoted British theatre critic Clement Scott, who shared his belief: "In every class of life women are exposed to dangers and temptations but far more in the theatres than elsewhere." As far as young men were concerned, in the Reverend Meader's opinion, the stage presented lascivious behavior as being "most alluring." Young men, he contends, are easily seduced by this portrayal.

With an official statement from the Methodist Episcopal Church that was similar in content and language to the Continental Congress resolution issued 139 years earlier, Meader concluded his four-letter paper storm with a warning against "harmful amusements—particularly against theatre-going, dancing, and such games of chance as are frequently associated with gambling."

"[We've Got] Elegance"

Hello Dolly!, lyrics and music by Jerry Herman, 1964

Historically, musical performances seldom suffered from the same negative bias as theatre. In Europe, by the eighteenth century, opera, performed at court and in opera houses, was a socially acceptable form of entertainment. It was often supported and, on occasion, commissioned by members of royalty—in other words, endorsed by people of culture and influence.

In the late nineteenth and early twentieth century, many Americans considered Europe to be the seat of culture and worthy of emulation. Most of the growing Midwestern communities that had started as lumber or mining camps, shipping ports, or agricultural centers were rapidly becoming legitimate towns. The time had come to proclaim that these towns had evolved from their rugged, "rough and ready" origins to the point that they were civilized and eager to embrace culture. How better to announce this fact than to open an opera house?

Perhaps a Red Jacket Common Council member best summed up this concept when the village officials were considering the advisability of erecting an opera house in what was then a thriving mining community. Allegedly, the councilman stood up at the meeting and declared, "What Red Jacket needs is an opera house. This isn't a Klondike boom town!"

The quest for cultural recognition brought about the Golden Age of American Opera Houses, 1865–1915. It was during this fifty-year period that hundreds of opera houses were constructed across the country. The opera-house-building boom began after the Civil War and continued until opulent movie palaces began to replace opulent opera houses as the style of theater most frequently constructed in the United States.

"What's in a Name?"

Romeo and Juliet by William Shakespeare, ca. 1597

A negative bias toward theatre and an attempt to create a cultural environment in the community are the two prevailing theories most often given to explain the use of the opera house euphemism. There is a significant precedent for this tradition as well. In 1778 Congress passed another, more adamant, resolution once again discouraging theatrical performances throughout the country. Although Congress was not empowered to compel the states to adopt its recommendation, it could dictate to individuals employed by the federal government. The resolution included the decree that

> any person holding office under the United States who shall act, promote, encourage or attend such plays shall be deemed unworthy to hold such office and shall be accordingly dismissed.

In those states that did not comply with the resolution, theatre touring companies found more or less hospitable venues in which to ply their trade. Foremost among these traveling troupes was the American Company, which later became the Old American Company, originally headed by actor-manager Lewis Hallam and then by his son, Lewis Hallam the Younger (1740–1808). One of the first professional theatre troupes to perform in North America, the American Company played, where they could, up and down the eastern seaboard from New York to Charleston, South Carolina.

Pennsylvania was one of the states that followed Congress's recommendation and passed a law prohibiting all theatre performances. The younger Hallam made the decision to breach that state's antitheatre law. First, in 1784 he petitioned to have the law repealed, but his petition was denied. Undaunted, in January 1787 he decided to test the waters with what turned out to be a successful two-week run of presentations that he advertised as operas, concerts, and lectures at Philadelphia's Southwark Theatre. That theater, the first permanent playhouse in America, had opened in 1766, but it had been closed due to the prohibition.

Encouraged by their successful first foray into hostile territory, Hallam brought his company back to Philadelphia in June and again took up residence in the Southwark Theatre. The irony is that at the same time drama as theatre was banned in Philadelphia, there was drama in another form being played out in the "City of Brotherly Love"—it was called politics. From May 14 to September 17, 1787, Philadelphia played host to the federal convention that was attended by representatives from every state in the country who, during those four months, hammered out the U.S. Constitution.

The prospect of capturing the attention of a potentially appreciative audience consisting of some of the best educated and most cultured men in the nation may be exactly why Hallam chose that moment to assault the city and the law. Whatever his motives, Lewis Hallam was no fool. He knew not to buck the Philadelphia authorities and, consequently, renamed the Southwark Theatre the Opera House in Southwark.

From the original playbills referenced by George O. Seilhamer in *History of the American Theatre during the Revolution and After*, Hallam advertised works that were comic plays with songs as "operas" and "concerts." In some cases, "concerts" appear to have been what the name suggests: a series of musical presentations both instrumental and vocal. He also advertised "poetical addresses," "moral poems," and "illustrated lectures" that were often scenes from a play. However, the word "play" never appeared on a handbill.

While in Philadelphia, the American Company presented Richard Brinsley Sheridan's five-act comedy *The School for Scandal*, first performed in London ten years earlier. The advertisement for this event read:

> At the Opera House in Southwark, This evening, the 30th of July, will be Performed A CONCERT; Between the Parts of the Concert will be introduced a COMIC LECTURE in five parts on the PERNICIOUS VICE OF SCANDAL.

If the definition of a concert can be expanded to include "a series of musical interludes performed intermittently throughout a scripted entertainment," then Hallam could be credited for employing a degree of truth in advertising as a concert of sorts was being presented between the five acts of Sheridan's comedy.

An Olio Is Not Oleo, a Butter Substitute

During this period, it was not uncommon for musical interludes, or olios, to be performed between the acts of a nonmusical play. Often members of the company would come to the stage and sing a song, do a dance, or play the fiddle or other musical instrument. The term "olio" derives from *olla podrida*, a term for a "hodgepodge" or a mixture of random items and also the name of a highly spiced Spanish stew of assorted ingredients. The purpose of the olios was to cover scene changes, to provide an opportunity for company members to display their special talents, and to introduce new songs and dances from Europe to folks throughout the country. These mini performances were one of the precursors of vaudeville—a series of short, unrelated, often musical presentations.

The olios became so popular that not only were they advertised along with the title of the production, but they often received top billing. A handbill for the February 14, 1878, performance at the Opera House in Adrian exclaimed, at the top of the bill and in large, bold print, that the offering would include a "Grand Spectacular and Original 'Pantomimic Olio'" and below that was the name of the Valentine's Day play, *Stupid and Cupid*.

Eventually, the term "olio" was replaced with the less esoteric and more descriptive word "specialties." These disparate, brief interludes continued to be a draw into the early part of the twentieth century. In September 1903 a journalist writing for the *Manistee Daily News* stated, "Lovers of melodrama regret that there are so few musical numbers and specialties introduced in the plays." The article went on to report that the upcoming production was an exception as the managers "have secured artists who have some very clever specialties. They are interspersed through the acts with good effect and give an added zest to the production." In a review of *The Man from Sweden* that was the 1903 Christmas attraction at Manistee's Ramsdell Theatre, the reviewer remarked, "The specialties were all good, particularly that of the Falkner family in hoop rolling."

Back to Lewis Hallam, the Younger vs. the City of Philadelphia

Albeit by subterfuge, Hallam was successful in achieving his goals. By calling it an opera house, he managed to keep the Southwark Theatre open during the prohibition in spite of the fact that he was presenting material that the city authorities deemed taboo.

In addition, he was successful in garnering the attention of at least one prominent gentleman. From the diary George Washington kept while in Philadelphia presiding over the Constitutional Convention, it is known that he attended three performances at the Opera House in Southwark. Thanks to young Lewis Hallam and the American Company, playhouses that seldom, if ever, produced opera came to be called opera houses.

Do You "Stand-Alone" or Are You "Upper-Floor"?

Chesley's *National List of Historic Theatre Buildings*, published in 1979, categorized still-standing Michigan playhouses using the following criteria:

A. A theatre or opera house built originally as a single use performance space, having a proscenium, and with the stage area equipped for theatrical performance. Often includes balconies, dressing rooms, scenery and equipment.

B. A theatre or opera house within a multiple use structure. Often an "upstairs house." Sometimes related to lodge use or as a performance space within a town hall or commercial building.

Of the 107 facilities listed in the 1904–5 edition of *Julius Cahn's Official Theatrical Guide*, fifty-nine were "stand-alone" opera houses designed as traditional theater spaces with a fully equipped stage house and a street-level entrance. The stand-alone opera house building was occupied by the theater only and did not house any other commercial or municipal enterprise.

The other forty-eight spaces were "upper-floor" opera houses that could range from a bare-bones assembly hall with a minimally equipped stage at one end and a flat floor with moveable seating to a more elaborate space with an auditorium two stories high, a balcony, and a fully equipped stage. As the name implies, the upper-floor opera houses were located on the second and/or third floors of a building the first floor of which was used for other, non-theater-related purposes. Opera houses of both configurations were venues for town meetings, lectures, and concerts as well as for professional touring theatre productions. Because of their flat floor and flexible seating, the upper-floor variety provided a suitable space for receptions, dances, and even boxing and wrestling matches.

"Let Us Take the Road"

The Beggar's Opera, lyrics and music by John Gay, 1728

By the early twentieth century, most of Michigan's playhouses were open for business and offered a combination of professional bookings and community events. Coldwater's location halfway between Detroit and Chicago on southern Michigan's major east–west route made it a convenient stop for thespians on the road. On the other hand, cities such as Manistee and, especially, what is now Calumet were not situated on a beaten path. In time, improved train service with more railroad routes made touring large productions to out-of-the-way places possible. In December 1899, first-class, overnight train service from Chicago through Milwaukee to Keweenaw's Copper Country was established, allowing theatre troupes to more easily access Michigan's remote Upper Peninsula.

On April 10, 1900, Houghton's *Daily Mining Gazette* reported that 1899–1900 had been the most financially successful theatre season in this country's history. Receipts from New York City accounted for approximately one fourth of the total while the remaining three-quarters came from cities outside the glow of the Great White Way. The figure was based on the estimated income of approximately one thousand touring companies performing seven times a week during the forty-week theatre season.

The practice of sending out a number of companies simultaneously presenting the same play in different parts of the country became enormously popular when Steele MacKaye (1842–94), actor/playwright/producer/inventor, revolutionized the touring business by exporting from New York City multiple road companies of his play **Hazel Kirke.* Written and produced by MacKaye, *Hazel Kirke* opened in 1880 at the Madison Square Theatre that he had purchased and renovated for the play's premiere.

In the two years after its successful New York run, MacKaye had fourteen *Hazel Kirke* companies on tour. Other producers were quick to follow MacKaye's lead. They realized that multiple productions of a popular attraction on the road garnered greater profits. If a show was successful in New York, several productions of that show were created and sent to different regions of the country.

"Stock Report"

Put It in Writing, lyrics by Fred Ebb, music by Norman L. Martin, 1963

In addition to those companies that toured with a single production that played at a given theater for only one or two nights, there were also touring stock companies. They traveled throughout the country taking up residence at an opera house for a week or more with a group of actors and a well-rehearsed collection of plays. Both single production and stock companies carried their own costumes and, in many cases, also had their own scenery, properties, and orchestra musicians. Some troupes relied on the host theater's stock scenery and local musicians to service their productions.

The typical schedule for a stock company was to arrive at an opera house and settle in for a predetermined length of time, often five days. During that period a different play was presented each evening with a matinee on Saturday—six plays in five days.

The plays presented were usually a combination of classics, proven hits, and contemporary melodramas and comedies. For example, in 1885, when Waite's Union Square Comedy Company was in Adrian, they performed six plays that included two proven hits, **Rip Van Winkle* and **Ten Nights in a Bar Room*; two contemporary melodramas, *The Shadow of Life* and *The Hidden Hand*; and two that have been long forgotten.

By the early twentieth century, touring stock companies had become a staple in opera house programming. It was not uncommon for as many as six companies, each scheduled for a week, to perform at one opera house in one season.

Many stock companies promoted special offers to entice

FIGURE 3. A jack-of-all-trades when it came to the theatre, Steele MacKaye invented folding theater seats and held the patent on numerous other theatrical inventions. In 1885, he provided a home for America's first drama school at his new Lyceum Theater in New York City. He is pictured here during his days as an actor at which time he played Hamlet in London. (Photographer unknown, ca. mid-nineteenth century. The Miriam and Ira D. Wallach Division of Art, Prints, and Photographs: Photography Collection, the New York Public Library Digital Collections.)

FIGURE 4. Sarah Bernhardt (*front*) standing with her party before her first appearance in a five-thousand-seat canvas circus tent set up outside of Dallas, Texas. With her tent in tow, she continued on to perform in Waco, Texas, and Kansas City, Missouri. (Photographer unknown, 1906. Retrieved from the Library of Congress.)

prospective audience members into the theater. They often advertised a "Ladies' Night" when women were admitted free of charge as long as they were accompanied by a paid ticket holder. One company advertised that at their production of *Lady Audley's Secret* there would be gifts of a silver cake basket and tea set, as well as a drawing for a gold watch. Another stock troupe presented a gift to the "prettiest lady" one evening, to the "handsomest man" the next, and to every child at the Saturday matinee.

"Since My Linda's in the Syn-de-cate"

Hodge, Podge & Co., lyrics by Walter Ford, music by John W. Bratton, 1900

In 1896 a small group of managing producers led by New York booking agents Marcus Klaw and Abraham Lincoln Erlanger created the Theatrical Trust (aka the Syndicate). For nearly twenty years the Syndicate controlled the majority of playhouses from New York to California. Klaw and Erlanger determined where each attraction would perform and on which dates. Their clients, the producing managers of touring productions, were required to do business with them exclusively.

In opposition to the Syndicate was the Shubert Organization led by the brothers Lee and J. J. Shubert, who were producers and theater owners. They advocated a more flexible policy regarding the booking of theatrical attractions. It was under the auspices of the Shubert Organization that *Sarah Bernhardt crossed the country in 1906 on one of her many "Farewell, America" tours. The Syndicate controlled all of the legitimate theaters in many cities throughout the states; shows sent out by producers not affiliated with that organization were denied access to Syndicate theaters. Consequently, when Bernhardt and her company reached Texas they pitched a tent.

— **HEADLINE** —

Circus Tent with Which Sarah Bernhardt Is Outwitting Theatrical Trust

On March 27, 1906, the *Chicago Daily Tribune* published the news that the French actress, on tour with a show managed by the Shubert Brothers, was barred by the Syndicate from appearing in any of their legitimate houses. Therefore, the "Divine Sarah" Bernhardt appeared as Camille under a circus tent set up in Dallas, Texas's Cycle Park. "An audience of 5,000 overwhelmed ushers and police in a scramble for seats."

As the Syndicate represented many of the most desirable attractions, opera house managers were eager to do whatever was necessary to ensure that Klaw and Erlanger would send the big sellers to their theaters.

> We are to have the first . . . syndicate attraction ever brought to Coldwater. If the engagement here proves a financial success we are promised "Babes in Toyland" and "The Wizard of Oz." (*Coldwater Daily Reporter*, February 6, 1905)

Managers of venues not on the East Coast began to organize in an effort to break the grip that the New York City–based Syndicate had on the touring business. In 1910, when the National Theater Owners' Association was created, the organization issued the following press release:

> Theater owners have been overwhelmed with questions as to why they could not have certain stars and plays that had become favorites in the theatrical centers. For days, and even weeks, at a time their houses have been kept dark simply because Klaw and Erlanger . . . refused to book the attractions of certain producers who demonstrated their right to freedom and independence.

By 1910 the Syndicate had begun to lose its reign over the touring business, and three years later, on May 26, 1913, the Syndicate and the Shuberts resolved their conflict, and theaters across the country could present productions from both organizations.

"Machine Age"

All in Fun, lyrics by June Sillman, music by Baldwin Bergersen, 1940

For years, the appearance of major theatre personalities had guaranteed enthusiastic audiences wherever they played. But by the late 1800s, for many ticket buyers, the magnetic draw of star power was matched by a fascination with theatre technology. In advertising, star billing was given to dazzling special effects as often as it was to dazzling personalities.

Laura Keene (1826–73) may be best remembered as the actress who was performing in *Our American Cousin* at Ford's Theatre the night that Abraham Lincoln was assassinated. One of the most influential theatre personalities of her time, she is considered to have been the first female theatre company manager in America.

When she appeared on Broadway in an extravaganza titled *The Seven Sisters*, which had the longest run of any production in her distinguished career, highly regarded Miss Keene felt obliged to share the spotlight with technology. For this production, advertised as "An Operatic, Spectacular, Diabolic, Musical, Terpsichorean, Farcical Burletta," equal billing was given to Miss Keene and to the show's technological marvel, "The Birth of the Butterfly in the Bower of the Ferns."

FIGURE 5. Actress Laura Keene managed a theater in New York City where she produced and acted in both classical and contemporary plays. (Photographer and date unknown. The Miriam and Ira D. Wallach Division of Art, Prints, and Photographs: Photography Collection, the New York Public Library Digital Collections.)

FIGURE 6. This print illustrates the fascination with trains on the part of people living in America's rural areas. The name of the train, *The Fast Mail*, is also the name of this print and became the title of one of the most produced railroad plays of the late nineteenth century. (Artist unknown, ca. 1875. Retrieved from the Library of Congress.)

In an attempt to cater to and cash in on the theatergoer's fascination with the magic of theatre technology, producers began to take shows with spectacular effects on the road. In the late 1860s, when a traveling theatre company was touring the melodrama *Under the Gaslight*, an express train, which was an integral element in the resolution of the plot, rolled onto the stage. During the course of the drama, the hero had been tied to a railroad track but was rescued a split second before the speeding train reached him. The action was a sensation wherever it played, which resulted in managers of touring companies presenting a number of railroad plays, *The Lightning Express*, *The Midnight Express*, and *The Cannonball Express*, to name a few.

Years later, the railroad melodrama was still the rage. Over a period of ten years, *The Fast Mail*, advertised as "The Finest, Foremost, and Best Railroad play ever written!," traveled up and down the state of Michigan. It began its journey at Coldwater's Tibbits Opera House in 1891, and after making tracks all around the Lower Peninsula for a decade, *The Fast Mail* was delivered to the Calumet Theatre in 1901. The advertisement announced that the audience would see "The Full-Sized Practical Locomotive and 14 Cars" carrying the mail at "lightning-fast speed," which was forty miles an hour!

The public's transportation obsession was not limited to railroad trains. Plays that exhibited realistic effects involving automobiles were popular as well. *The Governor's Pardon* offered "an actual Automobile Race, between Racing Automobiles over two miles of country roads through a blinding blizzard." For those patrons with nautical inclinations, the publicity for *The Tornado* promised "the collision of two ocean liners creating mountain-like waves."

As If by Magic

Many producers advertised that their productions included one or more transformation scenes. These were scene changes, a kind of metamorphosis, that took place right before the audience's eyes. Without closing the curtain, the setting would change from one spectacular environment to another—from a mountain pass to a marble palace, from a canal in Venice to a castle in Spain.

The transformations were accomplished with flying and collapsing scenery, hinged flats, pivoting props, and lighting effects. They were designed to take the audience's breath away. By using every stage mechanism available at the time, including traps, grooves, winches, and "smoke and mirrors," they did just that.

The use of calcium lights, an early version of the spotlight, turned into a marketable attraction to entice prospective patrons as well. The intense light was created when calcium oxide in the form of a block of lime was heated to incandescence in jets of burning oxygen and hydrogen. When attached to the balcony rail, in addition to spotlighting an individual performer, they provided a more natural illumination than that created by footlights. By the 1860s, advertisements for upcoming attractions exclaimed that in addition to the prestigious stars, the costly costumes, the sensational scenery, and the spectacular special effects, the production would be enhanced by the use of calcium lights.

Although theater managers were eager to book these spectacular productions, not all of Michigan's available facilities were large enough or well enough equipped to handle several carloads of scenery. One of the incentives for replacing the Red Jacket Opera House, built in 1887, with the Calumet Theatre only thirteen years later was that the original theater space was essentially a ballroom on the second floor of the town hall. It did have a small stage and a musicians' gallery, but it could not accommodate the technical demands of most traveling theatre productions.

Six weeks after the opening of the Calumet Theatre, a reporter compared the current production of *Devil's Auction* to previous presentations of the same play when it was presented at the upper-story Red Jacket Opera House.

> For the first time Calumet has seen a genuine spectacular show, and for the first time in the history of the Copper Country have traveling theatricals been offered the opportunity of displaying a carload of scenery upon a stage. "Devil's Auction" has appeared here before but was always obliged to leave its scenery in the railroad yards. (*Daily Mining Gazette*, May 3, 1900)

"It Happened in Chicago"

Casa Manana, lyrics by Irving Kahal and Billy Rose, music by Dana Suesse, 1936

Chicago's Iroquois Theatre fire on December 30, 1903, had an immediate impact on theaters across the country. That holiday-time tragedy claimed approximately six hundred lives, making it the deadliest single-building fire up to that time in this nation's history. The reaction to that disaster may have accounted for the survival of many opera houses and may have contributed to the demise of others. A constructive

FIGURE 7. This cartoon by DeMar asks the question, "How Many More Like It?" and hints at the dangers inherent in attending performances at upper-floor opera houses. It was first published in the *Philadelphia Record* and reprinted in the *Manistee Daily News*, January 31, 1908.

result was the upgrading of fire preventative features in facilities throughout the United States. At theaters everywhere, asbestos curtains were hung at the proscenium arch creating a fireproof barrier between the stage and the auditorium. To expedite evacuation in case of an emergency, the number of seats between aisles was limited and all exit doors were required to open outward.

On the other hand, the Eagle Opera House in Marshall, which opened in 1868, has remained vacant since 1904, only inhabited by pigeons. One theory to explain the closing is that as a third-story theater with a balcony but with limited egress, it was deemed too great a fire hazard to remain open in light of the tragic event that had occurred in Chicago the year before.

"The Picture of Real Life"

Countess Coquette, lyrics by Melville Alexander, music by Anatole Friedland, 1913

As early as 1867, the Adrian Union Hall began presenting "illuminated lectures"; the first was advertised as "Stereopantascopic Views of the Holy Land and Egypt." More photographic presentations or "magic lantern" shows followed with greater frequency at theaters everywhere. They were sometimes attached to another form of entertainment such as a vaudeville or minstrel show, but were often the evening's only offering.

Before the silent-film era, the illusion of moving pictures was created with the use of the stereopticon that was an early slide projector with two lenses. A series of still photographs projected on a large screen was manipulated to create the illusion of movement. The two lenses also enabled one image to dissolve into the next. These showings were often billed as "dissolving view stereopticon presentations." Fade out, fade in.

Stereopticon slide technology was quickly perceived to be a visual revolution that could not only entertain, but also educate and inform. The *Coldwater Daily Reporter* speculated, "The day is not far distant when the perfected moving picture will be a part of the college and high school system."

By the 1890s, there was an increased interest in and, therefore, output of pictures that moved; the most popular subjects were current events and foreign locations. With the outbreak of the Spanish–American War in 1898, picture presentations primarily consisted of photographs of that conflict. The Edison Manufacturing Company produced *Remember the Maine*, and other companies limited their presentations to war scenes. The Marks Brothers Company was a double threat as they presented vaudeville with moving pictures of the war between the acts.

When the images were arranged sequentially so as to create a through-line, it opened the door for storytelling by nonoral means. Plot-oriented motion pictures replaced both nonnarrative films and live theatrical performances as the people's entertainment preference. In 1898, the Edison Manufacturing Company released what is often credited as being the first narrative feature film, *The Passion Play of Oberammergau*, a photographic version of the seventeenth-century stage play presented every ten years in Bavaria.

"If I Had a Talking Picture of You"

Sunny Side Up, lyrics by B. G. DeSylva and Lew Brown, music by Lew Henderson, 1929

Lyman H. Howe, billed as "America's Traveler," frequently traveled to opera houses throughout Michigan. In the 1890s he created his own projector, the animotiscope, and by 1901 he was producing both travelogues and newsreels.

His policy: "A complete change of program at each appearance."

His motto: "If it happened, L. Howe has it!"

FIGURE 8. Phoenix Stereopticon, Dissolving View Apparatus, 1894. Slide shows of photographed images were introduced in this country around 1850. The stereopticon did not project pictures in three dimensions, as did the hand-held stereoscope. (*Illustrated Catalogue of Stereopticons*, McIntosh Battery and Optical Company.)

That claim was confirmed when he presented moving pictures of subjects such as Theodore Roosevelt's inauguration in 1901 and the Wright brothers' flight in 1903, both part of "Two Hours of World Travel." Presentations by Howe's Travel Festival became annual featured attractions at many opera houses.

You Ain't Heard Nothin' Yet!

adlibbed by Al Jolson, *The Jazz Singer*, 1927

With the use of a phonograph, Howe was the first motion picture producer to add a soundtrack to his presentations.

FIGURE 9. A newspaper advertisement for Lyman H. Howe's Travel Festival that announces the various foreign locales and exciting events to be presented as moving pictures in the current edition of the popular travelogue series. (*Coldwater Daily Reporter*, October 10, 1910.)

Each picture was accompanied by sound effects that the advertisement claimed "makes the spectator imagine he is seeing actual life itself."

On August 30, 1910, the *Adrian Daily Telegram* announced that Edison had given a public demonstration of his newest invention that provided the "Voice of Moving Pictures." The Edison Kinetophone made it possible to incorporate sound and to synchronize it to movement. The fact that pictures could talk was a major game changer—not only for opera houses but also for the entire entertainment industry.

"As the Years Roll By"

Her Regiment, lyrics by William Le Baron, music by Victor Herbert, 1917

Until motion pictures flooded the entertainment industry like a tidal wave, opera houses across the country served as the cultural and civic center for their region. But by the mid-twentieth century many had been razed or abandoned and neglected until, for some of those that were still standing, there was a rescue accomplished at the eleventh hour by a group of concerned citizens. Recently, several towns in Michigan have become aware of the architectural, cultural, and historic importance of their opera houses, and restoration projects are underway or have been completed.

On April 27, 2013, the Tibbits Opera House hosted a dedication celebration, the culmination of a campaign of several years' duration that raised several million dollars. The facade of the building was entirely restored to its original French Second Empire glory. In addition to champagne, the dedication ceremony featured speeches by local and state officials and a film that documented the restoration of the exterior of the opera house.

Opera houses in Adrian, Elk Rapids, Calumet, Howell, Traverse City, and other towns across the state have recently completed or have ongoing renovation and restoration projects. And, they all have a common mission: to provide their communities with a venue for professional musical and theatrical entertainment and/or to be a home for locally generated events.

Act I

TIBBITS OPERA HOUSE

Coldwater (1882)

Scene i

Building Going Up!

"Let our citizens do all in their power to encourage Mayor Tibbits in building this beautiful opera house, second to none in the state." —*The Coldwater Republican*, March 10, 1882

Let's Start at the Very Beginning / A Very Good Place to Start

The Sound of Music, "Do-Re-Mi," lyrics by Oscar Hammerstein II, music by Richard Rodgers, 1959

The city of Coldwater is situated in what was once a region of prairie and forests inhabited by the Potawatomi Indians. In 1821, Chief Topinabee sold the area to the U.S. government, and eight years later, the Territorial Legislature of Michigan designated it as Branch County. Originally, the town of Masonville was selected to be the county seat; however, in 1831 that distinction was transferred to the village of Branch. In 1842 the county seat was moved to Coldwater, where it remains today.

The invasion of settlers began in 1822 with two trading posts that opened in the area. They in turn attracted homesteaders to the region, and the first log house was built in 1830. The following year, a hotel was erected on an old Indian trail from Detroit to Chicago that is now US 12 (aka the Heritage Trail).

Soon the settlement evolved into the village of Lyons that was platted by Joseph Hanchett and the Reverend Allen Tibbits. Tibbits, a Methodist minister, was born in Lyons, New York. His youngest son, Barton Smith Tibbits, was the man behind the opera house that bears his name.

Lyons underwent a name change in 1833. Two theories have been put forward to explain the decision to name the settlement Coldwater. One story is that the original settlers were Methodist teetotalers, and perhaps cold water was their beverage of choice. A somewhat more credible reason is that the city's name is the English translation of a Native American term for the region that means either "lake water" or "cold water."

By the early 1830s, when what was a settlement had become a proper village, the first store and sawmill opened for business. The first schoolhouse was built in 1834, and two years later the first church was constructed. The following year, 1837, a newspaper, the *Observer*, commenced publication.

The population of Coldwater increased, and in 1837 it was incorporated as a village. Following a malaria epidemic that claimed the lives of thirty-two citizens, the village once again experienced a steady growth and became an incorporated city in 1861.

Early businesses included the manufacturing of pig iron, barrels, sleds, gloves, wheelbarrows, and cigars; there were also cement companies, grain mills, and breweries. Soon, horse farms were added to the list of successful local enterprises. Branch County became known as a center for horse breeding and training and supported a number of racetracks. During the Civil War, the U.S. government bought over three thousand horses from area stables to be trained as warhorses. By the early 1880s, the city could claim several new industries, the arrival of the Bell Telephone Company, and approximately six thousand residents. Coldwater's population peaked in 1970 with over 12,500 inhabitants. Today, there are approximately 10,750 citizens living in town.

The *Coldwater Sentinel* began publication in 1841, and other newspapers followed; the *Coldwater Republican* was first established in 1868, the *Courier* in 1882. They joined forces in 1897 to become the *Courier and Republican* for a short time, after which "Republican" was dropped from the masthead and the paper operated as the *Courier* until 1912.

"City on Fire!"

Sweeney Todd, the Demon Barber of Fleet Street,
lyrics and music by Stephen Sondheim, 1979)

A fire destroyed eight buildings in the downtown area in 1851, and three years later more businesses were consumed by fire. These two disasters provided the impetus for a decree from the village board that in the future no wood construction would be allowed in the commercial district of town. Four decades later, authorities suspected arson when more structures went up in flames. Several firemen were arrested when they admitted that they had started the fires to encourage the acquisition of new fire equipment.

Arts and Entertainment

One of the first cultural organizations to be established in Coldwater was the Ladies' Library Association. Not only did the association distribute books, but it also sponsored literary and scientific lectures. The E. R. Clarke Library (now the Coldwater Branch District Library) was dedicated in 1886. In addition to the library, there was an art gallery and a range of activities that included amateur theatrical presentations, concerts, lectures, and dances. They were presented in private homes, churches, and small meeting halls that were located on the second or third floor of commercial buildings. The most suitable venue for theatrical performances and large gatherings was the Armory Hall. In 1881, it was destroyed by fire and left the city void of a space large enough to accommodate a variety of events including the productions of touring theatre companies.

The *Coldwater Republican* bemoaned the demise of Armory Hall and on July 8, 1881, observed that "no dance can be had without climbing two pairs of stairs; no dramatic representation can be seen at all." The journalist went on to encourage someone to come forward and solve the problem: "Where is the citizen who wants fame and fortune?"

The first person to pick up the gauntlet was the former mayor of Coldwater, Henry Clay Lewis, who was a successful banker with a strong passion for the arts. In 1870, he opened an art gallery in Coldwater that housed a collection of sculpture and over seven hundred paintings. His collection was considered to be the largest art treasury west of New York City.

The Lewis Art Gallery remained open until 1895 at which time, in accordance with his will, all paintings and statuary were donated to the University of Michigan Museum of Art in Ann Arbor. Many of those art pieces have found their way back to Coldwater on permanent loan; eighteen of them are currently displayed on the walls of the Tibbits Opera House auditorium, and others are housed in the Coldwater Branch District Library.

"Brother, Can You Spare a Dime?"

Americana, lyrics by E. Y. Harburg, music by Jay Gorney, 1930

Henry Clay Lewis determined that an opera house could be constructed for approximately $16,000. He intended to contribute half that amount himself and to solicit the remaining portion from one or more of the city's prominent citizens. To that end, he sent a letter to the man who was, perhaps, the city's most prominent citizen, Barton S. Tibbits, a cigar factory owner who, at that time, was also the city's mayor. Lewis stated that he was prepared to invest $8,000 in the project if Tibbits would assist in procuring the remaining half from "property owners of the city."

Apparently, the property owners considered the endeavor to be too great a financial risk and were reluctant to jump on board. Of the $8,000 Tibbits had agreed to raise, after three days of soliciting he had donations from thirty-eight individuals that totaled only $2,441.25. There were contributions of up to $200 and one person gave just $6.25 to the enterprise, but Tibbits was not deterred from his newly acquired mission. He decided to fund the entire enterprise himself without Lewis's $8,000 and announced, prophetically, that he would "build a opera house if it bust my factory."

By November 23, 1881, just three weeks after Lewis had initially approached him about the project, Tibbits had purchased land across the street from his cigar factory on Hanchett Street, hired an architect, and was ready to break ground. The final price tag for the opera house is estimated to have been between $25,000 and $30,000 and includes the cost of construction as well as the purchase of equipment

FIGURE 10. Coldwater mayor and entrepreneur Barton S. Tibbits's long-lasting legacy is the Tibbits Opera House. (Photographer and date unknown. Photograph courtesy of the Tibbits Opera Foundation and Arts Council.)

and furnishings necessary to create the state-of-the-art playhouse. Barton S. Tibbits picked up the tab.

— **INTERLUDE** —

We interrupt our story for a Barton Smith Tibbits biography:

> Mr. Tibbits was a hustler by nature . . . He was outspoken in his sentiments and sometimes gave offense where none was intended. But those who knew him best appreciated his many sterling qualities, and knew that beneath the rough exterior was a nature kind and sympathetic. (*Courier and Republican*, September 1, 1899)

Barton Smith Tibbits (1841–99) was the youngest child of the Reverend and Caroline Starks Tibbits. "Bart," as he was called, grew up and was educated in Coldwater. At the age of nineteen, he enlisted in the First Michigan Calvary, and during the Civil War he participated in fifty skirmishes or battles including the Battle of Gettysburg. After the war, he and his new bride settled in Coldwater where he became a major player in both the local business and political arenas. In 1874, still in his thirties, he opened the B.S.T. Cigar Company, which became the largest cigar manufacturer in the state outside of Detroit. The company employed 175 men who turned out six million cigars a year.

Barton S. Tibbits was never one to avoid visibility: his cigars came with his portrait on both the box and the wrapper, and his initials, nearly a full story high, were attached to the top of his Chicago Street store. The cigar business was just one of many commercial enterprises in which he was engaged during his lifetime.

At the time the opera house opened, the *Coldwater Republican* acknowledged his generosity and achievement:

> For a long time a serious need has been felt in our city for a first-class place of amusement. Although Coldwater is the home of so many wealthy citizens, no one has seemed to possess sufficient courage to embark in so hazardous an undertaking until Mr. B.S. Tibbits, with his accustomed energy and "push" . . . took the matter in hand . . . and the result is a beautiful building, an ornament to our city of which we may justly be proud and an honor to Mr. Tibbits that will endure after the curtain has fallen on the last act in the drama of his life.

Two years after the opening, the opera house became a money pit, and as the sole owner, Tibbits began to feel the drain on his finances. An editorial published in the *Courier* on December 27, 1884, attributed the problem to the fact that the investment and the facility itself were too large for the potential income that could be expected from the audience base in a city the size of Coldwater. The newspaper also observed that citizens "who made the loudest request for such a facility" did not seem willing to financially support it. In conclusion, the journalist predicted that the opera house "will undoubtedly be converted into a roller mill by summer of 1885."

Through the sale of real estate and other assets, Tibbits tried to keep the opera house afloat, but he began to consider it an albatross. By 1885, he had depleted his fortune and was forced to unload the property and reportedly stated,

> I attribute to this enterprise, the Opera House, my downfall, and the sacrifice of a business which, had I been selfish, would today have made me a millionaire. (Marjorie Cline Glesmann, *Coldwater Daily Reporter*, October 11, 1979)

Barton S. Tibbits was an inveterate entrepreneur who was not to be defeated by the loss of an opera house and his wealth; he went on to pursue other business ventures, none of which were as successful as his cigar enterprise. He died at the age of fifty-eight. The newspaper reported that a very large crowd attended his funeral, held at the opera house. "The auditorium and balcony were filled to the outer walls . . . the casket seemed almost submerged in roses." It went on to characterize Barton S. Tibbits as

> a genial, whole-souled man, generous to the poor, lavish with his intimates, a loyal friend and comrade. Mr. Tibbits gave much to the community, but perhaps no gift so well-remembered as the opera house. (*Courier and Republican*, September 1, 1899)

— *And now, back to our story.* —

— **HEADLINE** —

The Mayor Has Sand

> This was proven yesterday when B.S. Tibbits signed the papers and paid the money which conveyed to him the property . . . where will stand . . . a building of which every citizen will be proud, the B.S.T. Opera-house. (*Coldwater Republican*, November 11, 1881)

According to Mayor Tibbits, the lot was acquired "for five hundred dollars less than the property was worth."

Tibbits hired architect Mortimer L. Smith (1840–96) to design his pet project. Smith served in that capacity on such Detroit landmarks as Campus Martius, the J. L. Hudson

FIGURE 11. Tibbits Opera House, 1903. The facade, the detailing, and the shape of the building make it a textbook example of French Second Empire architecture. (Photograph from the Randall Hazelbaker Collection. Courtesy of the Tibbits Opera Foundation and Arts Council.)

Department Store, and, in 1869, the original Detroit Opera House. On November 11, 1881, the *Coldwater Republican* reported that "Mr. Smith drew the plans for the Detroit and Ypsilanti Opera-houses both of which are pronounced perfect." Tibbits charged Smith with the mission to design an opera house smaller than the one in Detroit, but equally grand.

For what the press dubbed Coldwater's "temple of the muses," Mortimer L. Smith chose the French Second Empire architectural style. It was the most popular and, therefore, one of the most prevalent styles employed in the design of buildings that were erected between 1860 and 1890.

Typical of a French Second Empire structure, the building is square and symmetrical with a mansard roof. The use of assorted textures and colors defined by three-dimensional molding, cornices, and pediments is also characteristic of the style. Entrance doors and windows are usually arched and tall.

> The front elevation is in the modern style of architecture. . . . The facing is of pressed red brick with cut stone and black brick united in excellent taste. The galvanized ironwork of the cornices, window frames and caps are of new and handsome design. (*Coldwater Republican*, September 19, 1882)

In a niche below the domed roof is a bust of Shakespeare and underneath it, printed inside a golden arch, is written "Tibbits Opera House" (see figure 11).

Tibbits wasted no time getting the project off the ground or, perhaps, in the ground. A notice went up at the post office: "Wanted: Day laborers and teams to dig Opera House cellar." Ground was broken on November 23, 1881, just thirteen days after Tibbits had purchased the property.

According to the press, several weeks of labor were lost in March because of inclement weather that resulted in Tibbits pushing the project rapidly forward. Sometime later, an updated news item announced that more than thirty people were employed to help with the construction. By June, things were back on track, and the newspaper reported that the timbers for the roof were being placed in position.

> Special attention has been paid to the timbering of the entire building, rendering it one of the safest and most stable structures in Southern Michigan. (*Coldwater Republican*, September 19, 1882)

"On and Off the Stage"

The Golden Widow, lyrics by Edward Madden,
music by Melville Gideon and Louis Hirsch, 1909

— **TIBBITS OPERA HOUSE** —

Seating Capacity & Stage Dimensions

AS RECORDED IN *JULIUS CAHN'S OFFICIAL THEATRICAL GUIDE*, 1897

Seating Capacity	823
Proscenium Arch	Width 30′ / Height 30′
Depth of Stage from Footlights to Back Wall	40′
Width of Stage Between Side Walls	55′
Height from Stage Floor to Rigging Loft	75′

The Tibbits Opera House proscenium is truly an arch as opposed to a square or rectangular picture frame. The *Official Theatrical Guide*, 1897, indicated that the height was thirty feet, which is the distance from the stage floor to the topmost point of the proscenium curve. It went on to state that the width was also thirty feet; however, in the literature published today the opening is listed as being just over twenty-five feet wide (see Plate 1).

There were three traps in the stage floor that were used for elevating set pieces from the basement to the stage. The center trap, called the "vampire trap," was also used for actors to make quick, sudden entrances and exits. One journalist cautioned, "All you have to do is to step on it and . . . you find yourself doubled up on the basement floor with a broken wrist."

Located in the backstage area were speaking tubes and bell signals so that the stage manager could directly communicate with the box office, orchestra, and the stagehands. Offstage was the pin rail with hemp lines that were part of the counterweight system used to raise and lower draperies and drops, and there was a paint bridge with a movable frame.

A nine-foot-wide corridor behind the stage gave access to a scene storage room at one end and an actors' lounge or "greenroom" at the other. Between them were three carpeted dressing rooms—one was intended for the star. On the second floor were several more dressing rooms, and beneath the stage was a band room for the orchestra as well as a large room appointed to accommodate minstrels.

The orchestra pit, located in front of the stage, was lower than the auditorium floor. According to the 1897 *Theatrical Guide*, the opera house had a seven-piece orchestra on standby under the direction of S. Whitlock, but the pit could accommodate as many as twelve musicians.

Bring Up the Lights!

Although Mayor Tibbits ordered electricity for his entire cigar factory, for his opera house across the street he had electrically illuminated only the facade. The interior of the theater relied on gas fixtures for light. Located backstage were the gas table and the lighting control system that enabled one technician to instantly manipulate the 306 gaslights distributed throughout the building.

Low-pressure steam heat distributed through decorative radiators warmed the facility; the stage roof and the dome above the auditorium contained ventilators that released hot air.

"It's Only a Paper Moon"

The Great Magoo, lyrics by E. Y. Harburg and Billy Rose, music by Harold Arlen, 1933

When the Tibbits Opera House opened, the stock of scenery and properties was considered to be the largest and finest in Michigan. In addition to numerous drops, borders, wings, flats, and step units, there were doors and windows, four fireplaces, as well as assorted houses, huts, and cottages. The inventory also included trees, fences, bridges, an arbor, a fountain, a gondola, a rowboat, a chandelier, a throne, and a set of black and gold upholstered furniture.

Nationally known as a portrait, landscape, and scenic

artist who also created political cartoons, L. B. Chevalier was the supervisor for all of the scenery and was the scenic artist responsible for the painted flats and drops. The drop curtain, which was in audience view before the show began, depicted a broad flight of stairs that led to a terrace, and in the center of the terrace was painted a young man in court dress.

> One gives an involuntary start of surprise on entering at sight of the life-like figure, and believes for one moment that the play has begun. . . . The design is original with Mr. Chevalier and attracts great admiration, both from the novelty of the devise and the admirable manner in which the artist has executed his work. (*Coldwater Republican*, September 19, 1882)

As the house lights dimmed and the orchestra began to play, the drop curtain flew out to reveal the act curtain that was a painting of the Grand Canal in Venice filled with gondolas, barges, and fishing boats occupied by workers in colorful garments. Behind the boats was a cityscape that included, among other landmarks, the Palace of the Doge of Venice.

> This work is considered by Mr. Chevalier the best effort of his life. . . . Coldwater is to be congratulated in having secured so good a work of art. (*Coldwater Republican*, September 19, 1882)

Unfortunately, those drops no longer exist.

Gilding the Lily

the condensation of a metaphor from *King John* by William Shakespeare, ca. 1590s

Over the years, numerous remodeling projects have been executed. Although the facade has been restored to replicate the original, the inside of the playhouse has not. When the theater was renovated in the 1960s, new red cushioned seats were installed, and red-flocked wallpaper was attached to the auditorium walls to cover cracks in the plaster. Today, it looks as it did at that time (see Plate 2).

"Castle of Dreams"

Irene, lyrics by Joseph McCarthy, music by Harry Tierney, 1919

Back on September 21, 1882, when the Coldwater opening night patrons, filled with anticipation, approached their new playhouse, what did they encounter? From the street, a few steps led to an area approximately two feet above the sidewalk. There were four sets of wooden and glass double doors across the front of the building; two sets led directly into a vestibule with the box office and manager's office on the left and a smoking room on the right. Two stairways, one on each side of the lobby, led to the balcony's dress circle and gallery seats. Heavy wooden doors covered with dark terra cotta leather trimmed in gold separated the vestibule from the auditorium.

To be certain that patrons knew the identity of the gift horse that had provided this treasure to the city, B. S. Tibbits had his initials emblazoned on the opera house's glass doors as well as displayed on the roof of the building. If that weren't enough, his portrait was printed on every ticket.

In the auditorium, the parquet circle, which embraced the parquet or orchestra section, was in the shape of a horseshoe with the seats arranged in tiers. The parquet was separated from the parquet circle by a low wall.

Located on either side of the proscenium were private boxes draped with curtains of cardinal silk plush lined in gold fabric and trimmed with broad antique lace. Large beveled plate-glass mirrors decorated the front of the boxes. The floor of the boxes and the aisles was covered with Brussels carpet in a rich red hue.

Pastel or cameo tints accented in cardinal red, green, and gold were used throughout the auditorium. The walls were painted in the soft tints down to the decorative wainscoting. The newspaper reported that the color choices gave the auditorium "a bright and airy appearance."

The stage was framed with an ornate tin and plaster proscenium arch topped by a portrait of Shakespeare. The grand gas chandelier in the auditorium, known as an opal glass reflector, was made of semitransparent opal glass that distributed a subtle, soft light on the dome above and provided a uniform light for the audience below. Painted on the ceiling of the dome, encircling the chandelier, were cherubs bearing trailing garlands of flowers. According to the newspaper, the child-angels and their bounty were so well executed that

> one may almost imagine them floating in space and inhale the odor of their fragrant burden. It is impossible to give a description of the decorations which will convey an adequate idea of their beauty. They must be seen in order to be appreciated. (*Coldwater Republican*, September 19, 1882)

At the time of the 1960s renovation, plaster and paint were applied to the ceiling dome, obscuring the chubby cherubs with their garlands of flowers.

Gentlemen, Be Seated!

said the interlocutor to the minstrels

> Mr. Tibbits has decided to go to still further expense . . . upholstered chairs, a sample one of which can be seen at his office. (*Coldwater Republican*, June 6, 1882)

Folding chairs, known as grand opera chairs, were placed in the parquet, parquet circle, and dress circle. Each chair had a footrest and a hat and umbrella rack. They were upholstered in dark cardinal plush with the monogram B.S.T engraved on the back. The chairs, which cost a total of $3,000, were praised for "the selection and make-up of the material used and the neat manner in which the work has been done."

"You're the Top"

Anything Goes, lyrics and music by Cole Porter, 1934

> The plan will be similar to the Ypsilanti Opera-house, with inclined floor, and seating with folding chairs.

> A false canvas covered floor will be used for dancing. (*Coldwater Republican*, November 11, 1881)

One month after the opening, a canvas-covered portable floor was ready for use, which rendered the opera house a multipurpose facility. It extended from the front of the stage over the inclined floor of the parquet section to the low wall that divided the parquet seating from the parquet circle. The false floor could be quickly installed once the opera chairs were removed. The purpose of the portable deck was to create a level surface for those activities that could not take place on the raked floor. For the next ten years, when a theatrical production was not being presented and with the flat floor in place, the space was used for dancing parties, banquets, receptions, and wrestling matches.

"There'll Have to Be Changes Made"

My Darlin' Aida, lyrics by Charles Friedman, music by Hans Spialek based on Giuseppe Verdi, 1952

In June 1908, the opera house season closed earlier than usual so that various renovation projects could be accomplished. The improvements to the facility were ongoing. In 1909, a new sign was installed over the entrance to the opera house; it was eighty-six inches in diameter, studded with forty sixteen-candle-power incandescent lamps, finished in gold leaf, and read "Opera House."

During the summer of 1911, a major renovation to the balcony area was undertaken. A large rail was installed to divide the upper and lower galleries each now accessed by separate stairways. The new arrangement not only improved the flow of patron traffic to and from the upper regions of the auditorium but also better facilitated the evacuation of the theater if necessary. The new configuration of the space made it possible to add more opera chairs in the galleries, thereby increasing the total seating capacity of the playhouse.

A Changing of the Guard

From 1882 until 1885, Barton S. Tibbits and his staff enjoyed some degree of success:

> Manager Tibbits was made happy again last evening, his opera-house being filled with a large, fashionable and appreciative audience. (*Coldwater Republican*, April 10, 1883)

Success was fleeting, as on June 24, 1885, Tibbits had no choice but to sell the opera house. The buyers—a German saloon owner, Joseph Henning, and his wife, Amelia—purchased the playhouse for $13,000, about half of Tibbits's initial investment. Soon after they signed the bill of sale, Henning began to exploit the building's potential. He converted the basement into a saloon, with an attached billiard parlor and bowling alley.

> Henning's new saloon under the opera house threw its doors open to the public last Thursday evening. Lovers of ten pins will soon have an opportunity to exercise their

muscle, as Mr. Henning will lay a single alley, 85 feet long, on the north side of the basement. (*Courier*, July 1885)

When the saloon and gaming rooms proved to be unsuccessful in providing sufficient revenue to support the opera house, the saloon was converted into a tearoom with Mrs. Henning in charge of that enterprise.

Henning also expanded the range of events by offering wrestling and boxing matches, circus acts, and marionette shows, but continued presenting lectures, concerts, and amateur talent shows. He also continued to book professional minstrel shows and numerous touring theatre productions.

Who's Minding the Store?

Soon after Henning had acquired the property, C. L. Hunter, the theater manager who had been hired by Tibbits, resigned. Henning replaced him with George W. Klock, a music professor. When Klock assumed the position of theater manager, he essentially switched hats since he had previously been the leader of the Opera House Band. On July 2, 1889, the *Coldwater Republican* announced that Klock had resigned, and "hereafter the proprietor, Mr. Henning will have entire charge."

At that point, Henning took over the management of the facility himself and recruited his teenage daughter, Huldah, to be the box office manager. He assured patrons that the previously announced attractions would still be presented with one possible exception: "Vernona Jarbeau has canceled, and Manager Henning proposes to make trouble for her if the date is not filled."

As a manager, Joseph Henning did not always "make trouble" for the entertainers; he sometimes tried to solve their problems. The *New York Dramatic News* published a story as told by actor/manager Harry Webber. When Webber arrived in Coldwater to present his show, he informed Henning that a scene in the play required some revolvers, and he wrote what was needed on a piece of paper: "2 32-caliber revolvers." According to Mr. Webber, Henning returned an hour later with a large basket three-quarters filled with revolvers of all descriptions and, in an apologetic tone, explained that Coldwater was a "quiet place" and he didn't think there were 232 revolvers in the entire city.

"Business Is Bad"

The Gingham Girl, lyrics by Neville Fleeson, music by Albert Von Tilzer, 1922

Despite Henning's attempt to diversify both the activities within the building and the programming of events, the opera house was still operating in the red. In July 1889, the *Courier* ran the following letter to the editor from Joseph Henning explaining his dire financial situation and suggesting a solution:

> Nearly five years ago I purchased the opera house for $13,000. . . . I am offered for the property nearly as much as I gave and should I sell Coldwater will be deprived of what she seemed to most need eight years ago . . . a first-class opera house. . . . I earnestly hope the men of

means in our city will form a stock company, purchase the opera house and use it for just what it was originally intended, a place of amusement for our citizens.

A few days after Mr. Henning's letter appeared in print, the *Coldwater Republican* reported that its readers had responded, and the consensus was that the opera house should "not be diverted to any other purpose as we need such a building and we should not soon get another."

The *Coldwater Republican* not only concurred with this sentiment, but also encouraged the plan to sell opera house stock at $25 a share. In the end, Joseph Henning decided to struggle on with the help of his daughter, Huldah.

"It Takes a Woman"

Hello, Dolly!, lyrics and music by Jerry Herman, 1964

> Probably the youngest opera house manager in the country and the only successful female one. (*Courier*, August 1, 1891)

By the time she was nineteen, Huldah Henning was managing the theater. Her responsibilities included, among other duties, scheduling the season, booking touring productions, negotiating contracts, and supervising publicity. Allegedly, she signed her father's name on contracts and business letters because some theatre company managers were unwilling to conduct business negotiations with a woman—especially one so young.

However, managers of other touring companies as well as audience members and the press were unanimous in their praise of her abilities. After Miss Henning completed her first season as theater manager, the *Coldwater Republican* offered the following evaluation of her performance:

> She is a dignified, affable and capable woman of business while still a young girl. A young lady successfully managing a big opera house is a rare case but we have it and we are justly proud of the fact.

"It's So Nice to Have a Man Around the House"

It's a Small World, lyrics by Jack Elliott, music by Harold Spina, 1950

In September 1892 John T. Jackson, a company manager and advance man, brought his troupe to Coldwater for a week's engagement. There he conducted both professional and personal negotiations with young Huldah Henning. Nine months later, on June 21, 1893, they were married. A year after that it was announced that he was the new Tibbits Opera House manager.

> Mr. Jackson has been in the theatrical business for years and is well known among the professional world, which will enable him to bring to Coldwater some of the best and leading attractions now on the road. (*Coldwater Republican*, July 20, 1894)

With his professional theatre experience and a sound business sense, he was able to achieve a degree of financial stability for the opera house.

During the 1890s Jackson made many improvements to the facility. He enlarged the box office, redesigned and increased the stage mechanics and electrics, moved girders to create more wing space, and installed electric fans in the auditorium.

> J.T. Jackson . . . invented a box office ticket rack . . . showing at a glance the row, section and number of every seat in the parquet, dress circle, and private boxes, thus avoiding the tedious handling over and over of bundles of tickets to find the right one. (*Courier*, June 30, 1894)

Following the 1903 Iroquois Theatre fire in Chicago, Jackson installed a fire curtain at the proscenium as well as a sprinkler system over the stage, backstage, and dressing room areas. With seven street-level exits, it was believed that the theater could be evacuated in from two to three minutes in case of emergency.

As the theater manager, Jackson exercised complete control over the selection of engagements to be presented. In June 1904 the *Courier and Republican* reported that the Cora Van Tassel Company was threatening to sue Jackson, claiming damages in the sum of $200 for breach of contract. It seems that Jackson had booked *Camille*, starring Miss Van Tassel, to perform at the opera house for three performances in May. When the troupe arrived in Coldwater, they found that Jackson had canceled the engagement without notice. He explained that by the terms of the contract the Van Tassel Company was to have furnished advertising material but failed to do so. Also, he had received unfavorable reports about the production from where it had recently played.

Throughout the years, there were other incidents when Jackson canceled previously booked engagements at the last minute because he discovered that the attraction did not measure up to the required standard.

"Fussin', Feudin', and Fightin'"

Laffing Room Only, lyrics and music by Burton Lane, 1944

At the beginning of his tenure as manager, Jackson advertised that for most engagements, "popular prices will prevail." Later, however, he thought it necessary to increase ticket prices, which resulted in the editor of the *Courier and Republican* chastising him in print. In his defense, Jackson explained that when he negotiated with performers and touring companies he offered minimum compensation, but some major stars and attractions would not perform in Coldwater for such a small fee. Consequently, in order to provide the patrons with the top touring talent, he claimed to have no choice but to meet their demands. To do so and, at the same time, to safeguard the opera house's financial stability, his only option was to increase the cost of admission.

The *Courier and Republican* editor didn't buy it. He accused Jackson of raising the ticket prices unilaterally with the result that theater patrons in Coldwater were paying more than those in other cities for the same events. Jackson then claimed that he had no control over the ticket prices as the various companies set them.

The *Courier* editor didn't buy that either:

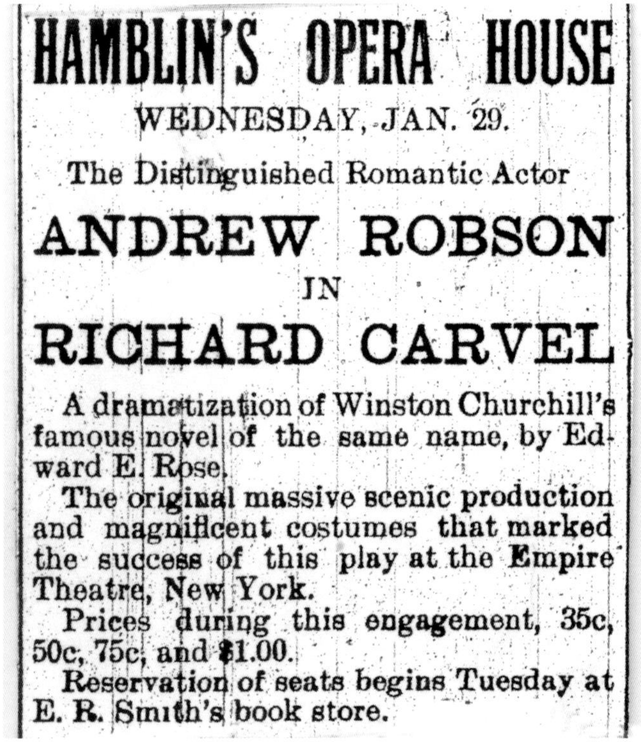

HAMBLIN'S OPERA HOUSE

WEDNESDAY, JAN. 29.

The Distinguished Romantic Actor

ANDREW ROBSON

IN

RICHARD CARVEL

A dramatization of Winston Churchill's famous novel of the same name, by Edward E. Rose.

The original massive scenic production and magnificent costumes that marked the success of this play at the Empire Theatre, New York.

Prices during this engagement, 35c, 50c, 75c, and $1.00.

Reservation of seats begins Tuesday at E. R. Smith's book store.

FIGURE 12. A Hamblin's Opera House newspaper advertisement for the play *Richard Carvel* as it appeared in the *Battle Creek Journal* proving that the top ticket price was one dollar, not one dollar and fifty cents. (*Courier and Republican*, January 1902.)

> Mr. Jackson a short time since played the Gus Sun minstrels here . . . the highest priced seats for that entertainment were 75 cents. This same company played at Nelson's opera house in Mt. Clemens with the highest priced seats 50 cents. Will Mr. Jackson explain why he was compelled by the Gus Sun manager to charge more than the Mt. Clemens opera house? (*Courier and Republican*, April 2, 1901)

The journalist added that he would take note of ticket prices advertised in other cities where productions on their way to Coldwater were playing. "This may possibly prevent him from being on the mercy of the managers as now he claims to be, but isn't."

The newspaper also complained that he promoted all events as being first-class and did not distinguish those that were truly top notch from those of inferior quality, and that he charged the same for both.

> Mr. Jackson says "The Royal Box" company is an all right attraction, and he also said that the "Quo Vadis" company was a strong one. One of the prominent ladies of the city said to "The Courier" . . . that she attended "Quo Vadis" because she thought from what Mr. Jackson said about it that the entertainment would certainly be worth seeing, but her disappointment was such that it would be a long time before she would go again. (*Courier and Republican*, April 2, 1901)

The reporter attended *The Royal Box* and admitted that it was worth the price of admission, but "the trouble is he makes no distinction and good, bad and indifferent companies are all playing at high prices."

When Jackson announced the ticket prices for the upcoming production of *Richard Carvel* starring popular leading man Andrew Robson, the *Courier and Republican* took exception:

> Mr. John T. Jackson . . . accuses "The Courier" with lying about the prices charged in Battle Creek . . . declaring the prices ranged from $1.50 to 35 cents. Here is the advertisement of the entertainment as it appeared in the

> "Battle Creek Journal," and if Mr. Jackson can find any reference to $1.50 seats he can do more than any one else can. (*Courier and Republican*, February 7, 1902)

In the same issue of the newspaper, Jackson was begrudgingly acknowledged for the manner in which he dealt with an objectionable incident that took place during the performance of a vaudeville show. Jackson had the curtain brought down on an act that employed inappropriate dialogue. He explained to the audience that coarse language was not tolerated at the opera house and that their money would be refunded at the ticket office.

> While "The Courier" and Mr. Jackson do not agree in many things it can commend his action in this instance. However, some people think he was only making a grand stand play because of a poor house. (*Courier and Republican*, February 7, 1902)

The Jackson–*Courier* feud escalated to the point that eventually no advertisements, press releases, or reviews that promoted the professional touring attractions booked at the opera house appeared in that newspaper. The only opera house information that the paper published concerned locally generated events. After twelve years, the *Courier and Republican* lifted its ban and once again began publishing publicity items pertaining to Tibbits's professional touring attractions.

The *Coldwater Daily Reporter*, on the other hand, did not have an issue with Jackson or the opera house. During the Jackson–*Courier* feud, in addition to the publicity the paper customarily provided, the *Daily Reporter* began publishing a column devoted to the activities at the theater under the byline J. T. Jackson. Three years later, in 1915, the byline disappeared, but a column called "Opera House Notes" appeared in almost every issue of the paper.

Manager Jackson was not the only object of the *Courier and Republican*'s scrutiny and scolding. The newspaper often took on the entire Coldwater theatergoing public. Patrons were reprimanded for leaving performances early and admonished for not appreciating fine music and drama.

In a review of a Parker Concert Company performance the audience was chastised for preparing to leave the premises before the conclusion of the concert:

> There was only one thing occurred to mar the pleasure of the evening. . . . "The Courier" is surprised that a Coldwater audience would be so thoughtless as to detract from the closing number on a musical program by undue haste in putting on wraps or leaving seats. (*Courier and Republican*, March 12, 1901)

It was not until three years later in a review of another concert that the newspaper reported that the problem had been solved:

> A greatly pleased audience left the opera house Friday night at the close of the Katharine Ridgeway Concert Co. entertainment and it is a pleasure to announce that "The Courier's" suggestion that the audience wait until the close of the entertainment before putting on wraps was acted upon. (*Courier and Republican*, February 8, 1904)

The *Coldwater Daily Reporter* also took Coldwater audiences to task. When it deemed that an event did not receive the patronage it deserved, the paper was quick to criticize the locals:

> It is evident by the attendance given Donald Robertson and his excellent company of players . . . that there is no very great demand for the best in this city. (*Coldwater Daily Reporter*, January 1, 1910)

"Two Ladies"

Cabaret, lyrics by Fred Ebb, music by John Kander, 1966

After considerable wooing on the part of John T. Jackson, he was able to convince *The Merry Widow* to waltz onto the Tibbits Opera House stage.

> Manager Jackson states that this is by far the biggest attempt that he has made in getting an attraction to Coldwater during the seventeen years of his management of the opera house. . . . If this attraction should get a lukewarm reception . . . it would damage the city to an alarming extent in the matter of getting attractions from New York. (*Coldwater Daily Reporter*, November 13, 1910)

Although the production of Franz Lehar's comic opera was touted as being "A New and Magnificent Production of the World's Most Famous Operetta," the turnout was disappointing.

> "The Merry Widow" played to a very poor house last evening and as a production it was the best that Coldwater has seen in years . . . the effort of getting such an attraction for Coldwater was fruitless as far as gate receipts are concerned. . . . In spite of the fact that "The Merry Widow" has been the rage of all countries for the last three years . . . Coldwater did not appreciate what it was getting. (*Coldwater Daily Reporter*, November 16, 1910)

When *_Madame Sherry_, advertised as "The World's Greatest Musical Sensation," made her appearance in Coldwater in May 1911, she endured a fate similar to that of *The Merry Widow*—disappointing attendance.

Several months later, at a conference of theater managers from the Michigan–Ohio region, it was decided that they should band together to book *Madame Sherry* for a return engagement at their opera houses. The question arose as to whether or not Mr. Jackson wanted to buy into the plan since when the show had first played at the Tibbits it lost money. The game Mr. Jackson replied that he knew no better place to look for money than where he lost it. On October 26, 1911, the *Coldwater Daily Reporter* announced that *Madame Sherry* was well attended the second time around.

The newspapers were not only frank when criticizing the audience, they also pulled no punches when it came to reviewing the productions. For example, *My Cinderella Girl* promised "A Whirlwind of Fun, Frolic, and Fascinating Music." However, the *Coldwater Daily Reporter* opined that they had not lived up to that promise and, in the following headline, shared that opinion with readers:

— HEADLINE —

Lacked Real Merit in Both Dramatic and Musical Qualities. Company Was Inadequate.

The local newspaper critics were not the only hard sell in Coldwater. On February 4, 1909, under the headline "Do Managers Fear Our Audience?" the *Coldwater Daily Reporter* ran an article that was a reprint of a piece that had appeared in the Chicago theatre magazine *The Green Book*. The author of the article contended that Coldwater was "the criterion of the entire country." Managers of touring companies that were scheduled to play Coldwater were warned "to watch out for the local audiences who are the most reluctant of any in the circuit to offer applause."

"Promises, Promises"

Promises, Promises, lyrics by Hal David, music by Burt Bacharach, 1968

To assure prospective patrons that they could attend a production on a no-risk basis, managers of touring productions began offering a satisfaction or money-back guarantee. The purpose of Jackson's October 1, 1913, column in the *Coldwater Daily Reporter* was to promote the upcoming production of *The Light Eternal*, a "big, powerful drama of the early Roman period—partly religious and partly romantic—but at all times an intensely interesting and inspiring play." Jackson went on to assure audience members that the manager of the production "guarantees his goods and the purchaser has the right to demand a refund of the purchase price if the

FIGURE 13. The producers alleged that the "clamoring demands" from cities across the country to see *Madame Sherry* was so great that they had no choice but to send out a special production with the original Broadway cast. Coldwater and Manistee were among the first cities outside of New York and Chicago to receive the megahit. (Newspaper advertisement for *Madame Sherry*. *Coldwater Daily Reporter*, May 3, 1911.)

guarantee is not fulfilled . . . absolute satisfaction guaranteed or your money refunded and no questions asked."

"As the Years Roll By"

Her Regiment, lyrics by William Le Baron, music by Victor Herbert, 1917

In 1904, Joseph and Amelia Henning sold the opera house to their daughter, Huldah, and her husband, John Jackson, for $4,000 and "other considerations." Jackson continued to manage the playhouse until 1919, when he and Huldah sold it to Dennis and Estella Vanes.

At the time of the sale, Jackson had been in control of the same theater longer than any other theater manager in Michigan—twenty-six years. After leaving show business, he started the Merchants' Outdoor Advertising Service that he headed until his untimely death in 1934 when he was struck by an automobile while crossing Chicago Street.

Two years prior to purchasing the opera house, Dennis "Denny" Vanes acquired a partial lease of the theater for the purpose of showing moving pictures. In that capacity, he booked all of the films that were screened there while Jackson continued to book and manage the live entertainment component. At that time, Vanes owned and managed the local Venetian Theater, a small venue that presented motion pictures and vaudeville. Vanes wanted a larger space to show popular films featuring popular movie stars that attracted a large turnout of patrons. The *Coldwater Daily Reporter* ran an advertisement that confirmed the marriage of the opera house to the Venetian. The readers were informed that on December 19 and 20, the film that would be showing matinees at the Venetian for ten cents plus a one-cent war tax could be seen in the evening at the opera house for fifteen cents plus a two-cent war tax.

The arrangement between Jackson and Vanes lasted only six months. The next year, on September 9, 1919, Dennis and Estella Vanes bought the opera house for $15,000. It was purchased on a land contract that extended until the buyers received title for the theater on March 8, 1921.

Dennis Vanes's intent was to make the opera house the most successful motion picture theater in southern Michigan outside of Kalamazoo, Battle Creek, and Jackson. His plans included remodeling the facility to make it more suitable for screening films and changing the name of the theater from the Tibbits Opera House to one that would indicate that it was now primarily a venue for motion pictures and under new management. The latter idea met with some resistance from the public, some of whom expressed the opinion that Barton S. Tibbits had done so much for the community that he deserved to have his name attached to his gift to Coldwater in perpetuity. A week after the sale Vanes came up with a compromise. He kept "Tibbits" but dropped "Opera House" and the Tibbits Opera House became the Tibbits Theater.

On August 20, 1934, Mr. and Mrs. Vanes sold the opera house for $40,000 to Schulte-Barrett Theatres, a company that owned and managed a Midwestern chain of movie houses. After purchasing the theater, William J. Schulte hired an architect to modernize the building. The project included removing the original 1882 French Second Empire architectural details, covering the front of the building with tiles to create an Art Deco facade, and adding a marquee.

FIGURE 14. The Tibbits Opera House was remodeled in the mid-1930s and became the Tibbits Theater, a venue for motion pictures. This photograph was taken in the late 1950s when the theater was closed and stood vacant. (Photograph courtesy of the Tibbits Opera Foundation and Arts Council.)

In contrast to the extreme makeover of the exterior, only minor changes to the interior were made. A concession stand was installed in the lobby, and in the auditorium, modern movie theater seats took the place of the elegant, embroidered opera chairs. The chandelier in the ceiling dome was headed for the dump but made a detour to the new armory for its use. When the opera house was renovated years later, the fixture was retrieved and reinstated. As the Tibbits Theater, the facility operated as a movie house until 1954.

The theater stood empty until the late 1950s when it was scheduled for demolition to make room for a parking lot. A community drama group, the Coldwater Players, approached William Schulte to ask if he would consider selling the facility to them and, while they were raising the money, allowing them to present plays there. He agreed and a campaign to save the opera house commenced.

In November 1959, with a down payment of $1,500, Schulte-Barrett Theatres and the Coldwater Players agreed upon an Option for Purchase of Land for $7,500. Four years later, on September 12, 1963, the Coldwater Players sold the property to the recently formed Tibbits Theater Foundation for one dollar, and the next week ownership was officially transferred from Schulte-Barrett Theatres to that organization.

FIGURE 15. "Help Restore Tibbits!" When this 2011 photograph was taken, the 1960s brick facade that replaced the Art Deco tiles had been stripped away, revealing the original exterior with indications of the placement of the French Second Empire architectural detail. (Photograph courtesy of the Tibbits Opera Foundation and Arts Council.)

Soon after the purchase, the deteriorating tile exterior was replaced with a simple, unrelieved brick facade, and in the lobby over the doors that lead to the auditorium a colorful mural was created. The montage depicts a jester as well as Shakespeare, members of his family and acting troupe, and characters from melodramas and minstrelsy (see Plate 3). It was designed and painted in 1964 by Alfred Parke, a Coldwater resident and former Disney animator who was one of the team of artists that was responsible for the artwork in the films *Pinocchio*, *Fantasia*, and *Dumbo*.

Nearly fifty years after the brick facade went up the campaign to take it down and restore the original French Second Empire facade was launched. The restoration was complete in 2013.

The restoration project garnered the opera house more than a half dozen awards including the American Institute of Architects' Michigan Building Award, the Michigan Governor's Award for Historic Preservation, and the Associated Builders & Contractors Award for "Excellence in Historic Restoration."

Today, the building is owned by the Tibbits Opera Foundation and Arts Council, Inc., founded in 1964. Their mission statement is "to engage all in arts, culture, education, and the preservation of the historic opera house." The Tibbits Opera House was designated a Michigan Historical Site in 1970.

FIGURE 16. The Tibbits Facade Restored!, 2013. (Photographer: SPI Photography, Coldwater, Michigan. Photograph courtesy of the Tibbits Opera Foundation and Arts Council.)

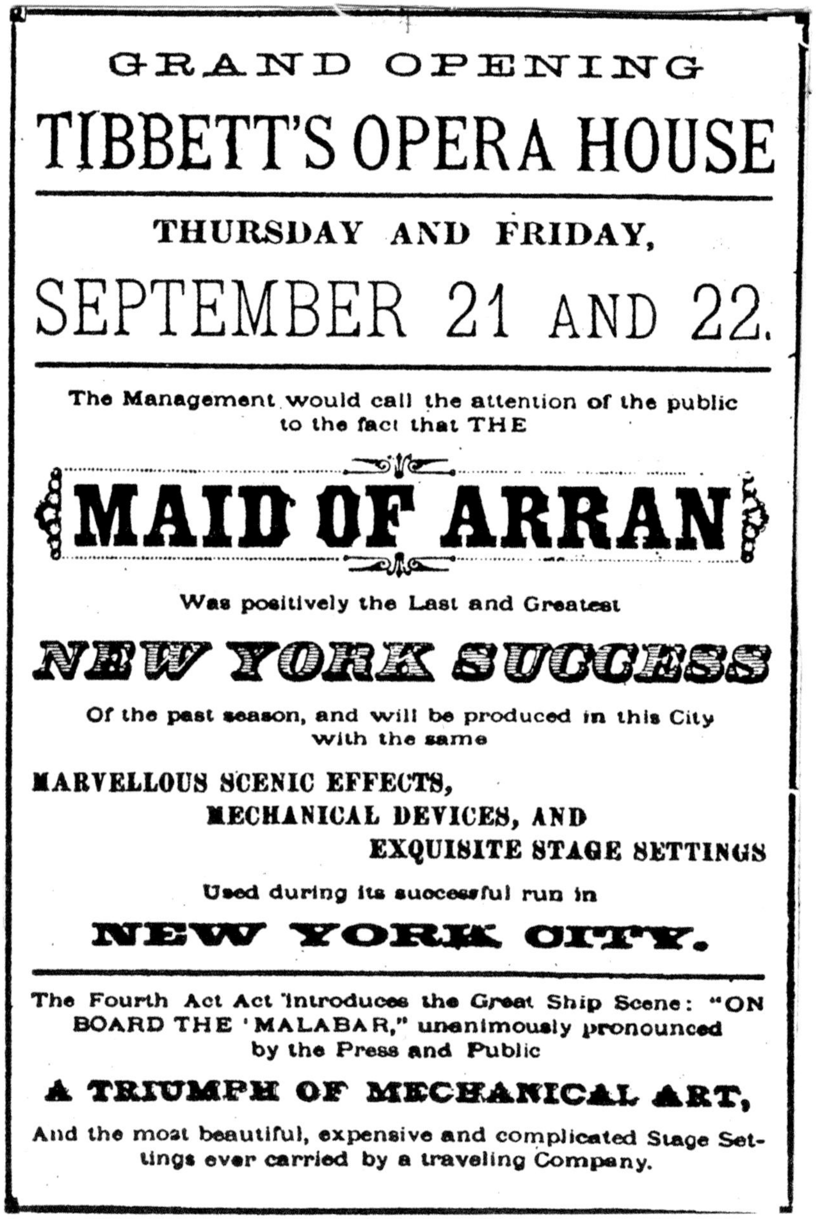

FIGURE 17. A newspaper advertisement announcing that the Tibbits Opera House will present a production of *The Maid of Arran* for its grand opening. (*Coldwater Republican*, September 21, 1882.)

SCENE ii

Curtain Going Up!

> The beautiful Opera house built by Mr. Tibbits, and to which the citizens of Branch County can point with pride, will be formally opened to the public Thursday evening. —*Coldwater Republican*, September 21, 1882

On opening night, which began with a parade and fireworks, the elegantly dressed patrons filled the theater from the parquet to the gallery. Mr. Tibbits personally welcomed those audience members holding tickets for parquet and parquet circle seats. The tickets for this special occasion had been sold before the opera house was completed with a money-back guarantee should the theater not open on the advertised date. Refunds were not necessary because the opera house opened on schedule, September 21, 1882.

The day after the opening, the *Coldwater Republican* gave a full account of the gala event:

> At eight o'clock the house was filled with the finest audience ever assembled at an entertainment in Coldwater. The ladies were in full dress and the brilliant hues of their dresses, the glittering lights, the handsome curtain and the elegant decorations of the house produced a tout ensemble seldom surpassed. The ushers, clad in their neat uniforms, performed the tasks allotted to them so well that no confusion occurred and the seats were found and occupied remarkably well for a first night. (*Coldwater Republican*, September 22, 1882)

The production booked for the official opening of the Tibbits Opera House was *The Maid of Arran*, advertised as an "Idyllic Irish Drama." However, before the audience could experience it, there was another presentation on stage that consisted of a series of speeches and testimonials delivered by prominent Coldwater gentlemen.

When it was Tibbits's turn to speak, he explained his motives in providing the city with what he hoped would become his legacy:

> It was my wish to erect a monument to my memory that every man, woman and child in Coldwater would appreciate, and secondly to show that I was not selfish, but ready to do anything in my power to beautify and ornament our city.

Before the curtain went up on *The Maid of Arran*, Louis F. Baum, the playwright and star of the production, was called onto the stage. He praised the attention that had been paid to the "comforts of the profession in the appointments of the stage and dressing rooms."

Louis F. Baum (1856–1919), also known as L. Frank Baum, but whose real name was Lyman Frank Baum, was the author of *The Wonderful Wizard of Oz* series of children's books. Years before the publication of his books he was a playwright and actor working under the stage name Louis F. Baum.

Baum was born in Chittenango, New York, where he grew up with his siblings on their affluent parents' estate, Rose Lawn. While still a young man, he developed a lifelong passion for the theatre. In 1880, his father built him a theater in Richburg, New York, and young Baum began to write, act, and direct.

One of his early efforts was *The Maid of Arran*, a drama with songs. The inspiration for the play was the William Black novel *A Princess of Thule*, published in 1874. Baum adapted the book into a five-act melodrama and added songs for which he composed the music and wrote the lyrics. In this period, many plays with music had songs randomly dropped into the storyline that might or might not have anything to do with the plot or the characters. Baum's songs, which did advance the narrative and reveal character, were published as a collection and sold as a songbook.

In the production, Louis F. Baum played Hugh Holcomb, and in a perfect bit of typecasting, Katharine Gray, Baum's real-life aunt, appeared as his character's aunt, Harriet Holcomb. *The Maid of Arran* opened in Rochester, New York, on May 15, 1882, where Baum's performance elicited the following comments from the Rochester *Democrat and Chronicle*:

> Louis F. Baum . . . impersonated Hugh Holcomb, a long, difficult character, in a manner that won for him many admirers. He has a fine appearance, a good voice under perfect control, and a manner that is at all times pleasing.

From Rochester, the show went on tour and garnered favorable reviews along the way. The *Detroit Free Press* described it as "Fascinating, Original and Comical," and the *Chicago Times* said it was "Certainly the Best Drama Produced Here This Season." The *Coldwater Republican*, however, expressed a dissenting opinion:

> The first act of the play dragged somewhat but improved materially as the play progressed. The song and dance might have been omitted with advantage. . . . The denouement is altogether too tame and should be rewritten.

From Arran to Oz

Despite his successful foray into show business, Baum abandoned that career to pursue a more stable profession. Years passed, and after several of his endeavors failed he began writing fairytales based on the stories he often improvised for his children. *The Wonderful Wizard of Oz* came out in 1900 and was an immediate success. Over the next twenty years, he produced thirteen Oz sequels. All told he wrote over fifty novels, as well as scores of short stories, poems, and plays including the libretto for the 1903 comic opera **The Wizard of Oz*.

For Michiganders, of particular note is Baum's novel *Tamawaca Folks: A Summer Comedy* that he wrote in 1907 under the pseudonym John Estes Cooke. In 1900, he bought a summer home in Macatawa Park near Holland, Michigan that he christened "The Sign of the Goose." The book is a comic parody of life in Macatawa Park, which he called a "fairytale" resort town.

"Another Op'nin', Another Show"

Kiss Me, Kate, lyrics and music by Cole Porter, 1948

> I shall make an earnest effort to place upon this stage a class of entertainments that shall be worthy your esteem and patronage. (Barton S. Tibbits, opening night address, September 21, 1882)

The program distributed the night of the grand opening of the Tibbits Opera House contained a notice that the next production would be the comedy *Cheek*, starring Roland Reed. The actor received considerable attention when he originated the role of KoKo in the American premiere of Gilbert and Sullivan's *The Mikado*. After that success, Reed could be counted upon to perform two songs from that comic opera, "I've Got a Little List" and "Tit Willow," as an encore following any and every production of any and every play in which he appeared.

Following Roland Reed, the opera house presented two minstrel shows, two plays, a political speech delivered by Governor William H. Gibson, and a stereopticon presentation titled "Illuminated Rambles in Foreign Lands."

On November 4, 1882, the eagerly anticipated production of **The Black Crook* finally arrived in Coldwater, sixteen years after it had opened in New York City. At the time of its opening in 1866, it was controversial: some of the press and public declared that it was stupendous; others thought it was scandalous. In Coldwater it was a bestseller. How did it hold up so many years after its premiere?

> The crowd of old baldheaded fellows on the front seats of the Opera House on Saturday evening last were sadly disappointed. The show wasn't as attractive as they expected. (*Courier*, November 11, 1882)

Apparently, spectacular scenery combined with the opportunity to ogle women's legs still sold tickets and continued to do so, as over a decade later, *The Black Crook* made a return engagement at the Tibbits Opera House.

The year ended with a visit from the A. O. Miller Company that was based in Blissfield, Michigan. It was in

FIGURE 18. Portrait of L. Frank Baum, actor-playwright (*The Maid of Arran*, 1882); author (*The Wonderful Wizard of Oz* series, 1900–20); and librettist and lyricist (*The Wizard of Oz* comic opera, 1903). (Photographer: Dana Hull, ca. 1908. Retrieved from the Library of Congress.)

residence for three days; its repertory included sentimental melodramas and mysteries. After a full year of extravaganzas and melodramas, the press suggested that plays with more substance be offered. On November 9, 1883, the *Coldwater Republican* stated, "It seems almost impossible to elevate the class of amusements in this city."

"On with the Show"

Pretty Faces, lyrics and music by Robert W. Cabell, 1990

Three of the melodramas that were most often produced at theaters everywhere before 1900 were seen at the Tibbits Opera House—**East Lynne*, *Hazel Kirke*, and **The Streets of New York*—along with the tried and true, ever-popular **Faust*, *Rip Van Winkle*, and **Uncle Tom's Cabin*.

Uncle Tom's Cabin was introduced to Coldwater audiences on January 11, 1883. In the thirty years since the play's premiere, it had been seen almost everywhere by almost everyone, and its message had been overpowered by the introduction of songs, dances, specialty acts, and spectacle. The imminent arrival of the drama that had been turned into a circus event was met with little enthusiasm by the gentlemen of the press among others.

> We knew it would come sooner or later, but have prayed that the calamity might be averted. Our prayers have been in vain and we will have to submit to the inevitable. (*Courier*, February 12, 1883)

To add insult to injury, *Uncle Tom's Cabin* made many return visits to Coldwater. On the Tibbits Opera House stage between 1883 and 1915, Eliza crossed the ice often pursued by real bloodhounds a total of twenty-seven times—sometimes twice in one day.

East Lynne, starring *Ada Gray as the ill-fated heroine, was first seen at the Tibbits Opera House in 1884. Miss Gray returned two more times as the same character; however, there were several other actresses who assumed the role of the doomed Lady Isabel at the playhouse. In 1910, in advance of a new production of *East Lynne*, the *Coldwater Daily Reporter* declared, "Ada Gray Lives Again!" The article claimed:

> Since the original Ada Gray production of "East Lynne" there never has been so complete a representation of Mrs. Wood's great love story. . . . The leading part is filled by no less a person than Miss Katherine Hathaway. . . . Miss Hathaway is said by critics to equal the art of Miss Ada Gray in all particulars. (*Coldwater Daily Reporter*, April 27, 1910)

Three days later, a two-column newspaper advertisement for this production of *East Lynne* proclaimed, "Not a cheap abridged stock company version but a complete and accurate enacting of the original text, with special scenery and wardrobe."

Rip Van Winkle was first performed in Coldwater in 1885 and was given two more showings that same year. The Waite's Union Square Comedy Company presented all three productions during three separate residencies.

Faust, another often produced favorite, made its Tibbits Opera House debut in 1893 and reappeared on that stage in eleven more productions over the next sixteen years. According to the local reviewer, the Porter J. White Company's production of *Faust* in 1898 was less than auspicious:

> Last evening "Faust" was presented . . . to a good audience but it was not up to the standard of previous productions. . . . Mr. White's presentation of Mephisto was fair . . . but Frank MacDonald as Faust did not look his part. The support was quite ordinary. (*Coldwater Daily Reporter*, November 1, 1898)

Thanks to technology, the Porter J. White Company redeemed itself when it came back the next season as the *Daily Reporter* pronounced that it was "the best spectacular scenic and electrical production of 'Faust' ever given in Coldwater."

FIGURE 19. Eliza crossing the ice was a popular image used on countless *Uncle Tom's Cabin* posters over a sixty-year period. This poster advertises George Peck's grand revival of *Stetson's Uncle Tom's Cabin* with preshow parades, brass bands, and a chorus of singers and dancers. (Publisher: A. S. Sear's Union Square Print, N.Y., 1886. Retrieved from the Library of Congress.)

"Are the Stars Out Tonight?"

Dames, "I Only Have Eyes for You," lyrics by Al Dubin, music by Harry Warren, 1934

Many of the touring productions that played at the Tibbits Opera House boasted the participation of well-known celebrities. Among the stars that appeared in Coldwater were *Francesca Janauschek in *Guy Mannering* and *Macbeth*, *Thomas Keene in *Richard III*, *Macbeth*, and *Julius Caesar*; *Robert Mantell in *Monbars*, *Secret Warrant*, and *The Dagger and the Cross*; and *Hortense Rhea in *Yvonne* and *Much Ado About Nothing*.

All but forgotten today, George L. Fox (1825–77) was a major celebrity in the mid-nineteenth century. Some historians consider him to have been the first major star of the

FIGURE 20. A lithograph featuring George L. Fox surrounded by caricatures of him in his *Humpty Dumpty* clown costume and makeup. (Publisher: Henry A. Thomas Artistic Litho. Co., N.Y., ca. 1875. Retrieved from the Library of Congress.)

American musical theatre. In 1868, Fox wrote and produced a uniquely American form of pantomime titled *Humpty Dumpty* in which he played a character called The Clown.

The show and Fox's performance were so popular that *Humpty Dumpty* managed to keep the ancient art of pantomime alive long after it had gone out of fashion as a form of popular entertainment. It was the most commercially successful pantomime ever presented in New York City.

The first act of *Humpty Dumpty* contains spoken dialogue and songs, but at one point the characters are rendered mute. In their silent state, they embark on a tour of New York City that is executed in pantomime. They occasionally regain their voices just long enough to perform a musical number.

George L. Fox died five years before the Tibbits Opera House opened. However, his creation lived on in touring productions that played across the country for the remainder of the nineteenth century and into the twentieth. Coldwater first saw the anachronistic work in 1883. Over the years, eight more productions of the pantomime were produced with various actors in the role of The Clown, each receiving star billing. George H. Adams, "America's Greatest Clown," starred in *Humpty Dumpty* in Coldwater, Red Jacket, and Manistee.

"Father and Son"

Modest Suzanne, lyrics by Harry B. Smith and Robert B. Smith, music by Jean Gilbert, 1912

Kit, the Arkansas Traveler, one of the most produced plays of the nineteenth century, was commissioned by and originally starred Francis "Frank" Chanfrau (1824–84). Chanfrau was already an established star when he came up with an idea for a new vehicle for himself, *Kit, the Arkansas Traveler*. The title was inspired by the familiar folk tune "The Arkansas Traveler." The play, a melodrama, begins when the villain kidnaps the wife and daughter of the hero, Kit Redding. Years pass during which time Kit has various encounters with the villain, not realizing that he is the kidnapper. Eventually, Kit is reunited with his daughter who tells him that her mother has died. She identifies the villain, Kit confronts his enemy, they struggle, our hero prevails, the villain dies, and Kit and daughter presumably live happily ever after.

Although Frank Chanfrau did not play Kit in Coldwater, in 1891 his son, Henry Chanfrau (1858–1901), did. Young Chanfrau stepped into the role after his father's death in 1884 and performed it throughout the country until 1899. According to the local press, the apple had not fallen far from the tree:

> At the opera house last evening Mr. Chanfrau appeared with his fine company in the laughable and thrilling comedy drama, "Kit, the Arkansas Traveler." The character of Kit as personated by Mr. Chanfrau was good. Mr. Chanfrau has many ways in his acting to remind one of the pleasant recollections of his father. (*Coldwater Republican*, December 11, 1891)

In its review of this performance the *Courier* pointed out that the play had been around for a while: "it has been before the public upwards of twenty years continuously—the play still retains its popularity and always attracts a crowd."

FIGURE 21. Three unidentified characters played by three unidentified actors in an undated production photo of *Kit, the Arkansas Traveler*. But what we do know is that Frank Chanfrau, who originated the role of Kit, performed it hundreds of times over a fifteen-year period and, for his efforts, earned an estimated $65,000 that today would be approximately $1,685,000. (Billy Rose Theatre Division, the New York Public Library Digital Collections.)

"Brush Up Your Shakespeare"

Kiss Me, Kate, lyrics and music by Cole Porter, 1948

Over the years, plays by Shakespeare were presented intermittently at the Tibbits Opera House, and when the production featured a major star business was better than when presented by a stock company without a well-known actor in the leading role. In April 1905, Manager Jackson had

FIGURE 22. From Storms, *The Players Blue Book*, 1901: "No American singer or comedienne has wider fame and favor than Miss Fay Templeton." She is seen here in a pose that is uncharacteristically demure. As a performer, she was known for her exuberant personality, comedic versatility, and throaty singing voice that, combined, catapulted her to stardom. (Photographer and date unknown. Billy Rose Theatre Division, the New York Public Library Digital Collections.)

an opportunity to book a stock company's production of *The Merchant of Venice*. The newspaper reported that the company needed "liberal patronage" because of the "investiture" it had made to create this lavish production. Consequently, Jackson threw down the gauntlet. The newspaper revealed that "Manager Jackson feels that if the support of a number of the better class of theatergoers is secured, success will be assured." The better class of theatergoers came through, and "their hearty cooperation have succeeded in securing a real Shakespearean treat."

The following month the Joseph Shipman Company presented *Twelfth Night*. Mr. Shipman, the New York manager, promised a sumptuous revival of the comedy and boasted that his was "the finest theatrical organization ever offered for the approval of the critical American public."

The 1912 theatre season at the Tibbits opened with the Ben Greet Players production of *A Midsummer Night's Dream* augmented with the music Felix Mendelssohn composed for it fifty years earlier.

"Only for You"

Hitchy-Koo of 1920, lyrics by Anne Calder and Glen MacDonough, music by Jerome Kern, 1920

Based on available production histories, there were performances by an emerging star and the matriarch of an acting dynasty as well as two popular plays presented at the Tibbits Opera House that were not seen in Red Jacket or Manistee. One play was an old warhorse and the other was hot off the presses.

An Emerging Star

Fay Templeton (1865–1939) began her long, successful career as a comic soubrette and later developed into a popular character actress. In 1883, at the age of eighteen, she made her only appearance at the Tibbits Opera House in *Mascotte*, a comic opera about a young girl who has the ability to bring good fortune to all she meets as long as she remains a virgin.

On December 15, 1882, the *Coldwater Republican* presented Miss Templeton with an early holiday present in the form of a testament to her talent:

> Fay Templeton steps upon the stage with a smirk and a smile and wins her way into our hearts. . . . Her metropolitan debut was made at the Grand Opera House, New York, when at nine years of age she gave the very best representation of Puck in Shakespeare's "Midsummer's Night" has ever been known. With pleasure we announce that this charming artiste is booked for Tibbits's Opera-house in February.

Two years after her appearance in Coldwater she was starring on Broadway in the 1885 revival of *Evangeline* playing the male lover, Gabriel, a performance that launched her forty-eight-year Broadway career. In 1898, when the comedy team of Joe Weber and Lew Fields opened their famous Weber and Fields Music Hall, they hired Templeton as one of their star attractions. Starting with *Hurly-Burly*, she introduced songs and participated in comedy sketches in five Weber and Fields productions, one a year until 1902.

In 1906, George M. Cohan wrote the leading role in the musical comedy *Forty-Five Minutes from Broadway* for her. The role of Buttercup in Gilbert and Sullivan's *H.M.S. Pinafore* became a staple in her repertoire later in her career. She played it on the road and in four Broadway revivals between 1914 and 1931, and in 1933, at the age of sixty-eight, she made her last Broadway appearance in Jerome Kern's *Roberta*.

The Theatre Matriarch

Georgiana "Georgie" Drew Barrymore (1856–93) came from a distinguished family of actors, the Drews. In 1876, she married Maurice Barrymore, and together they begat a dynasty of actors that included their three children, Lionel, Ethel, and John Barrymore; two grandchildren, Diana and John Drew Barrymore; and great-granddaughter, Drew Barrymore.

On February 29, 1889, "Georgie" Drew Barrymore came to Coldwater starring in the play *A Possible Case*. While the local critic gave her costumes a rave, he was less complimentary about the actress stating that her acting style was

> perhaps a trifle more of the Delsartian school of elocution than is requisite for the most pleasing and happy effects. In costuming the part, however, Miss Barrymore fully demonstrated her possession of a ravishingly beautiful and becoming wardrobe. (*Coldwater Republican*, March 1, 1889)

FIGURE 23. In 1927 Georgiana Drew Barrymore and her grown children, Lionel, Ethel, and John Barrymore, were the inspiration for the not-very-subtly disguised characters in the Broadway comedy *The Royal Family* by George S. Kaufman and Edna Ferber. The authors could never have offered a good-faith claim that "any similarity to persons living or dead is purely coincidental." The play enjoyed three New York revivals, the most recent in 2009. (Photographer: Sarony, Major, & Knapp, Lith. New York, date unknown. Billy Rose Theatre Division, the New York Public Library for the Performing Arts, Astor, Lenox, and Tilden Foundations.)

FIGURE 24. Fay Templeton, in a more characteristic pose than that seen in figure 22, as Gabriel, a "trouser role," in the 1885 Broadway revival of *Evangeline*. Young women playing young men dressed in tights or trousers was a popular theatrical convention at the time (Photographer: Napoleon Saron. Billy Rose Theatre Division, the New York Public Library for the Performing Arts, Astor, Lenox, and Tilden Foundations.)

The Moneymaking Warhorse

When the musical extravaganza *Evangeline; or, The Belle of Acadia* was presented at the Tibbits Opera House on November 6, 1891, it was already seventeen years old. It opened in 1874 at New York City's Niblo's Garden to negative reviews. The show then played in Boston where it was rewritten, recast, restaged, and became a hit. What followed were five New York City revivals and a series of tours that kept the show playing somewhere in America for thirty years.

The musical's creators—Edward E. Rice, music, and J. Cheever Goodwin, book and lyrics—decided to write an American burlesque that did not rely on the "spice of vice," as one reviewer put it. As the title would suggest, the plot was based on Henry Wadsworth Longfellow's poem *Evangeline, A Tale of Acadia*, but the finished product turned out to be more of a parody of the original poetic saga than a dramatic adaptation of it. When *Evangeline* played in Coldwater, the *Courier* stated that the show was "so far removed from Longfellow's pathetic lines that one could scarcely see the resemblance to the original."

Because the connotation of "burlesque" was moving from parody to "girlie show," Rice and Goodwin dubbed the work an "American Opera-Bouffe Extravaganza." *Evangeline* was intended to be family-friendly fare. However, the producers did succumb to the proven drawing power of the display of female limbs as seen in burlesque. Consequently, they cast a female soubrette as the male juvenile, Gabriel, Evangeline's beau, which required her to wear tights.

Longfellow's original tale is of two lovers in Nova Scotia who are separated and spend years in search of one another. In their version, Rice and Goodwin enhanced the sad story with the addition of exotic locations, a dancing heifer, and an amorous whale.

One of the most popular characters in the piece was the Lone Fisherman who never opened his mouth. James S.

Maffitt originated the role and played little else during the course of his career.

> James S. Maffitt in his great creation of that classic in pantomime, the Lone Fisherman, is still playing his old part, and creates as much mirth with his fishing line, telescope and toy boat now as he did seventeen years ago at Niblo's Garden on the opening night. (*Coldwater Republican*, November 3, 1891)

At some point, Goodwin left the show and Rice became its sole producer. *Evangeline* became his cash cow. Whenever one of his other projects failed, Rice would update the show, add new songs and comedy bits, and send *Evangeline* out on the road one more time.

Hot Off the Presses

In April 1912 Tibbits patrons had the opportunity to see a drama with a plot that was not only ripped from the national headlines, but also strongly connected to their own hometown. A stock company, the Alvarado Players, was in residence for four days presenting a series of contemporary plays including *Captured by Wireless*. The play recounted the saga of Dr. Hawley Harvey Crippen, a Coldwater native, who was hanged in 1910 after having been found guilty of the murder of his wife.

Crippen committed the murder in England, then with his mistress, who was disguised as a boy, boarded a ship headed for Canada. The ship's captain sent a communication

FIGURE 25. In *Evangeline*, James S. Maffitt performed the role of the Lone Fisherman in silence. He was the only mime to rival George L. Fox (*Humpty Dumpty*) in popularity. He played the fisherman in *Evangeline* touring productions and revivals for approximately two decades. (Photographer and date unknown. Billy Rose Theatre Division, the New York Public Library for the Performing Arts, Astor, Lenox, and Tilden Foundations.)

by telegraph to Scotland Yard reporting that he suspected the runaways were on board. Responding to the message a Scotland Yard inspector boarded a faster ship and was waiting for Crippen when he reached his destination. It was the first time that the relatively new wireless communication technology was employed to apprehend a criminal.

Take It from the Top!

Meanwhile, back in 1882, touring theatre productions often featuring marketable stars were not the only events that took place at the Tibbits Opera House. From its very beginning until the time when bookings were ruled by moving pictures, in addition to touring theatre company productions, the opera house presented stock companies, mystics and magicians, minstrel shows, animal acts, athletic events, concerts, and lectures. Following are some examples from the other entertainment and educational genres that attracted patrons to the opera house for more than thirty-five years.

"Stock Report"

Put It in Writing, lyrics by Fred Ebb, music by Norman L. Martin, 1963

Single, one-night-only productions were not the only theatre performances offered to Tibbits patrons between 1882 and 1919; numerous stock companies that were in residence for several days presenting several plays also frequented the opera house. In 1883, one year after the A. O. Miller Company performed at the playhouse, the second stock company arrived. It was the Bella Moore Combination that over three days presented three plays: *Fogg's Ferry*, *Pygmalion and Galatia*, and *Nan, the Good-for-Nothing*. Next to move in was Waite's Union Square Comedy Company that was in residence four times in 1885. Each visit was for six days during which time the company showcased six plays: contemporary comedies, melodramas, and a few perpetual crowd-pleasers that in addition to *Rip Van Winkle* and *Hazel Kirke*, included the temperance drama *Ten Nights in a Bar Room*.

The Canada-based Travernier Dramatic Company was in residence twice in Coldwater. The troupe toured Canada and Midwestern regions of the United States with its own costumes, scenery, and calcium lights. The company first performed at the Tibbits Opera House for six days in 1887, and returned for another week's visit two years later. The leading lady, Ida Van Cortland, was a highly regarded actress who could access a wide range of roles. Her repertoire on tour primarily consisted of comedies and melodramas with provocative titles such as *A Dangerous Woman*, *A Shadowed Life*, and *Caught in the Web*. The drama critic from the *Coldwater Republican* had great praise for the actress:

> Miss Van Cortland . . . is an actress of great versatility, appearing in a different character each evening, and seems to be at home in either heavy or light parts . . . all who fail to see Miss Van Cortland and her company will miss a rare treat.

The anticipated arrival of the Majestic Stock Company generated the greatest amount of hype to promote a stock company ever seen in the Coldwater press. It all began with a large, bold advertisement in the *Coldwater Daily Reporter* announcing that the company was to be in residence for a week beginning August 21, 1905:

> By far the greatest organization that has ever visited this city will be seen in the Majestic Stock Company. This attraction will long be remembered by Coldwater theatre-goers as being the best they have ever seen, and as they have been playing all summer, every member is letter perfect in his respective part.

In addition to the advertisement and the article there was also a two-column drawing of Mr. Oscar F. Cook, the stock company's manager. Two days later, in the same newspaper, there was a two-column drawing of Miss Louise Keene, "Leading Lady of the Majestic Stock Company," accompanied by a listing of the various artists and acts that the audience could expect to enjoy:

> Foremost among the list is Alice Alva, the lady with the clarinet. Miss Alva is the only lady in the world playing a "double bell euphonium" and renders difficult selections on a South American fiddle. (*Coldwater Daily Reporter*, August 14, 1905)

Over the next few days, in addition to announcing that band concerts will be given before each performance and ladies will be admitted for half price opening night, the newspaper ran a photo of Solora, "The Wonderful Electric Transformation Dancer," who used twelve large electric lamps to perfect her act.

All was for naught. The *Coldwater Daily Reporter* printed the last item pertaining to the Majestic Stock Company's imminent visit on August 22: "Owing to the failure of the Majestic Stock Company to reach town last night their further engagement has been canceled." Three months later, the company cashed in its rain check. Perhaps to mitigate the disappointment caused by their canceled performance, Manager Cook attempted to provide prospective audience members with more entertainment for their buck when the company returned:

> To avoid the long waits between the acts necessitated in the production, Manager Cook has secured a coterie of high-class vaudeville features, which will be introduced at each of the performances . . . headed by the three Ferguson Bros. and their dog. (*Coldwater Daily Reporter*, November 13, 1905)

So many of the stock companies presented the same plays that prospective ticket-buyers eventually became less enthused when a company's residency was announced. In a September 29, 1905, newspaper advertisement, Hyde's Theatre Party acknowledged that audiences were "tired of mediocre plays, badly acted and staged." Not even the ladies-free night and a promise of gifts enticed patrons to the theater to see a play they had seen many times before unless, of course, the play was *Uncle Tom's Cabin*. Consequently, several stock companies endeavored to present something new and unique and at popular prices.

In May 1910 the Powell & Cohan's Musical Comedy Company was in Coldwater for a week presenting seven musical plays. The Chicago-based musical theatre producers found themselves competing with both vaudeville (aka "the two-a-day") and the motion picture industry for audiences and income. To combat the situation, they sent out a company to play a different musical comedy every night for a week at reasonable prices. The managers claimed to have invested $10,000 in the enterprise.

The Edward Russell Players were in Coldwater in 1911 presenting "the latest Broadway plays—no melodramas. None of this high class repertoire has ever been seen before at cheap prices which should make it a strong inducement to the public to see them."

Culhane's Comedians presented a repertory of plays enhanced by "High Class Vaudeville Acts." They announced that the ticket price would be ten cents for any seat in the house, making it cheaper to go to the opera house than to stay at home.

By 1915, touring theatre companies were struggling to hold their own against the tide of films that were flooding venues that had traditionally featured only live entertainment. Movies were featured so prominently at opera houses that the company and the theater were obliged to make it clear what was on the stage as opposed to what was on the screen. When the Rolly Polly Girls Musical Comedy Company came to town the advertisement exclaimed, "This is Not a Picture Show!" However, "Motion Pictures Will Open and Close the Show."

If a combination of plays and vaudeville did not distract audiences from moving pictures or their "flicker fascination," perhaps a little magic might. In November 1915 the Nevison Comedy-Drama Tabloid and Vaudeville Company offered eight plays and, as an extra-added attraction, the appearance of Mysterious Marie. "The famous mental wonder will appear at every performance, answering any question concerning business, lost friends, missing articles, love affairs or anything you wish to know."

Something for Everyone

When it came to mystics and magicians, the Tibbits Opera House booked its fair share. Spiritualist Anna Eva Fay made two appearances, one in 1885 and one nine years later. There were séances with Vera the Medium and with the Mysterious Oneida, as well as performances by Reno, "The Great Magician"; Santanelli and Professor Sheppard, both hypnotists; Richards the Wizard, with "The Mystery Sensation of the Age"; and Herman the Great, whose act included both occult phenomena and vaudeville.

On December 26, 1910, Ita the Spiritualist took center stage. Five days prior to her appearance the *Coldwater Daily Reporter* explained, "Ita is the 15-year old California Mentalist, who has attracted attention all over the world and is still a problem for scientists and scholars to solve." Ita traveled with a vaudeville company that filled out the evening with a program of specialty acts.

In January 1884, "Buffalo Bill" Cody and his Cowboys rode into town to perform at the opera house. In addition to the usual reenactments of cowboy and Indian skirmishes, sharpshooter exhibitions, death-defying horsemanship, and rope tricks, they offered free camel rides. They were back in 1911, but this time on film. The audience could experience everything the cowboy company had to offer on screen, "realistic and true to life," instead of live on stage—everything but the free camel rides.

Professor W. W. Chapman's Animal Circus with his "school of educated animals" arrived for two days of performances in 1908. Ponies, dogs, and roosters were the pupils in his school. The Heber Brothers Winter Circus featured acting dogs and monkeys in a playlet titled *City of Dogville*. With the stage cleared of all scenery and paraphernalia, several equestrians brought their trained horses to Coldwater for exhibition at the playhouse.

With the opera chairs removed and the false floor in position, various athletic activities took place at the opera house: boxing and wrestling matches as well as roller-skating. The grand opening of the Tibbits Opera House Roller Skating Rink took place on June 5, 1883. The organizers of the event ordered a wagonload of skates.

A few boxing matches were booked into the Tibbits Opera House in the early years. Most of those events were traditional matches, but two famous pugilists did more.

FIGURE 26. John L. Sullivan, "Heavyweight Champion of the World," was one of the most successful bare-knuckle fighters of the period. He is pictured here in a characteristic pose. (Artist unknown, ca. 1887. Retrieved from the Library of Congress.)

"Two Handsome Men"

Mutt and Jeff, lyrics and music by Leroy Brown, Richard Carroll, Joseph Conoly, T. A. Hammel, Frank Montgomery, Phil Worde, 1922)

John L. Sullivan (1858–1918), a boxer turned actor, began his career in the ring in 1878. After forty-one bouts, he retired from boxing following his defeat to James J. "Gentleman Jim" Corbett in 1892—his only loss.

He was first seen at the Tibbits Opera House in 1885 when he was on tour with the Lester & Allen Minstrels. His act in the variety show was to assume classic postures of Greek and Roman statuary. A reviewer thought that Lester & Allen presented "an average minstrel performance," but "Sullivan was very good in his statue business that drew forth deserved applause."

He was back on the Tibbits stage in 1893, this time in a play, *The Man from Boston*. The last act was the main event.

It took place in a gymnasium complete with a boxing ring where Sullivan displayed his physique and his boxing skill.

> People took Mr. Sullivan's adoption to the stage as a joke at first, but his sincere efforts to become a painstaking actor soon won recognition . . . in the last act he appears in the familiar habiliments of the prize-ring . . . and the audience have a chance to howl themselves hoarse over the muscular development of the man who held the championship so many years. (*Coldwater Republican*, December 22, 1893)

His next trip to Coldwater was with *A Trip Across the Ocean* in 1898, and once again, in a scene set in a gymnasium, the former heavyweight boxer was able to demonstrate his pugilistic prowess.

The champ was back in 1905 to present a lecture-demonstration that included a six-boxer exhibition, a sparring match between Sullivan and James McCormack, as well as a full vaudeville program.

Nine years after Sullivan had appeared in *The Man from Boston*, Robert Fitzsimmons took a page from the Sullivan playbook and presented a production with a very similar last act. Trading on his celebrity as a prizefighter, Fitzsimmons toured the country in a play titled *A Fight for Love*. It was advertised as "A Dramatic and Scientific Event" starring the "Grand Old Man of the Prize Ring" and his wife, Julia May Gifford, "an actress of much emotional ability." In addition to his wife, Fitzsimmons traveled with his 190-pound pet lion that was said to be as gentle as a kitten and allowed anyone to pet it.

When *A Fight for Love* performed in Coldwater on January 26, 1905, it was apparent that Fitzsimmons was an athlete and not an actor—although he gave it his best shot. The highlight of the production was the last act boxing match that predictably resulted in "Fitz" besting his opponent.

By 1907, live boxers in the ring were replaced with live boxers on the screen. In February of that year the opera house screened a motion picture of the historic Gans-Nelson fight that awarded the largest purse ever given to any fighter up to that time, $32,500 that today would be approximately $809,000. The following month boxing enthusiasts could see moving pictures of the O'Brien-Burns twenty-round match. Tommy Burns was boxing on the screen again in 1909, this time against Jack Johnson in a match that was photographed in Sidney, Australia. A live commentator described every detail of the fight as it occurred on the screen.

Evidently, live wrestling matches were more popular with Coldwater citizens than filmed boxing matches as the opera house management booked them with great regularity. For a fifteen-year period, from 1885 to 1900, there was at least one wrestling match scheduled annually and, in some years, as many as three.

On December 11, 1913, the *Coldwater Daily Reporter* announced that everything was ready for the two big wrestling matches scheduled to take place at the opera house after a performance by the Jardin de Paris Girls. The first match was between Heinze and Bowser. Paul Bowser, called the wrestling demon, promised to pay $25.00 to any local man he could not throw in fifteen minutes. The other bout was between Miss Bryan and Miss Livingston, the champion female wrestler of the world. Cora Livingston (aka Mrs. Paul

Bowser) offered a similar carrot—"$25.00 to any lady athlete she fails to throw in ten minutes."

"Music in the Air"

A Hero is Born, lyrics by Agnes Morgan, music by Lehman Engel, 1937

Music was definitely in the air at the opera house even before it opened its doors for the premiere performance. Barton S. Tibbits was not only involved with the construction, furnishing, and decoration of his new playhouse, he also procured the musical support necessary to present first-class theatrical entertainment. He purchased a grand piano from C. J. Whitney of Detroit as well as instruments and uniforms for the opera house musicians. In January 1883, he hired local music professor George W. Klock to serve as music director.

Five days before the official opening of the theater, the twelve-member Opera House Orchestra presented a concert; the press observed that under Professor Klock's direction, the orchestra was the best music organization in the city. The following year, Klock was the music director and conductor for a production of *H.M.S. Pinafore* at the opera house featuring a fourteen-piece orchestra and a chorus of fifty, all local talent.

> At eight o'clock a large and fashionable audience had assembled, the orchestra took their seats, Prof. Klock waved his baton, and the music incident to the piece commenced. Miss Cora Ferris was greeted with rounds of applause as she appeared in the role of "Little Buttercup," her make up was very fine, and her singing . . . called forth much applause and many beautiful floral offerings. (*Coldwater Republican*, June 15, 1883)

When Barton Tibbits moved Klock from the position of music director to the position of theater manager in January 1884, the *Courier* announced that the Opera House Band had a new leader, James Rhodes, who had a mission:

> Mr. Rhodes says that while the new band will not number so many members he will labor hard to build it to a higher state of perfection—in fact, he expects to make it one of the best bands in the state if hard drill and thorough practice will effect the purpose.

The Tibbits Opera House was the venue for many locally generated music events including a concert that played on December 1, 1909, that must have been very hot as two female audience members fainted during the performance.

Among the nonlocal music groups that were seen and heard in Coldwater from 1883 to 1919 were the Children's Concert Company; the Dunbar Company, a male quartet who were both singers and bell ringers; the Silver Toned Quartette and Colored Company; and the Dixie Chorus Concert presented "Epic of the Negro, a Story of 300 years." The YMCA Entertainment Series sponsored many of these concerts.

Some of the nationally renowned music groups that performed at the opera house during that same period include the Boston Symphony Orchestra, the Chicago Symphony Orchestra, and the popular John Philip Sousa band.

FIGURE 27. While still a teenager, John Philip Sousa was an apprentice with the U.S. Marine Band. After his apprenticeship, he played in a theater pit orchestra and then returned to the Marine Band as the director, a position he held for twelve years before forming his own band. (Photographer unknown, ca. 1895. Retrieved from the Library of Congress.)

"It Must Be Great to Be a General but I'd Rather Lead the Band"

Miss Nobody from Starland, lyrics and music by Paul Rubens, 1910)

John Philip Sousa (1854–1932), "the March King," and his band became the best-known and most popular musical organization during the forty-year period that they toured the country and the world. It is estimated that during that period Sousa conducted over fifteen thousand concerts.

The maestro and his musicians were particularly welcome in Coldwater where, for a period of time, they performed annually. Over a three-day period prior to the band's September 22, 1905, appearance at the opera house, the *Coldwater Daily Reporter* ran three very short human-interest stories about Sousa. They relate how with charm and wit Sousa dealt with a neighbor who persistently practiced the piano badly; a dirty street urchin; and a spiteful, jealous fellow musician. The tales humanizing the military music man may have been total fiction.

As a composer, Sousa was responsible for 137 marches including a regional favorite, "Pride of the Wolverines," dedicated by the composer to the city of Detroit. He also composed numerous suites, overtures, and dances and provided the score for fifteen operettas; the one most often produced at Michigan opera houses and elsewhere was *El Capitan*.

The fifty-member John Philip Sousa band would often give a matinee concert at the Tibbits Opera House before moving on to Detroit or Toledo where it would present an evening concert the same day. Despite the fact that the Tibbits concerts were usually in the afternoon, they attracted an enthusiastic crowd.

> Sousa's band drew a very large audience at the opera house yesterday. Sousa's interpretation of musical numbers is distinctly an art of his own and a more graceful orchestra conductor or a leader who is more gracious to please is seldom seen. (*Courier and Republican*, February 23, 1900)

"Melody Makers"

Earl Carroll's Vanities of 1926, lyrics by Grace Henry, music by Morris Hamilton, 1926

Not all of the music groups were comprised of men only; the Cincinnati Ladies Cremona Orchestra, the Boston Ladies Symphony Orchestra, and the Swedish National Ladies Orchestra each made music on the Tibbits stage. Collegiate groups were also welcome to perform at the playhouse and included the Hillsdale, Oberlin, and Olivet College Glee Clubs, the University of Michigan Glee and Banjo Club, as well as the Harvard Quartette.

Among the world-famous performers booked into the opera house was Italian singer Giuseppe Campanari.

> Campanari the Divine," as he is called in Italy, his native country, is after all a most ordinary man to meet and for one of his prominence in the musical world is not the least bit set up over either his reputation or his attainments. (*Coldwater Daily Reporter*, November 13, 1910)

When the interviewer asked Campanari why he had given up his previous career as a celebrated cellist to perform as a singer, he responded:

> My voice is an instrument the same as is a cello. When I sing I play on my voice and the effect is far better than it is when I play on my cello . . . my voice can make you laugh and cry.

FIGURE 28. As a young man, Eduard Remenyi was exiled from Austria because of his participation in the Hungarian insurrection. According to his later press release, when he was in the army his superior officers so admired him as a national treasure that he was never assigned to an area or position that would put him in harm's way. (Artist and date unknown. Music Division, the New York Public Library Digital Collections.)

"He's Ravin', Let Him Rave"

Mother Goose, lyrics and music by George M. Cohan, 1903

Perhaps the most prestigious musical artist to perform for Coldwater audiences was Hungarian-born violinist Eduard Remenyi (1828?–1896). Remenyi began his musical education at the Vienna Conservatory, and by 1853 he was touring Europe presenting concerts with Johannes Brahms. The next year, he was appointed Queen Victoria's solo violinist, and in

1860 he accepted a similar position at the court of Emperor Franz Joseph of Austria.

Between the years of 1865 and 1879, he toured throughout the world and became known as a violin virtuoso with a unique performance style. One reviewer commented that Remenyi was "in love with his violin and we have seen him stroke and kiss it as he left the stage." The object of his affection was created in 1818 by an artisan of the Stradivarius school.

Remenyi eventually took up residence in the United States where he appeared on the Tibbits Opera House stage before an enthusiastic albeit small audience.

> Considering it the height of presumption for us to attempt a criticism of his playing, we simply content ourselves with saying that we look upon him as one of the best, if not the best violinist in the world. (*Courier*, November 10, 1883)

He performed in Coldwater again in 1896. This time, not only did he face another small audience, but he also had to deal with lost luggage and a disruptive child.

> The Remenyi Concert Company was much embarrassed Tuesday night by having their baggage missent. The members had to appear in their traveling dress. . . . Perhaps it was the baggage and not the disposition of Remenyi that made him appear sour and churlish when he was called upon for an encore, and his marked displeasure at a child that happened to make a slight noise while he was playing was really boorish. He deliberately put his fiddle under his arm and left the stage like a crusty old curmudgeon. Coldwater acknowledges his perfection of art but it don't approve of all the idiosyncrasies of a stuffy old crank. (*Courier*, January 25, 1896)

"Make Up Your Mind"

The International Revue, lyrics by Dorothy Fields, music by Jimmy McHugh, 1930

The *Coldwater Republican* reviewer was of two opinions when he considered local theatergoers' level of music appreciation. In the March 23, 1883, review of the operetta *Mascotte* starring Fay Templeton the reviewer applauded the public: "The large audience assembled at the Opera-house Tuesday evening to listen to *Mascotte* attested the fact that Coldwater is a music-loving city." However, in the review of Eduard Remenyi's violin concert presented eight months later, the reviewer admitted that he was disappointed at the small audience turnout. "Coldwater is evidently not a musical city."

Opera diva Jessie Bartlett Davis (1860–1905) performed in concert at the opera house on November 23, 1904. She had appeared in several operettas on Broadway and was best known for her performance in the original 1891 production of *Robin Hood* in which she introduced the iconic wedding song "Oh, Promise Me" (lyrics by Clement Scott, music by Reginald De Koven). The song sold over a million copies of sheet music in one year and for decades was the secular song most often performed at weddings.

True to form, the indecisive critic couldn't make up his mind, and his review of the diva's performance was mixed:

A very large audience assembled, occupying every seat in the house, the attraction being a concert by Jessie Bartlett Davis. . . . Miss Davis sang delightfully, and yet to those who had heard her in days gone by she was a disappointment. (*Courier and Republican*, November 28, 1904)

"Talk about This—Talk about That"

Sweethearts, lyrics by Robert B. Smith, music by Victor Herbert, 1913)

From the day the Tibbits Opera House opened it was a source of entertainment, education, and information. In addition to the theatre productions and concerts there were lectures and political rallies scheduled every season. One of the first lectures delivered from the stage was "The Origin of the Aborigines of North America," presented in 1883 by Barton S. Tibbits's father, Reverend Allen Tibbits.

On October 4, 1888, orator Anna Dickinson (1842–1932) delivered a speech on "Republican Issues of the Day" at the opera house. Unfortunately, the venue was not large enough to hold the crowd that had gathered, and many people were turned away.

As a lecturer she was nationally known and so admired that in New York City five thousand people attended when she spoke there on behalf of Republican candidates. In addition to supporting the Republican Party, her other lecture topics included antislavery, women's rights, and temperance. In 1864, she addressed the U.S. House of Representatives, the first woman to do so, and received a standing ovation from the congressmen.

FIGURE 29. American contralto Jessie Bartlett Davis made her stage debut as Buttercup in *H.M.S. Pinafore*. During her career she donned tights or trousers to play males in several operas. Among those roles were Siebel, the boy in love with Marguerite in Gounod's *Faust*; and Alan-a-Dale in the comic opera *Robin Hood*. She and her husband, theater manager William J. Davis, were part owners of Chicago's Iroquois Theatre at the time of its devastating fire. (Photographer: Morrison Studio, Chicago, ca. 1894. Billy Rose Theatre Division, the New York Public Library Digital Collections.)

The day before she spoke in Coldwater, she had delivered a lecture to a large crowd in Adrian sponsored by the Grand Army of the Republic, a fraternal organization of veterans of the Civil War's Union Army. The *Adrian Daily Times and Expositor* published an excerpt from that speech:

Someone said I have no right to wave the "bloody shirt." That I hide myself behind my woman's dresses and

FIGURE 30. Lecturer, actress, playwright, abolitionist, and suffragette Anna Dickinson, who played the title role in *Hamlet* in New York City, was one of the most eloquent and successful orators of her time. (Photographer and date unknown. Billy Rose Theatre Division, the New York Public Library Digital Collections.)

> should not talk to old soldiers. Is that so? Let us see. I was sent in '63 by the central committee of Pennsylvania, into the southwestern part of that state, among the northern wing of Lee's army . . . because no man would go. I was stoned, rotten-egged, and the hair on the right side of my head singed by a Minnie ball. I am an old soldier, and I stand before you to-night, old soldiers, because I have been under fire.

The Adrian newspaper went on to report that "Miss Dickinson closed amid loud and long continued applause and cheering." The Coldwater newspaper reported: "Though she had a severe cold, making it exceedingly difficult to talk, she held her audience to the close."

On February 20, 1892, a lecture titled "Abraham Lincoln" delivered by Robert C. Ingersoll drew patrons from communities outside of Branch County. The press described Ingersoll as a "matchless orator."

Talks about foreign countries and foreign travel were popular and frequent: "Travels in Equatorial Africa"; "Camp Life in Eastern Siberia"; and "Up the Rhine and Over the Alps with a Knapsack." "Hard Times, Their Cause and Cure," which was accompanied by a stereopticon presentation, was one of several lectures that dealt with social issues. The following lecture titles indicate that there were also talks of a more whimsical nature: "The Moon in Fact and Fancy"; "Peculiar People"; and "American Nuts, Cracked and Uncracked."

From November 1900 through March 1901, St. Agatha's Guild of St. Mark's Episcopal Church sponsored a series of eight entertainment programs that included both lectures and concerts. The YMCA Entertainment Series also sponsored both lectures and concerts that were presented at the Tibbits Opera House. On two occasions, James Whitcomb Riley gave poetry readings sponsored by the YMCA. Other events presented under the auspices of that organization include a demonstration by an accomplished crayon artist, a performance by an impersonator of great men, and a concert by the College Singing Girls. In a headline, the newspaper reported that the College Girls were "A Great Hit. This Number of the YMCA Entertainment Course was an Exceptionally Fine One."

On January 5, 1905, renowned poet Edmund Vance Cooke presented a monologue, delivered a lecture, and read several of his poems, and in 1909 the eminent attorney Clarence Darrow spoke from behind the Tibbits lectern.

The opera house hosted rallies for the Democratic, Republican, and Prohibition parties as well as political lectures delivered by governors, congressmen, and candidates for government offices.

"Father, Dear Father, Come Home with Me Now"

"Come Home, Father," lyrics and music by Henry Clay Work, 1864

Temperance was a hot topic in the late nineteenth and early twentieth centuries and elicited a number of lectures, plays, and a public discussion that took place at the opera house. In 1892 the talk was titled "The License Liquor Traffic and Its Attendant Evils." Twenty years later, in 1912, it was still an issue. That year there were two lectures: "Fighting the Liquor

Traffic" and "Should Saloons be Banished from the State?" Also in 1912, the Honorable John G. Woolley, a presidential candidate for the Prohibition Party, spoke to an enthusiastic audience.

Nationally known orator Sam Small spoke to the issue in 1916:

> Sam Small is the greatest temperance lecturer the nation affords at the present time and this vicinity is especially fortunate in being able to hear him. Manager Jackson is donating the time of the opera house for this lecture and the people of the city and vicinity are getting the benefit. The Coldwater Male Quartette will sing. (*Coldwater Daily Reporter*, November 1, 1916)

One year before the Eighteenth Amendment to the Constitution became the law of the land, F. B. Bale, a former juvenile court judge from Columbus, Ohio, spoke at the National-World Prohibition Rally at the opera house. The purpose of the talk was to convince citizens to vote "no" on the proposal to exclude wine and beer from the prohibition amendment. The state and national Anti-Saloon League sponsored the lecture. According to the *Coldwater Daily Reporter*:

> This is one of hundreds of National-World Prohibition rallies now being held throughout America. Uncle Sam who has been a chief factor in helping European and Oriental countries to civil and religious liberty will likewise help them in their struggle for freedom from the curse of strong drink.

"Homemade Happiness"

The Clinging Vine, lyrics by Zelda Sears, music by Harold A. Levey, 1922

With the flat floor in place, dancing parties became a regular event at the Tibbits Opera House. They began with two in 1882, the year the theater opened, and continued for a number of years. A grand masquerade ball was held in 1886, and for the Leap Year Ball in 1888 the music was provided by an orchestra from Kalamazoo and the boutonnieres were from Detroit.

The opera house has a long history of supporting the local high school. The first documentation of the theater being used as a venue for commencement exercises is from 1884. That arrangement continued for almost forty years until Roosevelt High School opened in 1923. In addition to commencement exercises, many class plays were seen at the theater. Among the shows produced by the high school were *H.M.S. Pinafore*; *The Art of Being Bored*; *Powhatan*, an Indian opera directed by William Baker of Chicago; and in 1917, in lieu of a scripted play, the junior class created a minstrel show. On December 18 and 19, 1919, proud parents and others enjoyed the musical comedy *Katcha-Koo*, advertised as "The Largest Home Talent Production Ever Staged by the High School."

Through the years the opera house was host to many diverse amateur theatre productions staged with local talent: Gilbert and Sullivan operettas, *An Evening of Dickens*, *The Rivals*, and *Ben Hur* with panoramas and tableaux. *Golden Hair and the Three Bears*, a juvenile operetta, was presented with a local cast in December 1885. The Presbyterian Sisterhood produced the comic opera *Ermine* and the Ladies Aid of St. Mark's Episcopal Church was responsible for *The Gypsy Rover*, "A Romantic Comic Opera."

The August 21, 1911, issue of the *Coldwater Daily Reporter* announced that "tomorrow evening John Wilson Dodge will begin rehearsals for the initial production of his newest and best opera, *Paul Revere*." The article also informed readers that "Mr. Dodge will bring his wife and daughter, Cynthia, with him . . . as the latter has quite a prominent part in the piece."

Five days later, another article was published in the newspaper reporting that Mr. Dodge had created the work with local musicians and vocalists in mind. Readers were also told that as the text was based on historical facts, "the result is that the opera is of educational value as well as being highly entertaining." Not only was it educational and entertaining, in its review of *Paul Revere*, the newspaper reported that it was a "big success."

> The production of last night went off with a smoothness that closely approached professionalism. . . . No one present was looking for such a successful performance in any sense of the word. (*Coldwater Daily Reporter*, September 13, 1911)

On May 27, 1918, a locally created and produced children's play, *Blue Boy*, was declared by the press to be "one of the most remarkable plays of its nature that was ever staged in Coldwater . . . some of the greatest surprises came in the special choruses of Will-O-Wisps, Elves, Wood Fairies, Fireflies and Frogs. The flower drill was also worthy of mention."

Minstrel shows were a popular form of entertainment for local audiences and performers. They were presented by the Coldwater Amateur Minstrels; the Elks Minstrels; the Fortnightly Ladies Minstrel Club; and in 1919 the Daughters of the American Revolution presented the Coldwater Elite Minstrel Maids and a feature film.

The Lady Minstrels of St. Agatha's Guild of St. Mark's Episcopal Church featured "50 Ladies of Local Prominence" who advertised that they would present "Local Hits, Puns, and New and Original Coon Songs." They promised that "Comical Arguments will Fly Between the Funny End-women. You Will Laugh, Roar, Scream."

"We Gather Together"

English lyrics by Theodore Baker, 1894; music based on traditional Dutch folk tune adapted by Adrianus Valerius, 1597

John Jackson was a very generous host when it came to providing space for community meetings whether the purpose of the gathering was religious, political, or patriotic. In November 1908 he opened the opera house on two consecutive Sunday evenings for special Baptist Church services. The purpose was to serve that church's congregation and to provide an opportunity for people who would be reluctant to attend a service in a specific church to attend one in a more neutral environment.

> By such an innovation scores who are strangers to a church and who would scoff at the suggestion that they attend an ordinary church service were drawn to these

> meetings, possibly from curiosity, but with a chance that untold good may be accomplished. (*Coldwater Daily Reporter*, November 2, 1908)

The experiment's success was headlined in the *Coldwater Daily Reporter* the day after the first service: "Tibbits Crowded to Capacity Last Evening." The Sunday Baptist services were continued annually for a number of years.

— HEADLINE —

Most Important Meeting Ever Held in Coldwater

In the February 4, 1915, issue of the *Coldwater Daily Reporter* a journalist urged everyone, whether for or against the proposed city charter, to attend the meeting that was to take place that evening—"Special invitation to ladies." The purpose of the meeting was to explain the difference between the old and the proposed new city charters.

The voting occurred the following Monday and attracted a large turnout; at noon many of the workingmen of the city took the opportunity to vote. The proposal was rejected by a small majority. The newspaper attributed the results to "the radical departure from our present methods. Coldwater is conservative in all matters to a great degree," and it advanced the theory that many voters did not understand the new charter and how it would be facilitated. "Had this feature been appreciated its adoption would have resulted."

In 1916 the opera house hosted a community meeting to encourage the citizens of Coldwater to become more involved with the development of the city through their enthusiastic moral and financial support. To entice people to attend, the newspaper pointed out that "Coldwater has many opportunities . . . that cannot be taken advantage of without co-operation on the part of all our citizens. The big meeting will make everybody a booster—get in harness—let no man stay away."

The day after the meeting took place the newspaper heralded the event's great success:

> The finest thing accomplished last night was the stirring up the spirit of those men in the large audience who gave sums of $5.00, $10.00, and $15.00 for the big booster fund. These sums were given by the common people and, after all, it is the common people who count in any project that goes for municipal benefit. (*Coldwater Daily Reporter*, April 28, 1916)

The following year, the *Coldwater Daily Reporter* commended Manager Jackson for making it possible to hold a patriotic demonstration at the theater. The event commenced with a band concert outside of the opera house. The principal speaker was the Honorable Joseph Hooper of Battle Creek. In his address, Mr. Hooper explained why the United States should support the war in Europe.

> It is our turn to lend aid and assistance to bleeding, torn France as did Lafayette when this miserable poor little country of ours was struggling for its life against the oppression of a tyrant. This war will never be ended until the Kaiser is pulled down from his tottering, bloodstained throne.

Caution: Attending the Theater May Be Hazardous to Your Health!

In 1918, the Spanish flu pandemic caused the state Board of Health to decree that all public gathering places close for a period of time. The Tibbits Opera House was dark from October 21 until November 9. When it reopened, the newspaper advertisements assured prospective patrons that "The Air in This Theatre Changed Every Six Minutes."

"Let's Go into a Picture Show"

Lyrics and music by Junie McCree and Albert Von Tilzer, 1909

In the 1893, 1897, and 1899 seasons, some kind of moving-picture presentation was part of the Tibbits Opera House programming. The first were in the form of stereopticon presentations that in succeeding years were followed by more sophisticated forms of moving pictures, some attached to an evening of vaudeville and others as the evening's only entertainment.

In 1916, the opera house announced that it had acquired four thousand feet of new moving pictures including *Sturgis Adopts a Baby*, a comedy made with local talent.

FIGURE 31. A poster for the motion picture *Through the Back Door* starring America's Sweetheart, Mary Pickford, one of the silent screen's most popular and prolific film actresses. From 1916 to 1921, when opera houses were transitioning into movie theaters, twenty-five films starring Pickford were released and made available to former live-theatre venues. (Publisher: The H. C. Miner Litho, Co., New York, 1921. Retrieved from the Library of Congress.)

The following note handwritten by John T. Jackson and sent to the Coldwater superintendent of schools was discovered in the Holbrook Heritage Room collection at the Coldwater Branch District Library:

> Next Saturday at 2:30 at the opera house we offer the modern fairy play "A Good Little Devil" in motion pictures with Mary Pickford. I believe the children would much enjoy seeing it. Send down as many as you desire. (August 17, 1916)

By 1918, movies had surpassed legitimate theatre as the public's preferred form of entertainment, which was reflected in the ratio of films to plays presented at opera houses everywhere. That year, customers had the opportunity to see thirty stage plays at the Tibbits Opera House and over eighty movies. The *Coldwater Daily Reporter* began to publish a feature article titled "Screenland" that consisted of movie news and movie star biographies with pictures. It appeared in the paper every Wednesday in March and intermittently thereafter. It replaced the "Amusement" column that featured opera house news.

When Dennis and Estella Vanes assumed ownership of the Tibbits Opera House in 1919, motion pictures became the major attraction. Most motion pictures were shown one night only, the exception being when the film featured a major star; Mary Pickford films usually played three consecutive nights.

As the new owner, Mr. Vanes initiated several updates to improve his patrons' moviegoing experience. First, he rearranged the seats in the parquet circle from their horseshoe configuration so that they all faced the screen, and he purchased a Boston pipe organ to enhance the live music that accompanied silent films. The organ pipes were installed in the boxes next to the proscenium arch, and the organ itself was in the orchestra pit. Eventually, the pipe organ was removed and found a new home at the Bronson Congregational Church. Later, when "talkies" became the rage, he purchased sound equipment that he upgraded twice over a seven-year period. The first talking picture to be shown at the new Tibbits Theater was *The Wild Party* starring Clara Bow in 1929.

Act II

CALUMET THEATRE

Red Jacket (1900)

SCENE i

Building Going Up!

One of America's finest turn-of-the-century opera house/theaters is to be discovered in a most unlikely, remote location . . . in the "ghost town" atmosphere of Calumet, a settlement of approximately 800 people in the abandoned copper fields of the U. P. —T. Kilgore Splake, "The Calumet Opera House and Theater," 1996

"Let's Start at the Very beginning / A Very Good Place to Start"

The Sound of Music, "Do-Re-Mi," lyrics by Oscar Hammerstein II, music by Richard Rodgers, 1959)

It is virtually impossible to tell the tale of the genesis and evolution of the village that is today known as Calumet without mentioning Douglass Houghton and the discovery of copper, Alexander Agassiz and the Calumet and Hecla Mining Company, the copper miners' strike of 1913–14, and the Italian Hall tragedy. So, here it is!

Thar's Copper in Them Thar Hills! #1

with apologies to Dr. M. F. Stephenson, Mark Twain, and Mulberry Sellers

It happens frequently that pieces of copper are found, weighing from ten to twenty pounds. I have seen several such pieces in the hands of savages . . . they esteem them as divinities, or as presents given to them to promote their happiness by the gods who dwell beneath the water. (Claude-Jean Allouez, Jesuit Missionary and Explorer, 1666)

It is widely recognized that Michigan is one of America's leading producers of automobiles and cherries. However, many people do not know that for nearly a century a northwestern section of the state's Upper Peninsula fulfilled the country's demand for copper. At one time, 95 percent of the nation's copper ore came from the mines in the Keweenaw region, an area that became known as Copper Country.

Historians believe that Native Americans first mined copper on the Keweenaw Peninsula between 5000 and 1200 BCE. However, this story begins in 1840 when Douglass Houghton set foot on the peninsula's northernmost tip and, allegedly, stumbled onto, or perhaps stumbled over, a forty-pound chunk of the metal.

Houghton's exploration of the Keweenaw Peninsula and discovery of copper led to the great migration to Michigan's most northern region. That in turn paved the way for the development of a community that would eventually build and support an opera house.

— **INTERLUDE** —

We interrupt our story for a Douglass Houghton biography:

Douglass Houghton (1809–45), often referred to as the "Father of American Copper Mining," was a jack of many trades. During his all-too-brief lifetime, he was the first professor of geology, mineralogy, and chemistry at the University of Michigan, the first Michigan State Geologist, a physician, and the mayor of Detroit.

His impact on Michigan cannot be overestimated as evidenced by the fact that in the state there are a city, county, and lake named Houghton as well as the Douglass Houghton Falls. There is also the Douglass Houghton Hall at Michigan Technological University and two memorial plaques honoring him, one on the Keweenaw Peninsula and one on the University of Michigan campus.

After discovering the copper, he made several trips back to the Upper Peninsula to document the extent of the deposits found there. His reports to the Michigan State Legislature detailing the quality and quantity of the metal were instrumental in initiating the country's first great mining rush—six years prior to the California gold rush. Prospectors found copper in rocks on the ground and in the peninsula's streams and rivers.

On the expedition of 1845, Douglass Houghton and a few of his assistants were canoeing on Lake Superior when a sudden storm capsized their boat and Houghton, as well as two of his crew, drowned.

— *And now, back to our story.* —

Whereas the region was referred to as Calumet, the village, which was platted in 1868 and incorporated in 1875, was originally called Red Jacket due to its proximity to the original Red Jacket Mining Company. The story is that the Red Jacket Mining Company had been named after a Seneca chief, Sagoyewatha, who had served as a guide, interpreter, and liaison for the British during the Revolutionary War. In gratitude for his services, the British presented him with a richly embroidered red uniform jacket, and he became known as "Red Jacket." Allegedly, he sported both the jacket and the moniker with pride.

The village was renamed in 1929, and Red Jacket became Calumet.

Thar's Copper in Them Thar Hills! #2

with apologies to Dr. M. F. Stephenson, Mark Twain, and Mulberry Sellers

Not unlike Douglass Houghton's experience eighteen years earlier, when Edwin J. Hulbert was conducting a survey of the Keweenaw Peninsula in 1858, he came across a huge boulder infused with copper. Upon further exploration and excavation, he discovered an enormous copper-rich conglomerate. He then went into the mining business for which he obtained financing from investors in Boston for two companies, the Calumet Mining Company and the Hecla Mining Company. They eventually merged to become the Calumet and Hecla Mining Company (C&H).

The major Boston investor in the Calumet and Hecla Mines was Quincy A. Shaw who contributed funds in exchange for shares of stock and power of attorney. In 1866, Shaw asked his brother-in-law, Alexander Agassiz, to go to the Keweenaw Peninsula and assess the profit potential of the mining enterprise. Agreeing to Quincy Shaw's request, Agassiz journeyed to Michigan's Upper Peninsula to observe the operation of the mines. He reported back to Shaw that the potential value of both the Calumet and Hecla mines was greater than could be imagined.

— **INTERLUDE** —

We interrupt our story for an Alexander Agassiz biography:

Alexander Agassiz (1835–1910) was born in Switzerland and was the son of renowned geologist and botanist, Louis Agassiz. After the death of his mother, young Agassiz immigrated to the United States. In 1855 he graduated from Harvard with the intention of pursuing a career in engineering and marine zoology.

When Hulbert sold his interest in the mines, Shaw convinced his brother-in-law to take charge of the operation. In 1867, the Agassiz family took up residence in the copper-rich wilds of Michigan. Agassiz became president of Calumet and Hecla, a position he retained for the rest of his life, and turned what was an unprofitable operation into the world's most productive copper mining company.

Once the operation of the mines was stable, Agassiz determined that it no longer required his full-time supervision; he and his family returned to Boston where he pursued his scientific interests. Twice a year he journeyed back to Michigan to attend to his administrative responsibilities there.

After he left Michigan as a permanent resident, he spent the next twenty-five years focused on his marine and coral reef interests. He participated in expeditions to various parts of the world where he collected scientific data and acquired artifacts for Harvard's Museum of Comparative Zoology. For twelve years Agassiz served as the curator and director of that museum and supported it financially with donations of an estimated total of $500,000 from his copper mine profits. Alexander Agassiz died in 1910, on a ship from Southampton, England, en route to New York. His son observed that it was only fitting that his father, a marine zoologist, should die at sea.

There is no doubt that Agassiz was instrumental in the realization of the Calumet Theatre, but there is no evidence that he conceived of its existence. It was the Red Jacket Common Council that unanimously agreed with councilman Michael Kemp, when, on November 15, 1898, he stood up at a council meeting and, allegedly, exclaimed that Red Jacket needed an opera house to dispel the notion that it was an uncivilized town.

FIGURE 32. Portrait of Alexander Agassiz, marine zoologist, oceanographer, mining engineer, and president of the Calumet and Hecla Mining Company, ca. 1900. (Photograph courtesy of National Park Service, Keweenaw National Historic Park, Wm. John "Jack" Foster Collection, Framed Photos.)

— And now, back to our story. —

Once "the suits" suspected that fortunes could be made by harvesting the copper, they arrived from the east eager to create empires by exploiting the treasure below the surface of the Keweenaw hills. Excavation began, and mines were created—some on the sites of the Native Americans' original copper pits. Among the most productive and profitable mines were those located along a rich, ore-embedded strip that ran the length of the Keweenaw Peninsula from Hancock to Copper Harbor.

Miners were needed to dig up the bounty, and as there was only a small local workforce, agents were dispersed and advertisements distributed across the country and in Europe broadcasting the employment opportunities available in Michigan's Upper Peninsula. Workers arrived at the Keweenaw Peninsula from Cornwall, Wales, Finland, Croatia, Germany, Italy, Sweden, Norway, Poland, Ireland, and Canada.

The Cornish were the first to arrive with their pasties and mining expertise, having left their homeland as the mines there began to fail. In 1900 there was a mass emigration from Finland brought about by Russia's oppression of that country. It is estimated that over fifty thousand Finnish refugees came to the United States with Minnesota, Wisconsin, or northern Upper Michigan as their final destination.

The new arrivals from various countries brought with them their language, traditions, and religion. In Red Jacket,

FIGURE 33. Copper miners hold their lunch pails as they are about to be transported down into the mine in a man car, 1910. (Superior View Photography, Marquette, Michigan.)

FIGURE 34. Calumet and Hecla compound (library at center, Agassiz home on right), 1904. (Photograph courtesy of National Park Service, Keweenaw National Historic Park, Wm. John "Jack" Foster Collection, Library Card Collection, #244.)

churches were established to serve specific ethnic groups where services were conducted in the native tongue of the congregation. The Finnish, German, and Swedish each had their own native-language newspapers.

"Life in a Northern Town"

Lyrics and music by Gilbert Alexander Gabriel and Nicholas William Laird-Clowes, 1985

As the village of Red Jacket developed, merchants, bankers, doctors, and lawyers descended upon the area. Soon educators arrived, and in 1885 the Michigan Mining School (now Michigan Technological University) opened in Houghton. Nine years later, Suomi College and Theological Seminary was established in Hancock. In 1958, the seminary and college separated, and in 2000 Suomi College became Finlandia University.

Although it had started as a rough-and-tumble mining camp, by the end of the nineteenth century, Red Jacket had evolved into a well-established community with stable governance and a sound economy. There were schools, hotels, business blocks, and long-distance telephone service.

On June 27, 1908, it was reported in the local newspaper that twenty-two passenger trains made a stop at the Copper Range Railroad Station in Red Jacket every day. The village had become the center of the copper mining industry in the United States.

The Calumet and Hecla Mining Company restricted all commercial or social establishments from opening on the company's grounds. Consequently, churches, meeting halls, stores, saloons, and brothels, along with other enterprises often found in an emerging community, had to be built on adjacent land that was owned by and leased from C&H.

The Red Jacket business district not only served the village's more than three thousand citizens but also all of Calumet Township with a population of over twenty-five thousand. That number peaked in 1910 when, according to the U.S. Census, there were more than thirty-nine thousand township inhabitants. The population base eroded exponentially as the mines began to shut down after World War II and the miners left the area in search of opportunities elsewhere. When the mines closed, so did the restaurants, the shops, the business and professional offices. The people who had worked in those establishments moved on, leaving a veritable ghost town in their dust. Today, just over seven hundred individuals call the village of Calumet home.

> Calumet has been a village and region which has been in steady decline, in terms of population and tax base. For many, the cost of maintaining a theater of this scale seems beyond their capabilities. (Kevin Harrington, *Red Jacket Theater and Town Hall*, 1975)

"Heigh-Ho, [Heigh-Ho, It's Off to Work We Go!]"

Snow White and the Seven Dwarfs, lyrics by Frank Churchill, music by Larry Morey, 1937

> This peninsula (Keweenaw) is cleft near its base by a valley in which lies a long sheet of water called Portage Lake. On the sides are the great stamp mills of the copper mines and a few miles north of it is the great Calumet & Hecla Mine which is one of the most notable establishments of the world. (*Harper's Magazine*, May 1882)

By 1913, three mining companies produced the lion's share of copper in the region. Calumet and Hecla became the largest and, over time, gained considerable power and autonomy. The company's relationship to its workers has been called one of "benevolent paternalism" or, by some, "benevolent feudalism." The company's policies both restricted and enhanced the quality of its employees' lives.

In addition to owning the land on which the mines existed, C&H also owned most of the surrounding property where it built over 1,750 houses that were rented to mine workers.

The company also built, owned, and maintained the schools, the public library, the hospital, and a bathhouse. Although it allowed commercial buildings as well as churches, the YMCA, and an opera house to be constructed by non-company-affiliated individuals, C&H owned the land on which these structures stood.

— HEADLINE —

Change in Time Begins at Noon

At noon today will begin what is known as "mine time," and all employees of the Calumet & Hecla as well as other mining companies in this district will go to work one half hour earlier . . . the mining companies are anxious to get as much daylight for their work as possible and such being the case they take their clocks and advance them just one-half hour. The public has always been looking forward to the time when the mining companies would do away with the practice . . . for it causes more than ordinary inconvenience. It is expected that the change back to standard time will come about the middle of February. (*Daily Mining Gazette*, October 14, 1906)

FIGURE 35. Low-Rent Housing. These homes built and owned by the copper mining company reportedly were rented to miners for five dollars a month. The houses pictured here were located in Kearsarge, three miles north of Red Jacket, date unknown. (Superior View Photography, Marquette, Michigan.)

"I Didn't Know What Time It Was"

Too Many Girls, lyrics by Lorenz Hart, music by Richard Rodgers, 1939

The influence of the mining company did not end with its owning the town; it extended to controlling time. Advertisements for events at the Calumet Theatre often included the curtain time with an indication as to whether that was "mine time" or "town time." The two-time policy also impacted transportation to and from the theater; information concerning the arrival and departure of carriages and trolleys that transported the patrons also had to specify at which of the two times they could be expected.

"Strike, Strike, Strike"

Sweet Little Devil, lyrics by B. G. DeSylva, music by George Gershwin, 1924

On July 23,1913, approximately nine thousand miners went out on strike, impacting every copper mine in Copper Country. The issues had to do with shorter workdays, higher wages, and the discontinued use of the one-man drill that was thought to be unsafe. The laborers initially requested that the company managers recognize the union, the Western Federation of Miners (WFM), and meet with their representatives to discuss wages, hours, and working conditions. For management, the idea of unionization of and negotiation with workers was unacceptable.

FIGURE 36. National Guard encampment during the copper miners' strike, 1913. (Photograph courtesy of the National Park Service, Keweenaw National Historic Park, Wm. John "Jack" Foster Collection, Glass Plate #113.)

The strikers, with the help of the WFM, organized parades, rallies, and picket lines and blocked access to the mines. In retaliation, the company managers asked the sheriff to deputize antiunion locals to patrol company property. For additional muscle, they imported professional strikebreakers, and they asked the governor to deploy National Guard troops to restore order. The governor called out the troops and the war began.

Soon the tension between the strikers and the strikebreakers escalated to violence. In 1913, there were two incidents of gunmen firing on boarding houses occupied by miners killing both miners and non-mine-affiliated persons. Finally, at the end of that bloody year, the president of the WFM was beaten, shot, dragged to the railroad station, put on a train to Chicago, and advised not to return to the Copper Country.

The strike impacted all aspects of life in the Keweenaw region, including the theater. During the 1913 theatre season, there were fifty-four events that took place at the Calumet Theatre between January 1 and December 23. During the 1914 season, only eleven events took place there. For the strikers, there was little money or inclination to attend any performance.

On April 13, 1914, the strike ended with the union unable to get a foothold into any of the Copper Country mines. Those miners who had not left the area to find employment in other industrial centers were invited to return to work if they turned in or destroyed their union cards.

"God Bless the Child"

Lyrics and music by Arthur Herzog Jr. and Billie Holiday, 1941

The most tragic strike-related incident took place on Christmas Eve, 1913. By that time, the miners had been out of work for five months, and the union's funds, intended to support the strikers, had diminished. The WFM Women's Auxiliary had organized a holiday party for the strikers' children that was held on the second floor of the Italian Hall. Santa was invited to hand out gifts to children who otherwise would receive little or nothing for Christmas.

At one point during the festivities, a man reportedly came up the stairs and yelled "Fire!" Panic ensued and in an attempt to escape children and adults rushed to the narrow stairway. It is assumed that some stumbled and fell with others falling on top of them. Seventy-three people either suffocated or were crushed to death; over sixty of them were children. There was no fire.

To accommodate the large number of bodies, a temporary morgue was set up in a room in the Red Jacket Town Hall adjacent to the Calumet Theatre. The last event to take place in the playhouse that year was a community meeting on December 25 to discuss the Italian Hall tragedy.

Eventually, the Michigan mines shut down partially because of the competition from the mines in the country's Western states where the ore could be more cost-effectively extracted from the ground, coupled with the diminishing demand for copper after World War II. In 1968, Universal Oil purchased the Calumet and Hecla Mining Company, but the next year, the once rich and powerful mine closed for good.

> Unemployment has become a way of life for many people living in the Keweenaw Peninsula. The jobless ranks never drop below 10-percent . . . and occasionally soar to more than twenty percent. . . . But this historic hamlet . . . still manages to support a year-round community theater that attracts programs ranging from the Detroit Symphony Orchestra to stage productions from Meadow Brook Theater. (James L. Kerwin, "A Cultural Landmark: Calumet's Goal—Coppertown, USA," 1976)

"Town Hall Tonight"

The Girl Friend, lyrics by Lorenz Hart, music by Richard Rodgers, 1926

Back in 1885, ten years after the village of Red Jacket had been incorporated but before the strike and Italian Hall tragedy,

FIGURE 37 (*above*). "Papa Is Striking for Us." The children of copper miners parading to demonstrate their support for their striking fathers, ca. 1913. In Mohawk, located north of Red Jacket, a sheriff's deputy shot a fourteen-year-old girl who was marching with her mother in a Labor Day pro-union parade. (Superior View Photography, Marquette, Michigan.)

FIGURE 38 (*left*). The aftermath of the Christmas party that took place on the second floor of the Italian Hall, a commercial building the first floor of which housed Vairo's Saloon and a Great Atlantic & Pacific Tea Co. store (A&P), 1913. (Superior View Photography, Marquette, Michigan.)

FIGURE 39. J. B. Sweatt designed the Red Jacket Town Hall, 1886. In 1900, by attaching a new facade to the original building, Charles K. Shand connected it physically and visually to the adjacent, newly constructed Calumet Theatre. (Photograph courtesy of the National Park Service, Keweenaw National Historic Park, the Andre Curto Collection, Album 14, #056.)

the city fathers thought it was time to erect a building that would accommodate the needs of the growing community. To that end, they petitioned Alexander Agassiz and the Calumet and Hecla Mining Company to lease a plot of land on Sixth Street.

The original lease was for five years at one dollar a year and gave the village permission to erect a building that would incorporate the town clerk's office, a council chamber, the jail, and the fire engine hall on the first floor and a public hall on the second. On February 19, 1886, the Red Jacket Common Council hired J. B. Sweatt, a Marquette-based architect, to design the new facility. During the same time period, 1886–87, Sweatt was also the architect for the First National Bank in Red Jacket and the Houghton County Court House.

The Red Jacket Town Hall, built for $14,272, was a two-story brick and brown Marquette sandstone structure that contained the separate spaces as specified in the lease. The second-floor space was originally referred to as a "public hall," and the lease stipulated that it was to be used "for no other purpose whatsoever." On Sweatt's architectural drawings, however, the second-floor space is labeled the Red Jacket Opera House.

The need for a venue dedicated to cultural events and entertainment arose with the arrival of the mining company executives and their families from the east where they were accustomed to having access to music and theatre presentations. Another incentive was to announce to the world that the remote Keweenaw Peninsula was now civilized and eager to embrace the arts. For these reasons, many towns in the area had a space called an "opera house," but few were adequately equipped to attract first-class professional theatre companies.

Although the Red Jacket Opera House had a small, permanent stage at one end of the room, when the space was used as a theater, all scenery and other production-related paraphernalia had to be hoisted up flights of stairs to the upper floor or, as often happened, left at the railroad station.

By 1896 the council members realized the limitations of their nine-year old facility; more space was needed for village-related activities. They made the decision to move the fire engines out of the town hall, to reassign the vacant space for other uses, and to construct an addition to the existing building.

> On motion the President was authorized to appoint a committee to wait on the Calumet and Hecla Mining Company in reference to building a fire engine house on Lot 4, Block 21. (Red Jacket Common Council Minutes, June 3, 1896)

The lot in question was across the street from the town hall. Within days they had their answer, and the call went out for architects to submit plans for the new firehouse. Four architects answered the call. Council members reviewed the submissions and selected the designs of local architect Charles K. Shand.

Once that project was well underway, the possibility of reimagining the town hall surfaced. The council decided to remodel the first floor only. With the fire equipment removed there was room for a large council chamber with

FIGURE 40. Red Jacket Fire Engine House, currently the Copper Country Firefighters' History Museum, 1904. Architect Charles K. Shand designed the building in 1898, one year before he was awarded the commission to remodel the town hall and design the Calumet Theatre. (Photograph courtesy of National Park Service, Keweenaw National Historic Park, Wm. John "Jack" Foster Collection, Library Card #053.)

FIGURE 41. Red Jacket Ballroom, originally the Red Jacket Opera House, on the second floor of the Calumet Town Hall, decorated for a wedding reception, November 2009. (Photograph courtesy of the Calumet Theatre.)

an adjoining committee room, a clerk's office, the marshal's office, a janitor's room, vault, and kitchen.

As far as the second-floor space was concerned, what was once the Red Jacket Opera House became the Red Jacket Ballroom.

> The second floor of the present building will be left just as it is and can be used for dances or public meetings. (*Copper Country Evening News*, January 1, 1899)

Over the years, in addition to "dances or public meetings," the Red Jacket Ballroom has been used as a play rehearsal room, a prop manufacturing studio, an auxiliary performance space for small music and dance concerts, as well as a hall for lectures, receptions, and banquets.

Onward and Upward

> Calumet boasts of 45,000 people and among them are two or three thousand who love the drama and opera, but they have been denied the pleasure of seeing either . . . because there was no playhouse wherein a company of standard reputation could be induced to appear. Now there is every probability that the higher class performers will visit our city, and be liberally patronized too. (*Daily Mining Gazette*, March 21, 1900)

At a November 15, 1898, meeting, Councilman Michael Kemp proposed that an addition to the town hall be built on the lot next door to the existing structure. Kemp moved that a delegation from the council approach the Calumet and Hecla Mining Company to discuss the possibility of leasing the desired lot. On motion, Kemp's proposed resolution was unanimously approved.

Apparently, there had been some closed-door discussion among council members about the possibility of constructing a grand opera house prior to Kemp's presentation of his proposal. A rumor of such a plan obviously leaked out of the council chambers as evidenced by a letter to the editor of the *Copper Country Evening News* signed "A Tax Payer."

> Would you mention in your valuable paper whether there is any truth in the report that the council of Red

> Jacket are proposing to erect an opera house on the vacant lot adjoining the present Town hall, whether they have had plans made to carry out such intentions, and last but not least whether the president and council have any power to build an opera house or right to spend taxpayer's money for such a purpose particularly after they have lately expended so much money to decorating and enlarging the accommodations at the present opera house.

This letter may have indicated to the council that it would be wise for them to proceed with caution as there could be some public opposition to the endeavor in light of the fact that the upper-floor Red Jacket Opera House had been enhanced with new stage lights and opera chairs only two years earlier. Therefore, a provision was added to Kemp's proposal that a special election be held on Saturday, November 26, 1898, to determine by the vote of Red Jacket's male citizens if "the village should borrow twenty-five thousand ($25,000) dollars or thereabouts to be expended for the enlarging of the present Town Hall." The loan amount was based on the council's expectation that it would cost approximately that much money for the construction. The common council meeting minutes of December 6, 1898, recorded the results of the election as "one hundred and fifty (150) votes contained the word yes and sixty-two (62) contained the word no."

On January 2, 1899, the common council assembled to discuss the town hall renovation and addition. Unfortunately, the meeting was adjourned before that business was concluded as the lights in the council chamber went out, and overhead in the Red Jacket Opera House, the performance of a vaudeville show elicited such enthusiastic foot stomping that it was not possible to conduct business on the floor below.

For reasons not explained in the common council meeting minutes, it was important to the members that the architect engaged for the town hall renovation and opera house construction project be selected from a totally anonymous pool of applicants. It was specified that plans and proposals be submitted without any information that would identify the person or firm that had generated them. Five architectural firms responded to the request.

> All the plans submitted were very good and provide for an addition which will be a model one and which would result in the village rooms being a credit to the city as well as providing an excellent Opera House in the new building. (*Copper Country Evening News*, January 6, 1899)

The common council decided to hold a special session on January 4, 1899, to scrutinize the plans and specification. At that meeting, two of the five submissions were selected as definite possibilities, the architect's identity still unknown. As the council members were unable to decide between the two, the meeting was adjourned for two days to afford the gentlemen of the council an opportunity to sleep on it.

As it turned out, the architect who had designed the Red Jacket Fire Engine House the year before, Charles K. Shand, had submitted the design that was selected by the council.

Six weeks after he was awarded the commission, the council accepted his final plans.

— **INTERLUDE** —

We interrupt our story for a Charles K. Shand biography:

Charles K. Shand (1867–1945) was born in Scotland where he trained for a career as an architect. Upon his arrival in this country in 1887, he first worked at architectural firms in the state of Washington. In the mid-1890s, he headed for Michigan's Keweenaw Peninsula to take advantage of the building boom in that area at that time. He opened offices in both Houghton and Red Jacket and advertised in the Houghton, Hancock, and Red Jacket city directories from 1895 to 1904. Shand worked for ten years in the Copper Country, and during that decade, in addition to the Red Jacket Fire Engine House and the Calumet Theatre, he was responsible for several other public and commercial buildings in Red Jacket as well as the Lake Linden Village Hall.

Eventually, Shand settled in Minnesota where he lived and worked until his death in 1945.

> G. [*sic*] K. Shand, pioneer Mesabi Range architect, was found dead this morning at his rooming house. . . . He had suffered a heart attack in the night . . . he was one of the architects for the famous Calumet theater, one of the first municipal theaters in the United States. (*Hibbing Daily Tribune*, October 22, 1945)

— *And now, back to our story.* —

"It Takes a Lot of Do-Re-Mi"

High Time, lyrics by Ray Golden, music by Philip Charing, 1953

With the approval of the voters, the council was permitted to borrow $25,000 for the project. But it became apparent that the final cost of the project would be greater than anticipated. From where would the additional funds to build the opera house the council envisioned be found? The minutes of council meetings of 1899 create the impression that, financially, the village sometimes existed "hand-to-mouth." According to existing financial records, in the spring of 1899 the town's bank balance was $5,614.48.

> On motion the Clerk was authorized to make arrangements with the Bank to pay village orders until there should be funds in the village treasury to pay them. (Red Jacket Common Council Minutes, April 4, 1899)

The council members made the decision to go back to the voters; they passed a resolution to hold a special election on July 12, 1899, to determine "by ballot whether the common council may be authorized to borrow twenty-five thousand ($25,000) Dollars additional to the $25,000 already authorized."

On the day designated for the election another resolution replaced the one that had been approved less than two weeks before. It proposed that the election be postponed until July 29 and that the proposal be amended to include a request to borrow a larger sum of money to underwrite the dream house.

> Shall the common council of the Village of Red Jacket be authorized to borrow forty-five thousand ($45,000) Dollars for the purpose of remodeling the present Town Hall? (Red Jacket Common Council Minutes, July 12, 1899)

The voters once again supported the council's proposal. The results were: Yes, 184 and No, 62. Ultimately, the project was financed through the sale of town bonds at 4.5 percent interest.

"You Can't Fool All the People All the Time"

Nancy Brown, lyrics by Frederick Ranken, music by Henry Hadley, 1903

Construction on the new opera house began in March 1899, and on December 1 the *Copper Country Evening News* reported that the shell of the building was in place. The prediction was that construction would be complete in time for the grand opening of the opera house to coincide with the turn of the century. Unfortunately, the century turned and the theater was three months away from completion. The delays were originally blamed on the construction crew; however, on January 18, 1900, the *Copper Country Evening News* printed an editorial suggesting that the blame should be shared with a group of citizens who vigorously protested being taxed for the proposed project.

> Many of the citizens who objected most strenuously to the city erecting the play house . . . raised the point that the council did not have the legal right to borrow money on the strength of the success they had at their first election.

The protesters suggested that the common council misled the population by claiming that the purpose of the first election was not to obtain approval for borrowing funds but rather to gage the people's interest in pursuing the project. According to the printed report, the protesters "had made such a kick" out of the alleged maneuvering on the part of the council that the contractors thought they may not be paid and suspended their work while maintaining the pretense that the construction was ongoing. However, after the voters approved the second proposal, in addition to following the previous construction schedule, work continued on weekends and holidays. Lamps were employed so that it was possible for workers to continue the construction after the sun went down. On March 20, 1900, a year after ground had been broken, the opera house doors were finally open to receive patrons.

How much the project cost the taxpayers is unclear as, depending on the source, the estimates vary. One document claims that the final bill was $51,300, and another reports that it was in the neighborhood of $78,000, but neither of those estimates specify if the figure is for the construction of the opera house only or if it also includes the cost of the town hall renovation. A third account states that the price for the remodeling was $23,150 and the cost of the Calumet Theatre was $65,200 for a grand total of $88,350. The village's indebtedness was paid back primarily with income received from renting the facility. By 1907, the opera house was not only debt free, it was making a profit!

FIGURE 42. Facade of the town hall and Calumet Theatre, 2009. Architect Shand's use of Italian Renaissance architectural detail succeeds in visually unifying two buildings into one. (Photograph courtesy of the Calumet Theatre.)

You Can't Judge a Book by Its Cover

> The building exterior is pretentious, but not distinguished. The theater interior is a glory of plaster rococo. (Kevin Harrington, *Red Jacket Theater and Town Hall*, 1975)

In an interview published at the time of the building's opening, Charles Shand referred to the architectural style of the exterior as Italian Renaissance. More recently, in her book *The Sandstone Architecture of the Lake Superior Region*, Michigan State Historic Preservation Officer Kathryn Bishop Eckert concurred: "The triple and paired round-headed openings, blind arcades, and a balustrade suggest Renaissance features." It has also been labeled Victorian-Romanesque, a style that combines the architectural shapes found on Ancient Roman structures with ornamentation that was popular in the Victorian era.

Despite the fact that all previous mention of the new facility in newspapers, council minutes, and architectural drawings called it an opera house, when it opened it was named the Calumet Theatre. New century, new names.

One of the objectives of the undertaking was to attach the new opera house to the existing town hall and to make the marriage of the two buildings visually compatible. To accomplish this goal, Shand replaced the town hall's Sixth Street facade and north wall with a new exterior in the same Italian Renaissance style that he employed for the front of the Calumet Theatre. According to the Historic American Buildings Survey issued in August 1975, Shand solved several design problems inherent in attaching an existing structure built for one purpose to a new building with a totally different purpose by covering both with one facade.

Seven months into the construction period, the newspaper printed a description of the emerging complex, informing the readers that the front of the buildings employed finely cut red Portage Entry sandstone from nearby Jacobsville that "creates a rich contrast to the buff-colored hydraulic-pressed brick on the upper floors." The article went on to report,

> The cornices will all be of copper and the top of the tower will also be of copper, so that in the copper and

> sandstone, copper country products form a conspicuous part of the building. (*Copper Country Evening News*, October 2, 1899)

The composition of the clock tower that topped the building consisted of a clock that was not installed until a few years after the building was complete, an open structure containing a bell, a cupola, and a flagpole with a weathervane and ball. In the fall of 1919, E. J. Hall, a former seaman known as "Sailor Jack" scaled to the top of the Calumet Theatre tower. Thereafter he was known as "the Human Fly."

The theater was closed for three weeks in 1961, during which time the cupola and bell tower were removed. They were in need of costly repairs, and some authorities believed that they might be vulnerable to lighting strikes. The Seth Thomas bell that had been hidden from sight in the tower has been on display in the park next to the theater since 1975.

Covering the Sixth Street entrance to the opera house is a portico of red sandstone beneath which three gray granite steps lead to two pairs of entrance doors that open into what, in 1900, was considered to be a state-of-the-art facility. In a period when gaslight, fireplaces, and outhouses were common, the Calumet Theatre boasted of electric lights, steam heat, and indoor toilets.

Although Charles Shand seemed to have been the common council's fair-haired boy in that he was awarded the Red Jacket fire engine house, town hall renovation, and opera house contracts, by the time construction was complete on the Calumet Theatre, the relationship may have soured. The council gave him strict orders not to proceed with any additional expenditures without permission from the building committee and passed a motion stating,

> Services of C.K. Shand be dispensed with and all further improvements to be made in and about the Town Hall and Opera House and public municipal property be supervised and managed by the Building Committee of the Council. (Red Jacket Common Council Minutes, December 29, 1900)

Who's Minding the Store?

John D. Cuddihy (1857–1929) was awarded a three-year lease to manage the opera house on February 6, 1900. That lease was continuously renewed for twenty-nine years. During his tenure, he was often referred to as the proprietor of the Calumet Theatre.

A self-made man, Cuddihy began his professional life as a bookkeeper for the Edward Ryan Store, and by the time he left their employment, he was the store's general manager. From 1886 until 1892, before his involvement with the Calumet Theatre, he served as the president of the Village of Red Jacket.

With his high standards and good taste, Cuddihy is credited for establishing the outstanding quality of performances that were presented at the theater. In 1905, he was elected to the executive board of the Northwestern Theater Managers' Association.

At the time of his death, in addition to his other

positions, he was also the president of two area banks and president of two mining companies.

> John D. Cuddihy ranks among the foremost business men of Red Jacket and belongs to that class of enterprising, progressive citizens to whom the West owes much of her present prosperity and greatness. (from *Our Michigan Friends, As We See 'Em*, 1905)

"Castle of Dreams"

Irene, lyrics by Joseph McCarthy, music by Harry Tierney, 1919

> The theater is elaborately and expansively decorated in a conflation of gilt plaster ornament . . . a theater and stage of stunning elegance. (Kevin Harrington, *Red Jacket Theater and Town Hall*, 1975)

When on March 20, 1900, the first patrons passed through the red oak entry doors of the playhouse, they stepped into a small vestibule or foyer. The area is the full width of the theatre, but with only ten feet between the entrance doors and the doors that lead to the auditorium. However, what it lacked in size it made up for in elegance with gilded plaster relief work, a mosaic tile floor, red oak veneered doors that opened to the auditorium, and, on both sides of the space, marble stairways with brass railings that led to the balcony and gallery above and to the restrooms below.

In the original design, there was no box office on the premises; tickets were acquired at Red Jacket's City Drug Store or at Barry's Drug Store in Houghton. Eventually, the marble stairway on the north wall of the lobby was removed, and a ticket office was installed in its place.

On December 2, 1899, the members of the common council reviewed the bids for decorating their new opera house. Two days later, they offered a contract to the William Eckart Co., Interior Decorators of Chicago. The Eckart Company was paid a total of $3,289, which included both compensation for the interior design of the theater and an additional $675 for redecorating the first floor of the town hall.

In the approved contract, the Eckart Company guaranteed,

> All work to be done in a first class, artistic and satisfactory manner in every respect and in accordance with architect's plans and specifications . . . and the work to be completed within any reasonable time you might mention.

The auditorium walls were painted Turkish red in an ombre technique, dark at the bottom and gradually working into lighter shades of the same hue toward the cream-colored ceiling. The columns, pilasters, and moldings around the proscenium arch were in the same dark red hue as the walls.

Rococo-style plasterwork designs employing floral and shell motifs finished in gold leaf adorned the cornices and column capitals. The same decorative treatment bordered the front of the boxes, balcony, gallery, and the main ceiling cove under the balcony (see Plate 4).

Gentlemen, Be Seated!

said the interlocutor to the minstrels

How many gentlemen could be seated? Originally, the theater boasted that it had room for 1,200 patrons: 400 on the main floor parquet including the four boxes that seated six people each, 400 in the balcony, and 400 in the upper gallery. Based on the tally published in the 1900–1901 edition of *Julius Cahn's Official Theatrical Guide* those numbers may have been rounded up. The *Guide* reported 385 seats on the main floor, 375 in the balcony, and 350 in the gallery for a total capacity of 1,110. In 1914, the seating capacity report indicated that there were 1,186 seats available. That number remained constant until 1921 when fifty seats were removed to accommodate the projection booth that was installed in the balcony. When the gallery was declared a fire hazard and permanently closed in 1961, seating for another 350 potential patrons was lost. Today, 711 occupied seats constitute a sold-out house.

Opera chairs of the latest design, which included a rack for a gentleman's hat under the seat, were placed in both the main floor parquet and the balcony. The chairs had a wooden frame and arms with a padded back and a seat that was upholstered in moss green mohair. They were purchased from a Chicago manufacturing company at a total cost of $3,734. The opera chairs, arranged in tiers, created a five-foot decline in floor elevation from the back of the house to the orchestra pit. The upper gallery contained narrow wooden benches. They were not the best seats in the house because of the steep angle created by the height of the gallery. However, tickets to sit in this area were relatively inexpensive and, consequently, on some occasions the gallery was sold out when the rest of the theater was not.

For those patrons who wished to be seen as well as to see, there were four ornate boxes, two on either side of the stage. They contained white wicker chairs that were purchased from Vertin's Department Store in Red Jacket (see Plate 5). There were brass rails around the boxes, the balcony, and the orchestra pit. The fabric that hung from the rails as well as the curtains behind the boxes was Roanoke tapestry. The color of the portieres, valances, draperies, and Brussels carpet was empire green.

"Nearer, My God, to Thee"

Lyrics by Sarah F. Adams, 1841, music by Lowell Mason, 1856

The balcony and upper gallery are horseshoe shaped and wrap around the rear of the auditorium. Situated on the main floor near the back of the parquet section are four cast iron columns that support the balcony. In the balcony, there are six smaller columns to support the gallery. The tale has been told that prior to the opening of the theater, an entire shift of the Calumet and Hecla mine was taken to the new building where they climbed up to the gallery and were told to jump up and down. The purpose of the drill was to determine if the six columns that held up the third-story structure would safely support the weight of a full load of miners and, by extension, a full load of patrons.

The orchestra pit in front of the stage was separated from the parquet by a brass rail. The 1900–1901 edition of *Julius*

Cahn's Official Theatrical Guide reported that the Calumet Theatre provided a seven-piece orchestra.

Gilding the Lily

the condensation of a metaphor from *King John* by William Shakespeare, ca. 1590s

> Because of the rather small size of the space and the depth of the proscenium arch, the effect is rather like being inside a Faberge Easter egg. Elegance, opulence, if not decadence, are brought to mind. (Kevin Harrington, *Red Jacket Theater and Town Hall*, 1975)

When the first-nighters entered the auditorium, their attention was immediately drawn to the decorative horseshoe-shaped proscenium arch that rose to a height of twenty-six feet and was thirty-two feet wide at the base (see Plate 6).

The notes that Shand submitted along with the construction and decoration plans for the theater stated that the proscenium arch was to be adorned with figures representing the arts. In the contract with the William Eckart Company, signed December 5, 1899, the specification for the artwork was confirmed:

> The proscenium arch . . . will be elaborately and artistically arranged with oil paintings representing the "Arts." These figures to be painted on canvas in a thorough artistic manner. Above work to be done for the sum of two thousand six hundred eighty dollars ($2,680).

The Frank Pentzold Company of Milwaukee is credited for the creation of the panels or murals. When completed, the five oil paintings on canvas that measured seven by eight feet were glued to the arch. Viewing from left to right, the murals represent painting, drama, music, poetry, and sculpture.

After more than three decades of adorning the proscenium, the paintings were removed in 1934 when the theater underwent a major redecoration in an attempt to create a more contemporary environment. The Civil Works Administration, a branch of the New Deal program, funded the project. Alfred Messner, a native of the area who was a graduate of the Chicago Institute of Arts and a nationally recognized interior designer, was selected to create the theater's new look. His plan was to obscure the curvilinear Victorian Rococo ornamentation with the clean lines and geometric shapes of the Art Deco. To that end, the decorative plaster, including the gold leaf, was painted over, and the murals were taken down from the proscenium.

On August 2, 1975, more than forty years after the removal of the paintings from the arch, the *Daily Mining Gazette* announced the good news that two of them had been found rolled up in the town hall. As only two of the murals were extant, both tattered and ripped, the decision was made to replace all of them. In 1996, the Calumet Theatre contracted Affiliated Artists of Wisconsin to duplicate the existing paintings and to research those that were missing so as to create new murals in the style of the originals (see Plates 7–11).

The cost of the replicas was twenty thousand dollars. They were secured to vinyl and then attached to the proscenium arch in such a way that they can be removed for cleaning. The installation of the new panels was complete on January 7, 1999, and the dedication ceremony took place a month later at a Chenille Sisters concert.

"On and Off the Stage"

The Golden Widow, lyrics by Edward Madden, music by Melville Gideon and Louis Hirsch, 1909

> The stage has been built with a view to accommodate the largest traveling performance, and it can never be said of the new opera house that a company was unable to use all their scenery on account of a small stage. (*Copper Country Evening News*, October 2, 1900)

— CALUMET THEATRE —

Seating Capacity & Stage Dimensions

AS RECORDED IN *JULIUS CAHN'S OFFICIAL THEATRICAL GUIDE, 1900-1901*

Seating Capacity	1,110
Proscenium Arch	Width 32′ / Height 26′
Depth of Stage from Footlights to Back Wall	38′
Width of Stage Between Side Walls	66′
Height from Stage Floor to Rigging Loft	60′

Cut into the stage floor were three traps located upstage right and left and downstage center. Not unlike the traps at the Tibbits Opera House, they were used for lowering wardrobe trunks and properties below the stage and to implement the magical entrances and exits of various characters. They have been sealed and are no longer in use.

Located under the stage were eight dressing rooms. There were also four "star" dressing chambers, as they were called, two situated on either side of the stage accessed from backstage by steep, narrow stairs. In 1979, one of the upper chambers was transformed into a museum-like installation designated as the "Sarah Bernhardt Dressing Room." It was appointed with appropriate artifacts and furnishings so as to recreate the look and ambiance of the early 1900s and was on display when the theater was open for tours.

Bring Up the Lights!

The Red Jacket Common Council meeting minutes of September 18, 1900, indicate that the Calumet and Hecla Mining Company presented a proposal to deliver three hundred electric lights to the theater from its electric light station for $633.05. The estimate included labor, wire, telephones, and other materials necessary to install the lights. The offer was accepted.

The Calumet Theatre was one of the first buildings in the area to employ electric lights exclusively. The building contained 1,441 incandescent lights, of which 275 were in the proscenium arch; eighty of them outlined its horseshoe shape and drew attention to the center circle of the domed ceiling that was surrounded by 512 lights. From the center of the ceiling hung a copper spheroid-shaped chandelier that could be raised and lowered by a pulley system. The chandelier contained over one hundred lights that created a brilliant pinpoint, starlight effect.

"It's Only a Paper Moon"

The Great Magoo, lyrics by E. Y. Harburg and Billy Rose, music by Harold Arlen, 1933

> The drop curtains for the new theatre are all of very fine design, the scenes are all new and original and of artistic beauty having been the admiration of all who have seen them. (*Copper Country Evening News*, February 4, 1900)

On September 31, 1899 the Red Jacket Common Council considered bids for the creation of opera house scenery. The contract was awarded to Associated Artists of Milwaukee under the supervision of Howard Tuttle, who received $2,600 for his elaborate settings and drops.

Good News, Bad News

The good news: During the 1904–5 season, the Calumet Theatre hosted over eighty professional touring company productions, more than in any previous year.

The bad news: In 1905, the newspaper reported that a large group of young toughs were standing in front of the theater spitting on patrons and blocking the doorway as they tried to enter.

More good news: For those male patrons who needed more refreshment during intermission than a breath of fresh air could provide, they had another option at two convenient locations. Next door to the theater was Shute's Saloon that, like the theater, opened in 1900. During the intermission, gentlemen could gather there under the leaded glass canopy mounted over the bar and enjoy a cigar and beverage. They would be informed that the intermission was coming to an end by blinking lights or a ringing bell controlled from backstage at the theater.

There was a similar arrangement in play at the bar of the Copper Range Hotel located across the street from the theater. Between the theater and the bar, a wire with two bells or buzzers, one at each end of the wire, had been installed. Just before the intermission, the stage manager would buzz the bar manager to alert him of the upcoming break. In the bar, two minutes before the intermission ended, the bell rang again informing the gentlemen that it was time to drink up and return to the opera house.

More bad news: The ingenious Copper Range Hotel intermission alert system was in operation until prohibition. In 1931, the connecting wire between the hotel and the theater was taken down.

And, finally, more good news: For the convenience of the patrons, after each performance, streetcars were lined up in front of the theater to take them as far south as Houghton and as far north as Mohawk. For those theatergoers with private transportation, doormen in livery summoned their carriages. According to Cousin Jack, a local storyteller (aka Jack Foster, now deceased), on the theater's side street stood a large, ornate claw-foot bathtub filled with fresh water so that those who came by horse and buggy could be sure their horses would not go thirsty.

Better Safe than Sorry

There were no fire escapes attached to the building at the time it opened. Over a year later, in May 1901, it occurred to the members of the common council that as a precautionary measure, they might consider fire escapes. The building committee was authorized to ask Alexander Agassiz for permission to use the area on the south side of the building to construct the escape stairs. On May 8, 1901, Mr. Agassiz granted his permission.

The Peninsula Heating and Plumbing Company was paid $829 to install the fire escape and create an outside door at the balcony level to provide access to it. The original contract was for the construction of stairs from the balcony to the ground only. It was assumed that in case of fire patrons seated in the gallery would exit down the interior stairs to the balcony and exit there.

A month after the 1903 Iroquois Theatre fire in Chicago, there was a review of the effectiveness of the fire safety measures at the Calumet Theatre. Members of the Red Jacket Common Council observed a fire drill carried out by the theater stagehands. Dissatisfied with the results of the drill, three days later the council called a special meeting with an architect to formulate plans for safety renovations to the playhouse.

A fire exit door was created between the first balcony and the second-floor ballroom of the neighboring Town Hall. In addition, new electric signs identified all exit doors, a sprinkler system was installed on the fly loft, a second fire escape was installed from the gallery independent of the existing one that serviced the balcony, and an asbestos fire curtain was purchased for $365. In April 1904, after the safety renovations had been completed and a fire drill had taken place, Manager Cuddihy estimated that in case of emergency, the theater could be completely evacuated in five minutes. In 1961, when the fire marshal declared that the gallery was badly in need of repair and a potential fire hazard, the gallery was closed and its fire escape removed.

"There'll Have to Be Changes Made"

My Darlin' Aida, lyrics by Charles Friedman,
music by Hans Spialek based on Giuseppe Verdi, 1952

The first major redecoration of the theater took place a decade after it opened. On June 6, 1910, the Panton and White Co. of Duluth, Minnesota, was awarded a contract to repair cracks in the plasterwork, repaint it in ivory, and highlight the scrollwork in gold. For the rest of the theater, the goal was to replace the Turkish red and empire green with shades of green and brown.

The lobby was painted a golden brown, the coatroom and lavatory a rich green, the stairwells a buff shade, and as stipulated in the estimate, "All to have elaborate and appropriate stenciling work." A sky effect was created on the ceiling in tints that complemented the proscenium paintings, and the company created a new front curtain that depicted a gold-framed Venetian landscape. The estimate included the promise that they would do all of the painting "for the sum of $1,290.00 in watercolor, and $1,690.00 in lead and oil."

The next year, 1911, the exterior of the building was given a boost. A sign with 160 electric lights that spelled out the name of the theater was attached near the entrance of the building.

Caution: Attending the Theater May Be Hazardous to Your Health!

The last quarter of 1918 was not a good time for the Calumet Theatre or for the country. The world was still at war and was fighting the Spanish flu pandemic. The edict from the Michigan State Board of Health that closed the Tibbits Opera House for three weeks impacted all theaters in the state. The doors of the Calumet Theatre were closed from mid-October until mid-November.

Nine days after the theater reopened for business, it had to be closed down again. After a performance on November 25, 1918, a pedestrian walking down Elm Street saw smoke billowing from the back of the building. Two factors definitely saved the theater and probably the town hall as well. First, the $365 spent on the asbestos curtain twelve years earlier turned out to be money well spent as it saved the auditorium when the fire broke out below the stage. Second, the fire engine house was located directly across the street.

The fire originated in the basement but quickly spread to the stage floor and on up to the fly loft. It destroyed all scenery and stage furnishings in its path. The heat was so intense that the spheroid chandelier melted and rained molten metal on the seats below. The cause of the fire was never determined, but the prime suspects were faulty wiring or a discarded cigarette. The restoration closed the theater for four months; it reopened with a touring production of the play *Parlor, Bedroom and Bath* on March 15, 1919.

As the 1920s rolled in, the theater's programming primarily consisted of a combination of stock company productions, vaudeville, and silent films. During the summer of 1929, the Calumet Theatre was closed for two months to install sound equipment, and from that time on, the films were no longer silent.

The End of an Era

> The Keweenaw copper boom began to fade as the ore deposits were either played out or the mineshafts had been extended too deep into the earth to make further mining profitable . . . the mining companies scaled back their operations and the economy and population in the area declined. Thus, the Calumet Theatre lost valuable support despite its popularity with the area and the summer tourist visitors. Sadly, the Calumet Theatre's glorious heydays were finished. (T. Kilgore Splake, "The Calumet Opera House and Theater," 1996)

The Calumet Theatre Company, an independent not-for-profit organization, was formed in 1983. Although the Village of Calumet owns the building, the Calumet Theatre Company is responsible for its management and maintenance. Their mission statement:

> The Calumet Theatre Company is committed to offering a quality entertainment experience that provides diverse

cultural and artistic opportunities while preserving the historic character of the Theatre.

The Calumet Theatre was added to the National Register of Historic Places in 1971. Ten years later, the theater was honored by the Michigan Society of Architecture in an exhibit as one of the fifty most significant structures in Michigan.

SCENE ii

Curtain Going Up!

> Mr. Cuddihy has not yet decided upon what he will secure for the first night in the new theater. . . . He wants something of an operatic nature, yet not too heavy along that line. —*Copper Country Evening News*, October 27, 1898

Mr. Cuddihy was successful in achieving his goal. He was able to book "something of an operatic nature, yet not too heavy." The production was the comic opera *The Highwayman* by composer Reginald De Koven and librettist/lyricist Harry B. Smith.

The operetta was a sequel of sorts to its successful predecessor, *Robin Hood*, created by the same team. *The Highwayman* opened on Broadway in 1897 and was the most successful musical entertainment of that season.

Following its New York run, the show went on tour traveling with its own scenery, costumes, orchestra, and a full company that included a real horse.

> The opening will be the greatest social event ever known in copperdom's metropolis. Never in the history of the Copper Country has there been such a gathering of fashionable folk as will be seen at the theater on this occasion. (*Daily Mining Gazette*, March 12, 1900)

Tickets went on sale at the City Drug Store in Red Jacket and Barry's Drug Store in Houghton for \$2.50, \$2.00, and \$1.00 with the boxes going for \$25.00 each. Management expected that the demand for opening night tickets would be strong, therefore a number of the best seats were held back and put up for auction at the fire engine house the day before the performance. The *Daily Mining Gazette* reported that the net proceeds from the auction would go to the Village of Red Jacket to be applied to the first year's interest on the

FIGURE 43. The Broadway Theatre Opera Company's production of *The Highwayman* that had premiered in New York three years earlier was the opening performance at the Calumet Theatre on March 20, 1900. (Publisher: A. S. Seer Print, N.Y., ca. 1898. Retrieved from the Library of Congress Prints and Photographs Division.)

town hall and opera house bonds. As the opening bid was set higher than the cost of buying a ticket from one of the drug stores, the auction turned out to be somewhat of a disappointment.

> Inside of two hours yesterday afternoon 250 seats for the opening performance at the new Calumet theatre were disposed of at an average price of $3.25 per seat. The seats sold were all in the parquet and first balcony . . . but there are still a large number of them to be had and most of the balcony circle is still unsold. (*Copper Country Evening News*, March 20, 1900)

On March 22, 1900, the *Copper Country Evening News* review of the opening night included an attendance update: "the top gallery had many vacant seats. . . . There were quite a few seats in the balcony circle and on the first floor that were unoccupied."

Despite the fact that it was not a full house, it was still a gala occasion. Special trains from Lake Linden and Houghton-Hancock brought patrons to Red Jacket for the performance. Before the curtain went up, John R. Ryan, president of the village's common council, stepped on stage and stated that it would be appropriate on this occasion to hear comments from someone who represented the interests upon which the village depended. He then introduced Captain William E. Parnall, of the Calumet and Hecla Mining Company, who stood up in his box and congratulated the people of Red Jacket on their magnificent new theater that he believed would be a lasting benefit for the city.

— HEADLINE —

'The Highwayman' Captured the Town

The day after the opening, the reviewer for the *Copper Country Evening News* had praise for the creators of the piece, the leading actors, and the production:

> Mr. Smith understands well how to touch the American funny bone and Mr. De Koven has never failed to appeal to the American love of tunefulness and light harmonies."
>
> Arthur Deagon, the highwayman, gives a strong interpretation of the part and . . . has a voice entirely adequate. Miss Thorne's stage presence is very charming and her costumes gorgeous.

For the plot of this comic opera, Smith borrowed from his earlier work, *Robin Hood*, as well as John Gay's *The Beggar's Opera*. A dashing young gentleman, Dick Fitzgerald, is cheated out of his fortune by the villain, Sir John Hawkhurst, and becomes an outlaw known as Captain Scarlet. He is eventually awarded a pardon, but Hawkhurst intercepts it. Fitzgerald's sweetheart, Lady Constance, saves the day when, with gun in hand, she convinces the culprit to relinquish the document. By the final curtain, the villain is bested, Fitzgerald receives the pardon for having been a highwayman, and he and Lady Constance live happily ever after.

One of the show's managers admired the theater as much as the reviewer admired the show. In a newspaper interview the Broadway Theatre Opera Company business manager was quoted as follows:

> Most new theatres are built to please what the audience sees . . . and the poor actors have to take chances on clumsy arrangements behind the footlights, but I have never seen any theatre with better or more convenient arrangements back of the drop curtain than you have right here in Calumet. It's a little gem. (B. T. King, Business Manager, Broadway Theatre Opera Company, *Copper Country Evening News*, March 20, 1900)

"Another Op'nin', Another Show"

Kiss Me, Kate, lyrics and music by Cole Porter, 1948

After the March opening, the Calumet Theatre had bookings of one kind of event or another on seventy-five of the days remaining in 1900; fifty-one of the presentations were plays or operettas produced by professional touring companies.

The Highwayman had no sooner left the building than *Faust* arrived the next day. *Faust* played to sold-out houses at normal prices that ranged from twenty-five cents to one dollar. In addition to reasonable ticket prices, patrons may have been lured into the theater by the advertisement for *Faust* that touted electric fireflies, electric owls and snakes, a burning barrel of wine, and "many other weird and dramatic effects."

"The Man of the Year This Week"

Top Banana, lyrics and music by Johnny Mercer, 1951)

The first leading man of note to perform in Red Jacket that year was the state-favorite star *Walker Whiteside. He was

FIGURE 44. Walker Whiteside, an actor born and raised in the Midwest, as Hamlet, a role he performed in New York and on tour. By the time he was in his early thirties, he had played the Danish prince in approximately 1,400 productions. (Photographer and date unknown. Museum of the City of New York.)

popular with Michigan audiences in general and particularly popular in Red Jacket. On his first visit he appeared as Hamlet and in *The Red Cockade*. Two days after Whiteside's initial appearance in the Keweenaw Peninsula, Manager Cuddihy received the following letter from the actor:

> Dear Sir:—I wish to express my sincere admiration of the Calumet theater in which my company and myself had the pleasure of appearing last night. The accommodations on the stage are Perfect . . . indeed from the foyer to the stage entrance the Calumet theater may rank with the best metropolitan play houses and is superior to many. My first visit to your city has been a most pleasant surprise and I hope to have the honor of being with you again.
>
> Sincerely yours, Walker Whiteside

He did "have the honor" of being at the Calumet Theatre again as later that year he was back to reprise his role in *Hamlet* and perform in *Heart and Sword*. He continued his association with the Calumet Theatre for six years. During that period, he played Hamlet three times as well as other Shakespearean characters such as Richard III and Shylock in *The Merchant of Venice*.

"A Couple of Clowns"

Nowhere to Go but Up, lyrics by James Lipton, music by Sol Berkowitz, 1962

Billed as "The Men Who Invented Fun," Charles A. Murray and Ollie Mack hit the Calumet Theatre boards with the first in their series of popular Irish American comedies, **Finnigan's Ball*, on May 21, 1900. The advertisement for their show claimed that they had "the largest, best singing, highest salaried, company ever seen in farce comedy" and promised "high class specialties, new and tuneful music, beautiful wardrobe, and pretty girls." They returned in September with the last of the series, *Finnigan's 400*.

In October 1900 audiences had an opportunity to see a second production of *Faust*, this one starring Porter J. White as Mephistopheles. The advance publicity for the production noted that it employed "16,000 feet of electric wire, eight calcium lights, and approximately 20,000 square feet of scenery."

"A Woman of Importance"

Coming Thro' the Rye, lyrics by George V. Hobart, music by J. Sebastian Hiller and A. Baldwin Sloane, 1906

In Red Jacket, citizens eagerly anticipated the stage appearance of the celebrated Polish actress *Madame Helena Modjeska. The demand for tickets was unprecedented:

> The rush for seats for the presentation of "Macbeth" by Modjeska when the sale commenced at the City Drug Store at 9:30 this morning exceeded anything of the kind that has ever been seen in this city. (*Copper Country Evening News*, December 3, 1900)

Mr. Cuddihy had extra chairs placed on the main floor and in the balcony to accommodate the overflow of patrons. Even with the added seats, many prospective ticket-buyers were turned away. Modjeska graciously agreed to do a special matinee performance of *Mary Stuart* for those who were not able to obtain tickets for *Macbeth*.

FIGURE 45. Madame Helena Modjeska in the title role of *Mary Stuart*, which she performed as a special matinee in Red Jacket for patrons who were not able to obtain tickets to her sold-out production of *Macbeth* the previous evening at the Calumet Theatre. High school students were excused from classes to attend the performance. (Photographer and date unknown. Museum of the City of New York.)

Mary Stuart was not reviewed by the local press, but the performance of *Macbeth* was:

> The production of "Macbeth" by Modjeska and company last evening was undoubtedly the greatest theatrical

> event that has ever occurred in the Copper Country . . . presented before one of the most brilliant audiences that has ever graced a performance in Upper Michigan. (*Copper Country Evening News*, December 7, 1900)

The newspaper did go on to report that the last two acts were disrupted by "hooligans and ruffians." Shortly thereafter an officer was placed in the gallery to keep troublemakers from spitting on the well-dressed patrons below. Despite the obstreperous elements in the audience, Modjeska returned to Red Jacket two more times. In 1902, she performed with the distinguished classical actor Louis James in Shakespeare's *Henry VIII*. Traveling with them were two carloads of scenery and fifty people.

A Ghost Story

Although Michigan's Upper Peninsula was only one of many stops on her tour, after her death Modjeska's spirit may have returned to the Keweenaw region, as there are those who believe that the ghost of the actress inhabits the Calumet Theatre.

Flash-forward: It is 1958 and a professional acting company has taken over the playhouse for a season of summer stock. The play is *The Taming of the Shrew*, and on July 22, opening night, a young actress named Adysse Lane is about to deliver Katharina's famous speech at the end of the play in which she outlines a wife's duty to her husband when suddenly the actress is distracted and appears to have forgotten her lines.

> Lane felt something pulling her up, pulling on her arm up toward the balcony. When she looked up that way, she saw Madam Modjeska and the madam gave her the lines. Lane later said she clearly saw the dark eyes and pale complexion of Modjeska's face atop a fuzzy outline of a body. The figure was looming near a spotlight stationed on the balcony. (*Lansing State Journal*, November 28, 1993)

Miss Lane quickly finished the speech, the show went on, and Modjeska had saved the day—and the play!

Since that time, there have been several other Modjeska sightings at the Calumet Theatre. Between 2007 and 2010, there were five paranormal investigations, and after each session the investigators presented their conclusion that confirmed the presence of paranormal activity in the facility.

It is curious that the ghost of a woman who died in California and whose body was shipped back to Poland for burial would take up residence in an opera house in Michigan's remote Upper Peninsula. Perhaps it's the pasties.

"On with the Show"

Pretty Faces, lyrics and music by Robert W. Cabell, 1990

After the 1900 inaugural season, the theater booked approximately forty professional touring productions a year until the copper miners' strike of 1913–14 when only eleven productions were booked.

Although still produced, after 1900 some of the most popular plays of the second half of the previous century began to disappear from opera house season schedules. On the other hand, at the Calumet Theatre, the old warhorse, *Uncle Tom's Cabin* was seen almost every year until December 26, 1924, when the Original Stetson Company, advertised as "the oldest existing *Uncle Tom's Cabin* company," brought the show to Red Jacket one more time with vaudeville performed between the acts of the play. The other titles that were most frequently advertised from 1900 until 1919 were *Faust*, seven times, and Charles H. Hoyt's *A Texas Steer*, six times.

And Now for a Word from Our Sponsors

Both the Klaw and Erlanger Syndicate and the Shubert Organization operated on the national level and dominated the touring business in most of the country. In 1910, the Syndicate began to boycott those theaters that were part of the National Theater Owners' Association, which was created in opposition to the control of the Syndicate. In support of and inspired by the National Theater Owners' Association, several small regional booking agencies were created. There were three that served Wisconsin, Minnesota, and the Upper Peninsula of Michigan. Their purpose was to bring first-class dramatic talent to cities north of Green Bay, Wisconsin. In Michigan that included, among other towns, Escanaba, Marquette, Iron Mountain, Ishpeming, and Red Jacket.

As the Syndicate exercised its boycott of not booking any of its productions in those theaters that did business with regional agencies, from 1910 to 1913, no Syndicate show played in Red Jacket. Finally, in the spring of 1913, when the Syndicate began to lose the strong hold it had on regional theaters, one of its productions, *The Prince of Pilsen*, played the Calumet Theatre. It was followed, three months later, by another Syndicate hit—*Peter Pan* starring *Maude Adams.

"Only for You"

Hitchy-Koo of 1920, lyrics by Anne Calder and Glen MacDonough, music by Jerome Kern, 1920

Many popular and, at the time, well-known actors trod the Calumet Theatre boards between 1900 and 1928. Some of them have been forgotten, but some have not. One hundred years after their final performances on stage, James O'Neill and Lillian Russell are still familiar names to many. They were only seen in Red Jacket—not in Coldwater or Manistee.

The Matinee Idol

James O'Neill (1847–1920) brought his most famous vehicle, *The Count of Monte Cristo*, to the Calumet Theatre in February 1902. He returned the next season in a play titled *The Manxman*. Today, he is probably best known as the father of playwright Eugene O'Neill and as the inspiration for the character of James Tyrone in his son's Pulitzer-Prize-winning play *Long Day's Journey into Night*.

O'Neill was born in Ireland and grew up in Cincinnati, Ohio. Early in his career, he played supporting roles to both Edwin Forrest and Edwin Booth. He was handsome, charismatic, and possessed great stage presence; he became

FIGURE 46. James O'Neill received acclaim for many of his performances including that of D'Artagnan in *The Three Musketeers*, but it was as Edmond Dantes in *The Count of Monte Cristo*, pictured here, that he was most famous. (Photographer: Bryon Company, New York, N.Y., 1900. Museum of the City of New York.)

a leading matinee idol while still in his twenties. His reputation as a "ladies man" resulted in a number of scandals that only enhanced his box office appeal.

In 1879, he garnered national attention when he portrayed Christ in the premiere of David Belasco's *The Passion Play* in San Francisco. As the city had an ordinance forbidding the "personification of any scriptural character upon the stage," he was taken to court and fined; the incident was reported throughout the country. Three years later, he was offered the leading role in the dramatization of Alexandre Dumas's novel *The Count of Monte Cristo*. For audiences O'Neill's performance was a sensation to the extent that over a thirty-year period he played the role approximately six thousand times, and by the time he retired had accrued an estimated one million dollars.

The Count of Monte Cristo was advertised as the "Most Magnificent Scenic Production Ever Seen on the American Stage." Even James O'Neill had to share top billing with the scenery.

"The Queen of Society"

Hoity-Toity, lyrics by Edgar Smith, music by John Stromberg, 1901

Lillian Russell (1860–1922) was born Helen Louise Leonard in Clinton, Iowa. When her parents separated, she moved to New York City with her mother who was an author, suffragette, and the first woman to run for mayor of New York City. As "Nellie Leonard," Lillian Russell made her professional debut in the chorus of *H.M.S. Pinafore* at the Brooklyn Park Theatre while still in her teens. She married the production's orchestra director who was the first of her four husbands. She went on to play leading roles in many other comic operas by Gilbert and Sullivan as well as those by Jacques Offenbach. At the age of nineteen, she was hired by Tony Pastor, "the father of vaudeville," who presented her as an English ballad singer and suggested the stage name "Lillian Russell."

In addition to her four marriages, she had dalliances with several famous men, including a four-decade relationship with wealthy business tycoon James Buchanan "Diamond Jim" Brady who showered her with expensive gifts. Apparently, she became so accustomed to having everything bestowed upon her that according to the celebrity gossip at the time, she was famous for never paying her bills.

From 1899 to 1904 she appeared in the musical revues produced by and starring comics Joe Weber and Lew Fields. Eventually, due to vocal problems, she switched from comic operas to nonmusical fare. One of her greatest successes was in the play *Wildfire* that she brought to the Calumet Theatre in 1909. In the play, Wildfire is the name of a prize racehorse whose owner is murdered early in the drama. The killer steals the horse, enters it in a big horseracing event, and pays a jockey to throw the race. The daughter of Wildfire's rightful owner, played by Miss Russell, tracks down the villain and exposes his plan. Wildfire wins the race.

The *Daily Mining Gazette* raved—especially about Miss Russell:

> She is first of all, a beautiful woman, queenly in figure and carriage, has a most expressive face and a magnetic personality. Her gowns made women in the audience gasp.

In 1922, following in her politically active mother's footsteps and at the request of President Warren Harding, she went to Europe on an immigration fact-finding mission. Her report was instrumental in the creation and passage of the Immigration Act of 1924.

"The Mystery Play"

Little Nellie Kelly, lyrics and music by George M. Cohan, 1922

Although George M. Cohan was not seen in any of these three Michigan towns, one of his few nonmusical creations was. *Seven Keys to Baldpate*, a successful comedy-mystery, opened on Broadway in 1913. Two years later the touring version was at the Calumet Theatre. The script was based on a novel by Earl Derr Biggers, best known for his books featuring Chinese American detective Charlie Chan. The Asian sleuth does not appear in the novel or the play. Instead, a writer, Billy McGee, has made a wager with a friend that he can write a one-thousand-word story in twenty-four hours. To be uninterrupted, his friend gives him what he says is the one and only key to an off-season, isolated inn, Baldpate. During the night, McGee discovers that there are six others with keys to the inn that have come to Baldpate to plan mischief, mayhem, and murder. It turns out that the other key holders are all actors that were hired by his friend so as to distract Billy from writing his story.

The dramatization was written, directed, and produced by Cohan. Although he usually starred in the plays he wrote and directed, he did not act in the New York or touring productions of this play. However, he did assume the leading

FIGURE 47. Lillian Russell in one of her many elegant gowns for which she was famous. One of her costumes for Weber and Fields's *Hokey-Pokey* was decorated with precious and semiprecious gems and allegedly cost $150,000. Miss. Russell had exact duplicates of her expensive costumes made to wear in rehearsal. Fact or fiction? (Photographer unknown, ca. 1904. Retrieved from the Library of Congress.)

role in the 1917 silent film version of the tale and in the 1935 Broadway revival. During a thirty-year period from 1917 to 1947, seven film versions of the play were released.

"Are the Stars Out Tonight?"

Dames, "I Only Have Eyes for You," lyrics by Al Dubin, music by Harry Warren, 1934

Although Red Jacket was one of the most remote entertainment sites in the state, during the first two decades of the twentieth century, thanks to improved railroad service, the national importance of the copper mining industry, and the presence of the copper barons in Red Jacket, the Calumet Theatre was able to attract more star personalities than many Lower Peninsula venues. Maude Adams, Helena Modjeska, James O'Neill, Lillian Russell, and Walker Whiteside were not the only stars to shine from the Calumet Theatre stage. Adding their presence to the dazzling firmament were Sarah Bernhardt in *Camille*, *Richard Mansfield in *Beaucaire*, *Otis Skinner in *Francesca da Rimini*, and *Eva Tanguay in *A Good Fellow*.

Business as Usual

By 1920, many opera houses were committed to booking motion pictures and vaudeville almost exclusively. There would be occasional performances by a touring or stock company, but they were few and far between. The Calumet Theatre, however, continued booking first-class professional productions for another eight years.

In 1921, *Irene* came to Red Jacket. The musical opened on Broadway in 1919 with a book by James Montgomery, lyrics by Joseph McCarthy, and music by Harry Tierney. The plot, essentially a Cinderella story, centers on a young Irish girl, Irene O'Dare, who works in a New York shop and is sent to a Long Island mansion on an errand. There, she meets and falls in love with the son of the estate owner. His friend, a fashion designer named Madame Lucy, who is really a man, convinces Irene to be a model in his/her fashion show. The fashion show is a success, and Irene sings a song about the "Alice Blue Gown" she is wearing—the song became a hit. There follow many complications and misunderstandings, but by the time the curtain falls, Irene has ended up with both the gown and the guy.

The show was praised for its intelligent plot and well-integrated songs. It broke the record held by **A Trip to Chinatown* as the longest-running Broadway musical and held that record for eighteen years. It was revived on Broadway twice; the second revival, in 1973, starred Debbie Reynolds. Although that revival had a respectable run of 594 performances, it couldn't outrun the original's 675 performances or claim seventeen national touring companies and two film adaptations.

The phenomenally successful 1919 Broadway hit comedy *Up in Mabel's Room* written by Wilson Collison and Otto Harbach was presented four times at the Calumet Theatre between 1921 and 1924. The farce concerns a young newlywed husband who is on a mission to retrieve a chemise that he had given his former girlfriend, Mabel, that was embroidered with both of their names. The piece of lingerie in question is, of course, up in Mabel's room—attempting to get it back generated all the fun.

For something completely different, the 6th Annual Edition of *George White's Scandals* played the Calumet Theatre in 1926. This glamorous revue that rivaled the *Ziegfeld Follies* boasted "100 Member Cast, The Famous George White Beauty Chorus—60 girls all under eighteen years old" and had a score by the popular 1920s songwriting team of Buddy DeSylva, Lew Brown, and Ray Henderson. The costumes were by artist and fashion designer Erté.

"Stock Report"

Put It in Writing, lyrics by Fred Ebb, music by Norman L. Martin, 1963

From the time the theater opened, residencies by stock companies were a significant part of the Calumet Theatre's bookings. The first year, two companies were in residence, the following year the number was four, and that number increased exponentially until it peaked in 1910 when fourteen companies took up fourteen weeks of the theatre season.

The Frank E. Long Stock Company must have been a particular favorite as between 1901 and 1913 it visited Red Jacket twenty-six times usually performing on six evenings per visit. In 1903 it performed seven plays with "vaudeville features," and the next year it was in town six days and had scheduled six plays. Unfortunately, that was a disappointing visit as one performance was canceled due to a blizzard and at another performance an actor was injured during the course of the play.

By 1905, the vaudeville component of the Frank E. Long Company's program became more prominent. In addition to offering six plays, it advertised the participation of a magician as well as singers, dancers, acrobats, and vaudeville numbers. The advertisement for its 1906 appearance referred to the troupe as "The Old Reliable Frank E. Long Company" and boasted of "16 People, 7 New Plays, 6 Feature Specialties" with the offer of "One Lady Free with each 30 cent ticket Monday night." The company's repertory primarily consisted of contemporary melodramas and Western sagas: *In the Shadow of the Gallows*, *The Cowboy and the Sheriff*, and *The Cowboy and the Girl*.

By contrast, the Tom Marks Stock Company, a 1905 booking, specialized in plays about the Irish: *The Irish Boarder*, *The Irish Detective*, and *Shamus O'Brien*. It advertised vaudeville features, illuminated songs, and moving pictures between acts. Also in residence in 1905 was the Courtenay Stock Company that presented Sir Arthur Conan Doyle's *The Sign of the Four* for which fifty local boys were cast to play Sherlock Holmes's junior detectives. In December of the same year, Pollard's Lilliputian Opera Company performed seven plays featuring fifty children from Australia between six and fourteen years of age. The highlight of its visit was the production of *H.M.S. Pinafore* featuring the all-adolescent cast.

Stock companies continued to be booked at the Calumet Theatre until 1928 when movies and vaudeville took over the playhouse. The most frequent visiting troupe of the 1920s was the Frank Winninger Comedy Company that performed during five seasons presenting seven to nine productions each residency. "Winninger" seems to have been a name synonymous with "stock company" as there was also the John D. Winninger Players that was booked three seasons and the Adolph Winninger Company that was seen once.

Something for Everyone

Spiritualists and magicians were seen less often at the Calumet Theatre than they were at other venues. In 1905, Adelaide Herman, "The Only Woman Magician in the World," as well as two hypnotists were on the Calumet Theatre stage. In addition, Madame Evelyn Fay, Exponent of Esoteric Philosophy, presented her show "Your Mind an Open Book to Madame Fay" that included Signor Blitz, "Europe's Greatest Wizard."

However, the dearth of mystery was compensated for by an abundance of muscle. Weekly wrestling and/or boxing matches took place at the facility in Red Jacket during its early years of operation. In 1904, the theater hosted a wrestling tournament, and the next year it presented the "Good Will Farm Athletic Show" that consisted of "Fisticuffs and Wrestling" as well as club swinging. During any given season, there were seldom fewer than four bouts of one kind or the other booked into the theater, and in 1909 there were seven matches—some live, some on film.

"Music in the Air"

A Hero Is Born, lyrics by Agnes Morgan, music by Lehman Engel, 1937

John Philip Sousa and his band were no strangers to the Upper Peninsula. They gave concerts at the Calumet Theatre in 1902, 1906, and 1912. The house was sold out for all performances.

> This evening two special trains will be run over the mineral Range Railway for the benefit of Torch Lake and Dollar Bay people wishing to attend the entertainment at the Calumet Theatre by Sousa's Band. (*Daily Mining Gazette*, March 15, 1902)

The Kilties, Canada's Military Band with forty musicians, ten soloists, a choir, highland dancers, bagpipers, and British military buglers, performed in Red Jacket on January 8, 1903. The band was on its "Eighth Grand Concert Tour." Previously it had toured Europe and performed before King Edward VII of England, and by 1912 the troupe had accrued four hundred thousand touring miles since it was formed in 1900.

Unfortunately, in their travels back and forth between America and Canada, they encountered some difficulty. Because the Kilties had not declared that their kilts were imported and had not paid the required duty, their garments were seized by custom officials leaving the Kilties kiltless. Until the matter was resolved, they were forced to appear at their subsequent performances in street clothes.

In addition to the Scottish music performed by the Canadian Kilties, other melodies from other nationalities were also heard at the Calumet Theatre: there were Norwegian Grand Concerts and National Croatian Concerts. The theater also presented concerts by groups and individuals from the region. During the first season, the Calumet and Hecla Band presented three "Grand Concerts." Between 1900 and 1919 the Calumet Temperance Band, the Northern Michigan Singers, the Michigan College of Mines Glee and Mandolin Club, and the Copper Country Choral Club were among regional and local organizations that performed on the stage and filled the auditorium with music.

"Finlandia"

Finland Awakes, music by Jean Sibelius, 1901

A large portion of the population of Red Jacket consisted of immigrants, and the largest ethnic group represented was the Finnish. Consequently, the Calumet Theatre hosted a significant number of events for or by that specific demographic. In the 1900–1901 season, there were two concerts by the Finnish Glee Club, a performance by the Finnish Opera Company, and a minstrel show sponsored by the Finnish Relief Committee.

Silvi, presented in 1904, was the first Finnish-language play to be produced at the theater. A Finnish-language musical, *At the Logging River*, followed it later that year and *The Workman's Wife*, also presented in 1904, was a Finnish-language temperance play.

The 1905 Finnish Society Jubilee was a celebration of the concessions granted by Russia to Finland. The evening consisted of speeches in Finnish and English as well as performances by the Calumet and Hecla Orchestra and the Finnish Glee Club. All told, there were more than thirty Finnish-specific events at the Calumet Theatre between 1900 and 1919 that included concerts, meetings, and lectures. There was even a performance by Finnish acrobats, a Finnish wrestling tournament, and several performances produced by the Finnish Dramatic Club.

"Talk about This—Talk about That"

Sweethearts, lyrics by Robert B. Smith, music by Victor Herbert, 1913

Various groups such as the Calumet Women's Club, the YMCA, the Copper City Odd Fellows Lodge, and the Calumet Lyceum Bureau sponsored lectures delivered at the theater.

The Lyceum Bureau originated in Boston in 1868 and expanded to become an organization that created a national circuit whereby orators and musicians presented lectures and concerts around the country. In 1911, a lecture at the Calumet Theatre titled "The World's Battle Ground" was the first event arranged and sponsored by the Calumet Lyceum Bureau. In its first year of operation the local branch of the bureau also sponsored the Castle Square Entertainers that performed songs, music, and readings. Other musical groups that appeared under the auspices of the Lyceum Bureau were the Southern Jubilee Singers and Players, the Mendelssohn Trio, and the Original Strollers Quartet with a vocal and instrumental program that included Swiss handbell ringing. In 1925, the local bureau presented their last event at the theater, the DeSellem-Folsum Operatic Quartet comprised of two singers, a cellist, and a pianist.

Titles of a few notable lectures include "Rascals and Saints—The Personality of American Men of Letters" delivered by Dr. A. E. Winship; Senator Benjamin Tillman from South Carolina had something to say about "The Race Problem"; Jane Addams of Hull House in Chicago explained "English and American Social Settlements and Their Present Tendencies"; A. Tresich Pavicich reported the "Conditions in Croatia"; and Anna Caulfield described "American Art and Mural Decorations."

Over the years the stage of the Calumet Theatre provided a platform for campaign speeches, rallies, caucuses, and conventions for the Democratic, Republican, Socialist, Prohibition, and Independent parties. In September 1900 telegraphed election returns were read from the stage between the acts of a play. That incident initiated an election-year tradition of announcing the voting results at the theater that continued until 1926.

"Homemade Happiness"

The Clinging Vine, lyrics by Zelda Sears, music by Harold A. Levey, 1922

The theater, owned by the Village of Red Jacket, could be rented by any community organization with the common council's approval. For a nominal fee, it became the venue for locally generated concerts, lectures, and other civic events. The Good Hope Temperance Society, the Norwegian Literary Society, the Knights of Pythias, and the Knights of Columbus were among the organizations that utilized the space for meetings and inductions.

In June 1900, the theater hosted the Calumet High School commencement and continued to do so for over a decade. The facility was also used for church services, suffrage meetings, the Croatian convention, and a presentation by a representative of the Bureau of Explosives for railroad workers and miners titled "The Safe Transportation of Explosives and Other Dangerous Articles."

Many local organizations including the Calumet Stock Company leased the theater to present theatrical productions. The Calumet Women's Club offered the play *Mother Goose Up-to-Date* as well as a vaudeville show with a chorus of 125 directed by Miss Alice B. Camper of Chicago.

The Calumet Elks Lodge presented the musical *In Double Harness* and a number of minstrel shows. However, the Elks' major undertaking was producing an original "juvenile opera" titled *The Golden Ball* in 1916 that was written by two local women who based their musical fantasy on *The Frog Prince* fairytale. Among the cast of characters were butterflies, fairies, tadpoles, and satyrs, all of whom, according to the reviewer, "charmingly executed steps and drills." The Calumet and Hecla Orchestra accompanied the production. The *Calumet News* proclaimed, "*The Golden Ball* is an unqualified success. Its future will extend beyond the confines of the copper country."

"If You Want to Be Successful in the Cinema"

Smiling Faces, lyrics by Mack Gordon, music by Harry Revel, 1930

When the Kinodrome Show was presented at the theater in 1902, Red Jacket was introduced to a state-of-the-art moving-picture machine. The company claimed that prior to its touring shows, rural communities had little exposure to "what is being accomplished in motion photography, the rapid advancement, and quality being obtained in the mysterious art." Other moving-picture presentations followed, and seven years after it had opened as a venue for legitimate theatre the Calumet Theatre ran an advertisement promoting "Moving Pictures That Talk."

At first, the movies were accompanied by vaudeville acts provided by the Coast-to-Coast Vaudeville Circuit. The acts disappeared from the weekly bill in less than a year when the agreement between the theater and the circuit was terminated. From that point on, the theater was a movie house that showed major first-run films on Saturday, Sunday, and two weeknights.

The Calumet Theatre made only minor adjustments to accommodate movies. In 1913, a movie projection booth was installed at the back of the first floor of the auditorium. Later, upgrading to an arc projector necessitated relocating the projection booth to a larger space in the balcony. In order to provide the beam of the projector with an unobstructed path to the screen, a notch had to be cut out of a decorative cornice.

By 1923, movies reigned at the Calumet Theatre. That season consisted of twenty-four films and only four live-action touring productions. In addition to the movies, on some evenings the theater was used for events that promoted local businesses such as demonstrations called "cooking schools" presented by the Houghton Electric Light Company and fashion shows sponsored by Vertin's Department Store, as well as the occasional amateur theatre production.

"As the Years Roll By"

Her Regiment, lyrics by William Le Baron, music by Victor Herbert, 1917

On November 7, 1928, the musical *Hit the Deck* that had opened on Broadway the year before was presented at the playhouse. It was the last professional touring production to play the venue for twelve years. During that interim, the bill of fare at the theater consisted of vaudeville, films, and local events. After the demise of vaudeville in the 1930s, the Calumet Theatre became a movie theater and continued showing first-run films until the early 1970s, after which time subsequent seasons primarily consisted of performances by both professional and amateur music groups and local events, with films scheduled intermittently.

Unlike many other opera houses that were built before the advent of movies and television, there was never a time when the Calumet Theatre went through a literal or metaphoric dark period. It was never closed for an extended period of time, nor was it threatened with demolition. It has served the area continuously since 1900.

Act III

RAMSDELL THEATRE

Manistee (1903)

FIGURE 48. Does this building look familiar? It is the Ramsdell Theatre and Assembly Hall in Manistee, Michigan, that opened in 1903. Compare it to the building in figure 49. (Photographer: Beverly Wilkens, Old Hippie Productions, Manistee, Michigan, 2017.)

FIGURE 49. The Calumet Theatre was built three years before the Ramsdell Theatre. They have almost identical footprints. (Photograph courtesy of the Calumet Theatre.)

SCENE i

Building Going Up!

I'd like to pick up this theatre and take it back to Broadway! —Tony Award–winning set designer Jo Mielziner, *Ludington Daily News*, July 22, 1971

"Exactly Like You"

The International Revue, lyrics by Dorothy Fields, music by Jimmy McHugh, 1930

Many basic elements of the Calumet Theatre and Ramsdell Theatre complexes (figures 48 and 49) are identical: a separate building attached to the left of the theater with a ballroom on the second floor, a portico over the theater entrance, and a bell tower. The major difference between them when viewed from the street is the style of the architectural detailing. The facade of the Calumet Theatre is Italian Renaissance whereas the front of the Ramsdell Theatre is Colonial in style.

The *Manistee Daily News* was religious about recording every move the owner, T. J. Ramsdell, and the architect, Solon S. Beman, made during the construction period. Every time Beman traveled to Manistee from Chicago to monitor the progress of the construction, it was noted. When Ramsdell went to Saginaw and later Sheboygan, Wisconsin, to select brick for the building, the local citizens knew about it thanks to the diligence of the newspaper. However, there is no mention or record to suggest that Ramsdell and Beman ever took a trip to Michigan's Upper Peninsula to check out the Calumet Theatre. Did the prevailing design for opera houses at the turn of the century always include a bell tower, a portico, and an adjacent building with a second floor ballroom all erected on a corner lot? Or could the similarity between the two facilities simply be a coincidence? An intriguing question for which there seems to be no definitive answer, so, instead . . .

FIGURE 50. Logs were floated down the Manistee River to a sawmill where they were sorted, cut, and shipped across Lake Michigan to Chicago, Milwaukee, and other destinations west, ca. 1900. (Photograph courtesy of the Manistee County Historical Museum.)

"Let's Start at the Very Beginning / A Very Good Place to Start"

The Sound of Music, "Do-Re-Mi," lyrics by Oscar Hammerstein II, music by Richard Rodgers, 1959

Before the first Euro-Americans walked the banks of the Manistee River, it was home to Native Americans. There may have been as many as fifteen Ottawa villages situated on the northeastern shores of Lake Michigan at the beginning of the nineteenth century.

With the opening of the Erie Canal in 1825, settlers from the east could more easily travel to the Great Lakes region to expand the American frontier. A Jesuit mission house was built on Lake Manistee by 1826, but it was not until fifteen years later that the first permanent non–Native American settlement was established. John Stronach and his son Adam arrived at the mouth of the Manistee River on April 16, 1841. They brought with them from southern Michigan more than a dozen men and the supplies necessary to build a sawmill. They constructed their first mill on Manistee Lake and later another on the Manistee River. The Manistee lumber industry was born.

Initially, the U.S. government offered the Manistee region's indigenous dwellers whatever land they desired for their reservation. The tribe selected a rectangular area that was six miles north and south by twenty-two miles east and west that included the Manistee River Valley. That large area was the Ottawa reservation from 1836 to 1848. The next year, a new treaty between the Ottawa and the United States that returned the land to the government was signed. The land was turned over to settlers who used the lumber from the acres of white pine forest to build their homesteads and, later, their mills, shops, churches, schools, and, ultimately, a city.

"I Talk to the Trees"

Paint Your Wagon, lyrics by Alan Jay Lerner, music by Frederick Loewe, 1951

At first, the exporting of lumber from Manistee was impeded by a 250-foot long sandbar at the mouth of the river with a water depth of five feet, preventing vessels' access to the harbor. The lumber had to be transported by rafts from the shore to the ship. In 1854, the situation was remedied when workmen excavated a channel across the bar creating a deepwater harbor entrance, and Manistee become one of the largest and busiest shipping ports on the Great Lakes.

Various advances in logging technology made in the 1870s allowed access to remote areas where trees were harvested and transported to the Manistee port on newly introduced logging wheels.

In 1899 the *Manistee Daily News* published a history of the area written by Mrs. Edward D. Wheeler, wife of a local lumberman. She wrote, "there were forty sawmills cutting millions of feet of lumber annually," making the region one of the top producers of lumber in the country. The workers lived in an encampment that included a large bunkhouse, a dining room, and a kitchen. They worked from sunup to sundown six days a week and on Sunday maintained and repaired tools and equipment. The workforce consisted of settlers from the east, Canadian and European immigrants, and Native Americans.

Although the lumber industry filled the coffers of the lumber barons, it decimated the white pine forests. However, by the mid-1930s, more than thirty thousand acres of trees had been planted to replace the forests cut down during the lumbering boom. The Manistee National Forest, established in 1938, now encompasses 538,756 acres and is one of the largest national forests in the central United States.

FIGURE 51. The logging wheels revolutionized the lumber industry in Michigan as they made it possible to transport logs from deep within the forest to the Manistee harbor twelve months a year, ca. 1895. (Photograph courtesy of the Manistee County Historical Museum.)

Salt of the Earth

Manistee, at one time known as "Salt City," had a second industry that was launched on February 7, 1881, when a well driller struck a bed of salt in the Manistee area 1,936 feet below the ground. The salt story actually began two years earlier when two county surveyors told Charles Reitz, a local lumberman, that they believed salt could be found in the area by deep drilling. Reitz, in turn, convinced a dozen potential investors that such a possibility existed. Each of

FIGURE 52. Salt block interior where workers shoveled salt into barrels for transportation, ca. 1910. (Photograph courtesy of the Manistee County Historical Museum.)

those men made a financial contribution to the project that resulted in a total of over eight thousand dollars. Reitz then hired a well driller who, when he hit solid rock at five hundred feet, reported that finding salt was unlikely. At that point, the money raised had been spent, and Reitz's investors dropped out of the enterprise. Reitz, however, was undeterred. With his own money, he hired another well driller, and after three attempts, each one at a greater depth than the one before, a thirty-two foot bed of solid salt was found.

Once the discovery was made, nearly a dozen companies, including existing lumber establishments, jumped on the bandwagon and began sinking wells to extract the salt. The most successful was the Buckley and Douglas Lumber Company that by 1905 controlled the largest salt block in the world. The Morton Salt Company eventually acquired the Buckley and Douglas business.

In the late nineteenth century a third industry emerged—shingles. Manistee was one of the leading shingle-manufacturing cities in the world. In her article on the area's history, Mrs. Wheeler reported that at one time there were over thirty shingle mills on the Manistee River.

And last, but certainly not least, during the summer months of the early 1900s, tourists from major metropolitan areas across Lake Michigan arrived on steamers to take advantage of the amenities Manistee had to offer such as fishing, swimming, and boating. The residents welcomed the visitors and embraced the new tourist industry.

"Show Me 'Round the Town"

My Home Town Girl, lyrics by Frank Stammers, music by Louis A. Hirsch, 1917

In 1846 "Manistee" became the official name of the community. In addition to being the name of the city, "Manistee" is also the name of a river, a lake, a county, and a national forest. There is some debate concerning the exact meaning of the word. Most historians believe it derived from an Ojibwe term meaning "the spirit of the woods (or trees)." Other translations put forward have been "whispering through the pines" and "river with islands at its mouth."

During the 1860s what had been a lumbering encampment consisting of numerous sawmills began to acquire some of the elements associated with a real town. Religious services had taken place in various secular venues until 1862 when the Methodist Episcopal Church was constructed. Other denominations followed the lead, and in the early 1870s German immigrants built the Trinity Lutheran Church and School with sermons delivered and classes taught in German.

Manistee was incorporated as a village in 1869. Two years later, on October 8, 1871, the day of the Great Chicago Fire, a fire swept through the village of Manistee. It destroyed much of the town, leaving hundreds of citizens homeless but undaunted—the city rose from the ashes. When it was rebuilt, replacements were constructed of sturdier stuff; the wooden shacks that had lined the main street before the fire were replaced with elegant brick buildings.

Only two years after the fire, the *Manistee Democrat* published a letter written on April 24, 1873, by a local citizen, Mr. B. C. Girdler, describing the city's attributes:

> Manistee has in all twenty saw mills, some of them the finest in the State which with its vast resources of pine makes it one of the largest lumbering towns in the west. Machine shops, wagon and carriage factories of almost every description are to be found here and each and all appear to be doing a fine business. Almost every religious denomination is represented here by fine churches. . . . This summer the city intends to pave Main street. . . . As the business portion of the city is built on this street it will add materially to the benefit and looks of the place.

FIGURE 53. The River Street Gateway that welcomes tourists to Manistee's historic downtown district, 2017. (Photographer: Beverly Wilkens, Old Hippie Productions, Manistee, Michigan.)

Today, Manistee is promoted as a historic "Victorian Port City," but back in the 1870s it was still a lumber town with a population of five thousand. Early in that decade, the Flint and Pere Marquette Railroad Company extended its line to bring service to the city. In the words of Mrs. Wheeler: "We listened eagerly for the first shrill screech of the iron horse, and all rejoiced when Manistee was at last united to the world by rapid transit."

The three-floor courthouse went up in 1877 containing the sheriff's office, the jail, offices for city employees, and a courtroom. It was during that decade that the "temperance war" was waged. Mrs. Wheeler told the tale:

> for thirty-five successive evenings people listened with the deepest interest to lectures and enthusiastic speeches, and more than 2,000 persons signed the pledge. Those who opposed this cause . . . resorted to many petty meannesses such as girdling trees, killing horses, injuring property in various ways, and even threatening life.

The Women's Christian Temperance Union (WCTU) was very influential at this time; it advocated closing every saloon in town and, to that end, was known to take violent action. WCTU members also championed women's voting rights and burned public school library books that in their opinion should not be in the hands of children.

By the 1880s the community was thriving; the telephone exchange was in operation, and the water company was established. During the last decade of the nineteenth century, Manistee experienced tremendous growth that resulted in the opening of eight drug stores, three dry goods stores, numerous grocery stores, a building and loan association, and a fire department with an electric alarm system. There were two daily and seven weekly newspapers; of the weekly publications one was in German and one in Swedish.

As a harbinger of the progress yet to come in the new century, on Christmas Eve 1900 for the first time the city was illuminated by electric light. By that time, four railroad lines serviced Manistee making it possible to bring to the citizens a level of entertainment not seen in the area before.

> Years ago a country town had little chance to secure first class productions but with improved methods of travel this condition has changed. (*Manistee Daily News*, December 3, 1901)

Today, the population of Manistee is just over six thousand, but at the time of the 1900 census, Manistee was the eleventh largest town in Michigan with over 14,250 residents. Thanks primarily to trees and salt, it was believed to be the home of more millionaires per capita than any other city in the United States. One of Manistee's wealthiest citizens was Thomas Jefferson Ramsdell.

— **INTERLUDE** —

We interrupt our story for a T. J. Ramsdell biography:

Thomas Jefferson (T. J.) Ramsdell (1833–1917) was born on a farm near Plymouth, Michigan, and attended the Normal School in Ypsilanti. Later, he began reading law and ultimately graduated from the National Law School at Poughkeepsie, New York. He returned to his home state where he served as a clerk of the Michigan Supreme Court. There, a judge suggested that he consider relocating to what was the emerging, albeit remote, lumbering community of Manistee, Michigan, as the inhabitants there were without a lawyer or legal services. Young Ramsdell followed the advice, and in 1860, with a sleigh full of legal books, his adventure began. The journey took him two weeks, as the last eighty miles to the lumber encampment was not a road but an Indian trail.

Here follows both versions of the tale of T. J. Ramsdell's arrival to the Manistee area. As the story goes, before he reached his destination he was stopped by a felled tree obstructing his path. (The variation on the tale is that it was not a tree but a steep hill that halted his journey.) At that moment, a party of boisterous lumberjacks appeared and began harassing the young man with his books and educated manner. However, when they learned of his profession their attitude changed, as they were eager to have a lawyer in town to negotiate contracts and represent them in court when they were charged with drunken and disorderly conduct. At the time, the closest attorney was in Traverse City, sixty miles away. The happy ending to this story is that they not only welcomed him but also carried his books, sleigh, and horse over the tree (or up the hill) and on to Manistee.

Upon his arrival, he set up his law office in a shanty, and as he was the only attorney in the area, he soon had a thriving practice. In 1867, after more lawyers had come to town, he went into partnership with E. E. Benedict and continued to work as a lawyer committed to public service. During his career he was elected to the State House of Representatives, served as the county treasurer, and held several terms as prosecuting attorney. He also opened the first hardware store in Manistee and was instrumental in the establishment of the first newspaper and the Manistee Water Works. He assisted in the creation of the first public school, was on the school board for eighteen years, and was named president of the First National Bank.

His fortune was made primarily in real estate. The story is that Ramsdell initiated his real estate empire by trading his horse and sleigh for forty acres of land in the southwest section of the city. Over the years, he acquired a great deal of property on which he constructed large buildings and entire commercial blocks.

When Ramsdell died, the *Manistee News Advocate* published his obituary on the front page of the April 23, 1917, issue:

> The death of Thomas J. Ramsdell takes from us a man to whom we owe much. He leaves as monuments for his city some of the finest buildings and most valued institutions. Manistee never lost a more distinguished leader among the men whose efforts of yesterday is our heritage of today than Thomas Jefferson Ramsdell.

FIGURE 54. This is a caricature of the "well-dressed, bearded, Victorian-looking gentleman," Thomas Jefferson Ramsdell seated in his theater box holding a program that reads "Ramsdell Opera House." The small scale-building at his side is a model of the First National Bank for which he was the founder and president. (*Our Michigan Friends "As We See 'Em"; A Gallery of Pen Sketches*, Newspaper Cartoonists' Association of Michigan and C. O Youngstrand [Detroit: Wm. Graham, 1905]. Retrieved from the Library of Congress. Photograph courtesy of the Manistee County Historical Museum.)

There is an anecdote, still told today, that years ago a man working in the basement of the Ramsdell Theatre saw a young girl in a white dress standing in a doorway. "Follow me to your fortune," she said, and then disappeared. Some people believe the White Lady, as she is called, is the ghost of Ramsdell's daughter. If that is true, then the well-dressed, bearded, Victorian-looking gentleman who reportedly has been spotted in the playhouse from time to time could be the ghost of Thomas Jefferson Ramsdell himself.

— *And now, back to our story.* —

Prior to the construction of the Ramsdell Theatre in 1903, there was another theater in Manistee built in 1876 by a Scandinavian society for the purpose of providing a space for presentations related to their heritage. Called the Scandinavian Opera House or Hall it was a multifunction facility that seated one thousand. Because it was the only large auditorium in the city, other organizations often rented it. It became a community-gathering place for meetings, political rallies, high school graduations, and theatrical productions. It burned down in 1882 and was immediately rebuilt in 1883. Fifteen years later, in 1898, that facility was purchased by a group from New York City and was completely remodeled with, among other things, the addition of a twenty-four-foot-high rigging loft. It was renamed the Grand Opera House; it was destroyed by fire in 1900.

After the fire, other venues in Manistee hosted many of the more intimate activities that had formerly taken place at the Grand Opera House, but there was no other facility that was appropriate for professional theatre productions. The local newspaper published an editorial stating that cultural opportunities had diminished in the city as there was no place for touring theatre companies to perform. Eleven days after the editorial appeared the newspaper reported the following:

> The old skating rink on Maple street which for some time has served no useful purpose . . . will soon be torn down. The property has been purchased and it is probable that the site will be used to much greater advantage in the near future. (*Manistee Daily News*, April 11, 1901)

Eight months later, the future of the property was known. On December 3, 1901, the newspaper reported that the two corner lots had been purchased by T. J. Ramsdell "who proposes to erect a thoroughly modern opera house thereon. Manistee has never had a first class stage."

In the same article, T. J. Ramsdell shared his vision with the readers:

> If I can build a good opera house for $25,000 I shall do so. My idea is to build a thoroughly modern theatre capable of accommodating any troupe. I should like the theatre to be of Grecian architecture and expect to build it of stone and rock-faced brick. There would be a large basement to be used as a dance hall and there would also be dressing rooms and lavatories on both floors.

Ramsdell's initial idea was to have a space for auxiliary activities on the first floor of the building with the theater above. However, after some consideration and given the size of the two adjoining lots, according to the January 3, 1902, edition of the *Manistee Daily News*, he decided "to double the size of the floor plan and make theatre and assembly hall side by side, neither encroaching on the other."

Although Ramsdell had originally allotted $25,000 for the project, he found it necessary to up the figure to $50,000, and in the end his investment was between $100,000 and $150,000. When the Ramsdell Theatre opened, it boasted the latest electrical, heating, ventilation, and fire protection systems. It was also exquisitely appointed.

"Castle of Dreams"

Irene, lyrics by Joseph McCarthy, music by Harry Tierney, 1919

As the sole benefactor of a gift to the city, Ramsdell did manage to garner some perks. On January 22, 1902, the *Manistee Daily News* reported that a deal had been made between Ramsdell and the city's common council:

> City should have free use of the buildings on Decoration Day, Fourth of July, Labor Day, and so forth for a period of ten years . . . the property should be assessed at not more than $2,500 (the value of the land) for a period of ten years.

In a 1962 interview, Ramsdell's youngest daughter, Ruth Ramsdell Campbell, said, "Father wanted the theater to be as fine as any in New York."

With that goal in mind, he began the task of identifying the best architect for the job. He first selected a Chicago architect, Henry Ives Cobb, who arrived in Manistee on February 19, 1902, to discuss the project. His architectural style of choice was French Renaissance. Perhaps the proposed style did not sit well with Ramsdell, for a week later his son Frederic Ramsdell was on his way to Chicago to consult with other candidates for the job. Shortly thereafter the news was released that Ramsdell had hired nationally known architect Solon Spencer Beman.

— **INTERLUDE** —

We interrupt our story for a Solon Spencer Beman biography:

Solon Spencer Beman (1853–1914) was born in Brooklyn, New York. In 1870, at the age of seventeen, he began to work and study at a well-known architectural firm in New York City. He remained with that firm until 1877 when he opened a practice in association with a landscape architect, Nathan F. Barrett.

His initial contact with railroad baron George Mortimer Pullman was in 1879 when Pullman hired Beman and Barrett to design a summer home on his property in Long Beach, New Jersey. Pullman was so pleased with the results that he invited the two young architects to come to Chicago to design the town of Pullman, a railroad car-manufacturing center with amenities for railroad employees. It turned out to be an enormous undertaking that included more than 1,300 houses, a factory, water tower, theater, church, hotel, market, and schools. According to Mrs. Duane Doty in her book *The Town of Pullman*, "Of all nineteenth century planned industrial communities, Pullman was the largest and most complete."

Some of Beman's other important commissions in Chicago were the Illinois Central Station, Studebaker Fine Arts Building, and several structures for the 1893 World's Columbian Exposition. He also designed office buildings and factories in Indiana, Michigan, Minnesota, Ohio, and Wisconsin, and more than a dozen Christian Science churches across the country. However, the town of Pullman, which is now an Illinois State Historical Site, remains the highlight of his very impressive career.

— And now, back to our story. —

In Ramsdell's eagerness to get the project underway, in January 1902, more than a month before Beman was scheduled to make his first visit to Manistee, he ordered lumber for the opera house. Soon after the lumber arrived gravel was delivered by ship from the Manitou Islands.

On March 12, Solon S. Beman visited Manistee to look at the site and discuss plans with Ramsdell. He then sent his new employer a partial set of plans from Chicago indicating "the style of architecture will be Colonial." In 1962, the *Detroit Free Press* referred to the Ramsdell Theatre as "a prize example of Greek Revival architecture." Thirty years later, the 1992 edition of *Theatre Classics*, the magazine published by the League of Historic American Theatres, stated that the building was in the "Classical style with Renaissance overtones." However, as a red brick structure with a center entrance and a portico supported by contrasting pale grey cement columns (original buildings in this style had wooden columns painted white), featuring small multipaned windows symmetrically arranged on the upper floors, it is generally thought to be what the architect intended it to be, Colonial.

"Diggin' Up Dirt"

Vamp Till Ready, lyrics by Richard Levinson and William Link, music by Ronald Lowden, 1955

> In excavating for the theatre several queer finds were made. In one place a wooden basement floor was uncovered . . . a sewing machine dating from the fire of '71 was also unearthed. (*Manistee Daily News*, April 23, 1902)

The newspaper went on to report that in addition to the items above, "a small six-shooter was dug up on the Ramsdell theatre site . . . and was excellently preserved," and that a silver watch charm had been discovered. "The inscription identified the owner who had lived in an adjoining house nearly 25–30 years before." C. A. Haskins claimed that he was in possession of an iron cannon that he found during the excavation.

The downside of the big dig was that the big hole created the possibility of an accident to happen, and on May 16, 1902, that possibility was realized. A horse fell into one of the deep ditches at the construction site and was extricated with difficulty.

"While Others Are Building Castles in the Air"

Lyrics by Jack Mahoney, music by Fred Fisher, 1919

> There is no better theatre in Michigan than the Ramsdell. It is substantially built, beautifully decorated, and possesses the latest electrical devices. (*Manistee Daily News*, December 5, 1903)

At the end of April, fifteen thousand red bricks for the building's exterior were transported by schooner across Lake Michigan from Sheboygan, Wisconsin, to the Manistee port. Grey concrete Doric columns were constructed to accent the red brick facade and to support the colonnade, or portico, over the entrance to the theater. The roof of the portico created a balcony where musicians could perform before the show.

Architect Beman made frequent trips to Manistee to check the progress and quality of the work. On one visit he had nothing but praise for the local masons and carpenters claiming that their work was better than that of Chicago builders.

The original intention on the part of T. J. Ramsdell was to open the theater before the end of 1902. Construction commenced in March, but due to inclement weather a great deal of time was lost and it became apparent that a year-end deadline for both the theater and the adjacent building was not realistic. In order to complete one portion of the complex before 1903, the focus became the assembly hall. A thirteen-hour workday was made possible by installing an arc light in the interior of the building. The assembly hall opened on December 18, 1902. In July 1903, theater manager Charles M. Southwell stated that he expected to open the theater the first week of September—which he did.

Five years after the theater opened, a reporter for the *Manistee Daily News* commended T. J. Ramsdell for his foresight, vision, and tenacity. He reminded his readers that in 1903, because of the diminishing supply of lumber, the city was experiencing an economic decline. The journalist went on to say that Ramsdell could have invested in many different causes that would have benefited the community, but he understood what the people needed most. He put his money where it would provide entertainment and education for his fellow citizens.

A number of Manistee residents questioned Ramsdell's priorities. To build an opera house with the sole purpose of presenting professional theatre productions at a time when some believed that the city was dangerously close to economic freefall was in their minds an inadvisable if not ostentatious expenditure of money. Unlike the Red Jacket Common Council member who said, "What Red Jacket needs is an opera house," Ramsdell's peers probably believed that the last thing Manistee needed was an opera house.

Ramsdell's daughter Ruth confirmed the existence of this attitude in a letter dated March 4, 1971. She recalled that at the time the theater was being built she had heard a rumor that some of the local businessmen referred to the project as "Ramsdell's Folly." When she asked her father about it, she quotes him as saying, "I think all those millionaires call it that but you will live long enough to hear the city speak proudly and gratefully of it and maybe you will be proud of your father."

While some locals may have questioned the advisability of the project, theatre people were enthusiastic in their support of it. On September 4, 1903, the *Manistee Daily Advocate* reported that in the opinion of the manager of the opening production, *A Chinese Honeymoon*,

> It is the best that ever happened for Manistee. It will make the town known throughout the country. No other

FIGURE 55. Frederic W. Ramsdell, son of T. J. Ramsdell, was a nationally recognized artist who designed the interior of the Ramsdell Theatre and was the creator of the dome and lobby lunette paintings. (Photographer unknown, 1895. Photograph courtesy of the Manistee County Historical Museum.)

> city of the size of Manistee has so good a theatre. . . . Manistee cannot be too grateful to Mr. Ramsdell.

Gilding the Lily

the condensation of a metaphor from *King John* by William Shakespeare, ca. 1590s

T. J. Ramsdell's son Frederic Winthrop Ramsdell (1865–1915), an established artist, was given considerable design responsibility and artistic freedom working in his father's new theater; this was due only in part to nepotism. Prior to undertaking the theater interior design and decoration project, he had been a student at the Art Students' League of New York followed by several years of study in Paris where his work was exhibited at the Paris Salon.

On January 3, 1902, the *Manistee Daily News* applauded the green and gold palette Frederic Ramsdell had selected for the interior design of the theater.

> Green is the most restful shade for the eyes, and it has a cleanness and dignity that no other color possesses. The use of gold to relieve the green will be carried out to a limited extent with brass railings and trimmings. It will lend an air of extreme richness.

Many months later the newspaper once again commended Ramsdell for his color selection: "The walls are being tinted a delightfully subdued green which will never clash with any kind of gown."

Frederic Ramsdell's paintings for both the ceiling dome and the lobby lunettes were Greek in subject matter and Victorian in style. It has been reported that he painted the dome by lying on his back on scaffolding high above the seating area below. The painting reveals Venus, naked from the waist up, draped in diaphanous gauze from the waist down, driving a gilded chariot drawn by doves surrounded by cherubs. The local scandal was that Frederic's wife was his model for the goddess of love dressed—or undressed—as pictured on the ceiling (see Plate 13).

If Frederic's wife posed for Venus, who were the models for the maids on the lunettes cavorting in bucolic bliss over the Grecian countryside? According to one journalist, Ramsdell's intention was to "immortalize several pretty Manistee belles of the day." A more popular theory is that the faces of the nearly naked nubile nymphs are intended to resemble the wives of the millionaires who had initiated the "Ramsdell's Folly" reference. The Ramsdells' revenge!

After completing the interior design of the playhouse, Frederic Ramsdell tried his hand at scene painting. Apparently, he so enjoyed the experience that he decided to turn it into a vocation. Ramsdell and Truman Curtis, a Chicago-based scenic artist, announced their plan to open a scene-painting studio in the Ramsdell Theatre. When reviewing the production of *We Are King* on September 8, 1903, the journalist acknowledged the contribution of Messrs. Ramsdell and Curtis's newly formed scene-painting firm.

> Not a little of last evening's success is attributable to the beautiful scenery. In fact the rising of the curtain on each new act was greeted with signs of appreciation. The garden scene is the prettiest ever seen in Manistee.

"It's Only a Paper Moon"

The Great Magoo, lyrics by E. Y. Harburg and Billy Rose, music by Harold Arlen, 1933

T. J. Ramsdell engaged the nationally acclaimed artist Walter Wilcox Burridge (1857–1913) and his firm to create the show drop and a set of stock drops for his new theater. Burridge was also known for his illustrations, his panoramic landscape paintings, and as a scene designer who created scenery for forty-two Broadway productions including his much lauded designs for the original production of the comic opera *The Wizard of Oz*.

> I would rather be a scene painter than anything else in this world. (Walter Wilcox Burridge, *Manistee Daily News*, May 19, 1903)

On May 15, 1903, Burridge arrived in Manistee to begin painting the scenery. One drop is used today as a show curtain and fills the proscenium opening before a performance begins (see Plate 12). It is believed to be the only example of Burridge's scene painting artistry that is still in existence. Burridge named it "A Grove Near Athens," and it depicts a statue of the goddess Flora with the Acropolis in the distance (see Plate 14).

The newspaper praised the scenic artist's accomplishments: "Walter Burridge's grand work on the foliage and landscape is enough alone to give the playhouse a reputation."

> And when I've had a particularly vexing day, I take myself out into the house of the theatre, set myself down, and let the nobility of Solon Beman's architectural lines and the glory of Walter Burridge's scenic painting lift me up and calm me down. (Ruth Cooper, former general manager, Ramsdell Theatre, Centennial Souvenir Program, 1993)

FIGURE 56. This is one of two lobby lunettes painted by Frederic Ramsdell. They are on either side of the lobby, one above the ticket office and the other above a door leading to an adjacent area. (Photographer: Beverly Wilkens, Old Hippie Productions, Manistee, Michigan, 2017.)

Gentlemen, Be Seated!

said the interlocutor to the minstrels

At the time the theater opened the seating in the auditorium was arranged in the shape of a horseshoe with a graded first floor and two balconies. At the back of the parquet section were two loges, small areas with moveable chairs behind an ornamental rail. There were six boxes, four on the orchestra level and two above. Each gilt-encrusted box with its heavy, plush draperies could accommodate six patrons. The balcony, which was ornamented in gilt and ringed with lights, mirrored the curved shape of the parquet seating below.

Upon viewing the auditorium, one of the most impressive architectural elements is the horseshoe balcony (see Plate 15). The second balcony or gallery was a late addition to the plans.

> It has been decided to put an additional balcony in the Ramsdell Theatre. This will provide seats for 400 more. It was found that ample room existed above the first balcony. (*Manistee Daily News*, November 29, 1902)

The second balcony was steep with uncomfortable wooden benches, but it provided an inexpensive entertainment opportunity; the *Manistee Daily Advocate* stated that the second balcony was clearly an afterthought but predicted, "It will be a favorite for small boys."

On August 13, 1903, the *Manistee Daily Advocate* announced that the theater seats were scheduled to be installed and that "a gang of workmen will arrive on Monday from Grand Rapids . . . to place them in position."

> In the parquet and dress circle the chairs have upholstered seats, and wooden backs, desirable for their coolness. . . . Practically every seat has an unobstructed view of the stage. (*Manistee Daily News*, August 22, 1903)

The American Seating Company of Grand Rapids furnished the chairs. During the 1990s when a major theater restoration project was underway, the original chairs were replaced with new upholstered seats provided by the same company. The wooden armrests from the original chairs were refinished and attached to the replacements.

Shortly after the opening in 1903, Robert R. Ramsdell, another Ramsdell son who was listed in the opening night program as the building manager, said, "there are seats for just 1,200 in the entire house, inclusive of boxes. The parquet and lower tiers of boxes will seat 450 and the two balconies take care of 750." Again, Julius Cahn in his *Official Theatrical Guide* begged to differ; he claims that there were only 1,100 seats available.

A section of balcony seats that had occupied an area designated as the "Family Circle" was removed in 1923 to make space for a modern projection booth. Currently, the theater can provide seats for around 465 patrons in the orchestra and balcony. The second balcony is no longer used because of fire safety concerns. There are twenty seats in the boxes as well as wooden benches at the far edges of the first balcony for a potential total capacity of 526. However, those seats are only used when the demand for tickets warrants selling them.

"On and Off the Stage"

The Golden Widow, lyrics by Edward Madden,
music by Melville Gideon and Louis Hirsch, 1909

When the theater opened, the stage mechanics were state-of-the-art. Four miles of rope were employed for the purpose of raising and lowering the scenery through pulleys in the gridiron. At the time it was built, the Ramsdell's grid was one of the highest in the country.

> All scenery will lift from the stage into a great scene loft some seventy feet in height. There will not be a single piece to slide in the old fashioned bungling way. (*Manistee Daily News*, August 22, 1903)

— **RAMSDELL THEATRE** —

Seating Capacity & Stage Dimensions

AS RECORDED IN *JULIUS CAHN'S OFFICIAL THEATRICAL GUIDE*, 1903-4

Seating Capacity	1,100
Proscenium Arch	Width 26′ / Height 26′
Depth of Stage from Footlights to Back Wall	38′
Width of Stage Between Side Walls	60′
Height from Stage Floor to Rigging Loft	72′

The installation of the rigging system was supervised by L. H. Savage, a stage carpenter who was on loan from the Illinois Theatre in Chicago. The *Manistee Daily News* identified him as "one of the men who make apparatus for the wonderful stage illusions that charm and bewilder theatre-goers."

The stage floor contained three traps located downstage right and left and upstage center. In addition there were six elevators upstage operated by counterweights. The downstage right trap is currently not operational; however, the other two still function. As they were deemed a safety hazard, the elevators are no longer used.

For fire protection in the scene loft, the top of the proscenium arch was filled with sheet metal lined with asbestos. An asbestos curtain was installed at the proscenium that could be lowered and entirely isolate the auditorium.

An orchestra pit was located in front of the stage, one and a half feet below the auditorium floor. Originally the theater orchestra consisted of seven members under the direction of Professor W. Church, but the pit could accommodate as many as twenty musicians.

On July 9, 1903, the *Manistee Daily Advocate* assured its readers,

> The actors and actresses have not been neglected, and nine dressing rooms, besides a chorus room, are provided. Six of the dressing rooms are beneath the stage, while the other three are reached by a spiral staircase from the stage. Each dressing room is commodious to a degree that is pleasing, and the furnishings of each are the best and most substantial kind.

At the end of the first season there was a summer hiatus when crews made upgrades to the facility. The theater reopened on August 1, 1904, for season number two, and the *Manistee Daily News* called it a "Grand Opening with more perfect equipment than ever before, greater comfort and safety for patrons."

Bring Up the Lights!

In August 1903, the largest electrical switchboard used in a theater north of Detroit was delivered to Lloyd and Smith, the lighting contractors for the Ramsdell Theatre. The solid marble switchboard contained sixty switches and was placed on a pivot so that the back of the board could be easily accessed. The electric lights that encircled the ceiling dome in the auditorium were turned on for the first time on August 12, 1903.

"We Gather Together"

English lyrics by Theodore Baker, 1894; music based on traditional Dutch folk tune adapted by Adrianus Valerius, 1597

> The idea of incorporating with the theater a large assembly hall has been an important consideration with Mr. Ramsdell from the beginning. (*Manistee Daily News*, January 3, 1902)

The assembly hall (aka Ramsdell Hall) is situated to the north of the theater physically separated on the interior by a thick masonry wall and visually separated on the exterior by a tall, square tower. The first floor of the hall consisted of an impressive reception area leading to parlors, a dining room, and kitchen. The press predicted that it "will henceforth be the center of Manistee social life." The second floor, accessed by a grand stairway, was designated as the ballroom. It is a 120-by-70-foot space with oak paneled wainscoting and many large windows. There is a slightly raised dais along two sides of the room on which seating is available for spectators to sit and observe the terpsichorean activity without the risk of their toes being trod upon by the dancers. At one end of the room is an imposing brick fireplace that faces a musicians' gallery at the opposite end of the dance floor.

"The Party Gets Going"

Pipe Dream, lyrics by Oscar Hammerstein II, music by Richard Rodgers, 1955

On November 8, 1902, Mr. and Mrs. T. J. Ramsdell traveled to Grand Rapids to select linen, silver, and china for the new Ramsdell Hall. They had the twenty dozen sets of china and silverware monogrammed with the initials "R.H." Their son Frederic designed the monogram.

> A flag floated from the tower of Ramsdell Hall today signifying that the hall will be used for the first time tonight. (*Manistee Daily News*, December 12, 1902)

The unofficial opening of the hall took place on December 12, 1902, with a ball hosted by the Manistee Retail Clerk's Union. The Manistee Concert Orchestra provided the music. The official opening, a gala dinner and dance, took place six days later on December 18 and was hosted by Ramsdell and his wife. Guests from Manistee's social register were served dinner in the first-floor dining rooms followed by dancing in the second-floor ballroom. The ball commenced with a grand march led by Miss Burrows of Saginaw and Mr. Carl Ramsdell, assisted by Miss Marinette Ramsdell and Mr. Harvey Larson.

Did the event go off without a hitch? Not quite. The *Manistee Daily News* expressed the hosts' concerns the day before the highly anticipated opening. "Some consternation has been caused by the non-arrival of the china and dining tables." Three days later the newspaper reported that the china arrived the night before the party, "When all hope had been abandoned." The tables, however, did not arrive on time.

The area's socially elite were not the only recipients of

FIGURE 57. The 100th Anniversary of the Manistee Chamber of Commerce was celebrated in the Ramsdell Assembly Hall's Grand Ballroom in 2016. The space is officially named Rotary Hall in honor of the service organization that saved the hall and theater from demolition in the 1920s. At one end of the ballroom is what was originally a musicians' gallery from where this photo was taken. (Photographer: Beverly Wilkens, Old Hippie Productions, Manistee, Michigan.)

Ramsdell Hall's hospitality. National Guard soldiers were also welcome. The newspaper speculated that no other company in Michigan's National Guard was as well housed. In an arrangement that had been negotiated with Ramsdell before the building was constructed, certain spaces in the assembly hall were designated for the use of Company F as their armory. There was a room on the first floor adjacent to the parlors that was the armory proper where the weapons were stored. In the basement were rooms for recreation—billiards, bowling—as well as a shooting gallery. The second-floor ballroom was used for drills.

A number of patriotic citizens donated ten dollars each to enable Company F to purchase a release from an existing contract for armory space in the Olympian Hall. The contributing citizens were given immunity from jury duty and poll tax for one year.

Although the Ramsdells' intent for the assembly hall was to be a space appropriate for balls, dinners, receptions, and other celebrations, over the years it was also a roller-skating rink, a basketball court, a dance studio, a lecture hall, and a rehearsal room. Today, the first floor that is now Hardy Hall and the second floor, the Rotary Ballroom, are used year-round for art exhibits, dance recitals, music concerts, proms, weddings, receptions, business meetings, and banquets.

"And Father Wanted Me to Learn a Trade"

Stop! Look! Listen!, lyrics and music by Irving Berlin, 1915

Ramsdell had fourteen children, six of whom, according to his obituary, outlived him. He obviously subscribed to nepotism as, in addition to Frederic's contribution as interior designer, mural painter, and scenic artist, father Ramsdell provided employment for a number of his other sons. The program for the opening of the theater confirmed that this was to be a family business: "Mr. T. J. Ramsdell, Owner; Robert R. Ramsdell, Building Manager; Ellis Ramsdell, Stage Manager; Lewis Ramsdell, Theater Physician."

Perhaps it was not just nepotism; Ramsdell was known to be thrifty. There are stories that when the stock scenery was being prepared he had his entire brood assist by cutting out of scenic fabric intricate leaf patterns needed for the foliage borders.

Who's Minding the Store?

As there is no evidence that any of the Ramsdells had prior theatre experience, it is to his credit that T. J. Ramsdell brought in a proven professional to oversee the inaugural season. He hired Charles M. Southwell, who had previously been employed by opera companies in Chicago. Mr. Southwell arrived in Manistee on May 4, 1903, and, as planned, booked and managed the opening season. However, for the 1904–5 season Robert Ramsdell assumed the managerial responsibilities.

"The Party's Over"

Bells Are Ringing, lyrics by Betty Comden and Adolph Green, music by Jule Styne, 1956

In 1922, five years after Ramsdell died, his estate considered razing the building due to the high cost of maintenance and the tax burden. An alternate proposal was made to sell the property to the Manistee Board of Commerce for $50,000—well below the original cost. Neither option was acted upon. The estate considered demolition of the Ramsdell Theatre complex again in 1925, but the local Rotary Club purchased the building for $25,000. The first floor of the assembly hall became quarters for the Rotary Club, and the second floor was used for basketball.

Butterfield Theatres, a Michigan-based chain that controlled over one hundred movie theaters, leased the auditorium portion of the Ramsdell complex from the Rotarians in the 1930s. At the time, rumor had it that, with the exception of some local events and occasional screening of films, Butterfield was keeping the playhouse dark so as to avoid competition with its new movie palace in downtown Manistee.

When the Ramsdell Theatre opened again in 1939, the newly formed Manistee Civic Players became the primary occupant. In 1941, the Rotarians made an agreement to sell the entire complex to the City of Manistee over a twelve-year period. The city took ownership of the property in 1953.

In 2016, the Ramsdell Regional Center for the Arts was formed. Their mission statement:

> To optimize an irreplaceable regional center for cultural, education and social activities through programming excellence, fiscal stability, strong community partnerships and committed volunteers.

The Ramsdell Theatre was added to the National Register of Historic Places in 1972.

SCENE ii

Curtain Going Up!

The fact that Manistee is somewhat isolated will make the booking of the best companies somewhat difficult. —Charles N. Southwell, Ramsdell Theatre Manager, May 5, 1903

Manager Southwell's prediction was unnecessarily pessimistic; for the gala opening of the Ramsdell Theatre he was successful in booking the biggest hit of the 1902–3 Broadway theatre season, *A Chinese Honeymoon*.

The show was a British import with music composed by Howard Talbot supporting a book and lyrics by Sir George Dance. It had opened at the Royal Strand Theatre in London in October 1901 where it became the first musical comedy to surpass one thousand consecutive performances in England. The show then crossed the sea to open at Shubert's New York Casino Theatre on June 2, 1902, where it played for an entire year.

After it closed on Broadway it launched a national tour and had played in Philadelphia just prior to stopping in Manistee on its way to Chicago. Two weeks after the Ramsdell Theatre performance the show played at the Calumet Theatre, and following the national tour it reopened on Broadway for a month. It then went on a second national tour that included the Tibbits Opera House in Coldwater.

As Manistee was not originally on the company's touring itinerary, the one-hundred-member troupe was transported from Philadelphia, along with two carloads of scenery, on a chartered train at a cost of $1,200. When the company arrived, the local hotels could not accommodate them all, and some cast and crew members were welcomed into private homes.

FIGURE 58. *A Chinese Honeymoon* arrived in Manistee by special train to open the Ramsdell Theatre in 1903. It had played in New York the previous season after breaking attendance records in London in 1901. (Publisher: Strobridge Litho Co., Cincinnati, New York, ca. 1902. Retrieved from the Library of Congress Prints and Photographs Division.)

A week before the show opened in Manistee, Manager Southwell announced that tickets for *A Chinese Honeymoon* were on sale and that the box office would be open daily from 9:00 a.m. until 8:00 p.m. He also informed potential patrons, "Tickets will be sold nowhere else." Opening night ticket prices for seats on the main floor ranged from five to ten dollars. The boxes sold for fifty dollars each.

According to a mention in the *Manistee Daily News*, business was booming. "Manager Southwell has received quite a large order for seats for the opening from well known parties in Ludington. They may charter a special train or one of the many excursion boats."

— **HEADLINE** —

Brilliant Opening of Ramsdell Theatre

> On the historic opening night of the theater Manistee's "400" turned out in white tie and tails, in jewels and hour glass gowns from Paris, to see a musical hit imported from Broadway. (*Detroit Free Press*, August 11, 1962)

The day after the opening, the *Manistee Daily News* provided a detailed report of the auspicious occasion:

> Judge McAlvay voiced the heartfelt feelings of the entire community last evening, when . . . he thanked Mr. T. J. Ramsdell for the public spirit and generous instincts that resulted in the founding of the noble building. . . . Turning to the box in which Mr. Ramsdell and his family sat, he concluded his remarks in a touching way

> expressing the hope that Mr. Ramsdell might live long to enjoy the beautiful structure and the many inspiring plays which will be presented upon the stage.

The article went on to describe the opening moments of the production and the reaction of the audience: "The drop curtain, said by competent judges to be Burridge's masterpiece, . . . was greeted by a round of applause."

After that, the audience was treated to

> a play that has delighted hundreds of thousands of theatre-goers in the greatest cities of the world. There for three hours the remainder of the world was forgotten for the charms of pretty faces, gorgeous costumes, catchy music, and all that goes to make a successful light opera.

According to the October 16, 1901, issue of the British publication *The Tattler*, *A Chinese Honeymoon* owed a great debt of gratitude to W. S. Gilbert's *The Mikado*. The journalist contends that if there had been no *The Mikado* set in a fanciful rendering of Japan there would never have been *A Chinese Honeymoon* set in a fanciful rendering of China.

A Chinese Honeymoon consists of three plots that unfold simultaneously. The first storyline revolves around the Emperor of Ylang-Ylang who wishes to marry but seeks a bride who will wed him for himself and not because he is the ruler of the country. To find the right woman he sends out an emissary, his Lord High Admiral, with instructions to tell prospective wives that the Emperor is really a billposter.

If the emissary is unsuccessful, which of course he is, the penalty is a lingering death. The Admiral tries many different solutions to his problem, all of them with comic consequences. Typical of the times, the native folk have musical-comedy-stereotypical, pseudo-ethnic names such as Soo-Soo, Sing-Sing, Yen-Yen, and Chippie Chop.

The second plot concerns a young American man in China who kisses a girl and then learns that according to that country's custom, when a man kisses a woman he must marry her. Filling out the cast of characters and providing the third comic plot is a newlywed couple, Mr. and Mrs. Pineapple, a cockney fellow with a jealous wife. She travels with her four bridesmaids who are charged by the bride with the task of keeping an eye on her husband. Comic compromising, albeit innocent, circumstances evolve.

The reviewer for the *Manistee Daily News* opined that the costumes worn by the bride and four bridesmaids surpassed in "brilliancy" any of the gowns worn by women in the audience. The costumes were recent replacements created at considerable expense. The fact that they were being worn for the first time on the Ramsdell Theatre stage was an indication to the reviewer that the professional theatre world considered the new Manistee playhouse a significant venue.

After the curtain came down, a reception and dance were held in Ramsdell Hall. There, members of the cast and crew of *A Chinese Honeymoon* mingled with the first nighters. Church's orchestra played waltzes and two-steps until two o'clock in the morning. During the performance earlier in the evening, several of the local musicians from Church's orchestra had augmented the professional orchestra that traveled with the show.

"Another Op'nin', Another Show"

Kiss Me, Kate, lyrics and music by Cole Porter, 1948

> It is expected to be able to bring in an average of two productions per week to play the new theatre. . . . None but the best attractions will be booked. (*Manistee Daily Advocate*, July 9, 1903)

The first season at the Ramsdell Theatre was very ambitious. Between the opening of *A Chinese Honeymoon* on September 4, 1903, and the end of the year the playhouse was the site of performances by twenty-five theatre companies, several minstrel shows, one music concert, and a presentation by Dr. H. J. Reynolds and his company of mediums demonstrating "Spirit Power in the Light" sponsored by the Religio-Psychological Society.

One evening during that season was devoted to a presentation from the International Bioscope Company that screened moving pictures in natural color. The program included motion pictures of the $10,000 Melies production of *A Trip to Mars*, an *Uncle Tom's Cabin* production, and three pantomimes. The audience also experienced the International Yacht Races and a day in the life of an American fireman.

Four days after *A Chinese Honeymoon* moved on, Walker Whiteside arrived in his popular comedy-drama *We Are King*. Then came *Quincy Adams Sawyer and Mason's Corner Folks*, advertised as "The Best New England Story Ever Written." It played the Ramsdell on October 9, 1903, for the first of three times over a four-year period. The show was also seen with the same degree of frequency in Red Jacket and Coldwater.

The newspaper advertisement for *Quincy Adams Sawyer* promised "one great big laugh from beginning to end and the sweetest love story ever told." Plays set in rural New England, sometimes referred to as "pastoral plays," were great audience pleasers.

Quincy Adams Sawyer, dramatized by Justin Adams, was based on the 1900 novel by Charles Felton Pidgin. It relates the adventures of a young Harvard graduate from a wealthy family who travels from Boston to the bucolic atmosphere of Mason's Corner to recover from an illness. There, he encounters many quaint characters, becomes embroiled in the life of the country village, and finds romance. The *Manistee Daily News* article promoting the show asked its readers, "Did you ever court a country girl? Did you ever sing in a country church choir? Did you ever go to a husking bee? Did you ever attend a town meeting? That is what the play called *Quincy Adams Sawyer* is all about."

In the last two months of 1903, Manistee audiences were treated to a popular Western play, *Arizona*; Knute Erickson, "the Swedish Dialect Comedian," in *The Man from Sweden*; and on December 30, Shakespeare's *As You Like It*.

"On with the Show"

Pretty Faces, lyrics and music by Robert W. Cabell, 1990

In 1904, fifty-three professional touring companies brought their productions to Manistee. In addition, the theater hosted performances by four minstrel companies and presented four music concerts, one stock company, and one opera—*Carmen*. The Bizet opera was presented by the English Grand Opera Company. The reviewer for the *Manistee Daily News* expressed the opinion that "it was in the nature of a privilege to hear *Carmen* sung with such clear, forcible, and dramatic enunciation of the English text."

The first show of the new year was a return engagement of Walker Whiteside and his hit *We Are King* on January 14 followed by Henrik Ibsen's *Hedda Gabler* on February 2. Later in the season, Ibsen was represented again with a production of *A Doll's House* starring Clara Thropp as Nora. After the curtain fell on *A Doll's House,* so as to provide "a dainty dessert after the heavy meal of Ibsen," Miss Thropp came to the stage and sang Rudyard Kipling's famous barrack-room ballad, "On the Road to Mandalay."

More fun than an Ibsen drama was Weber and Field's "Festival of Mirth and Music," *Hoity-Toity*, that played the Ramsdell Theatre on February 10. The show was the original $25,000 production from the Weber and Fields Music Hall in New York City and consisted of a company of fifty—"Mostly Girls." The advertisement announced that the *Hoity-Toity* Company's stop in Manistee was the only one it made in the state between Bay City and Grand Rapids.

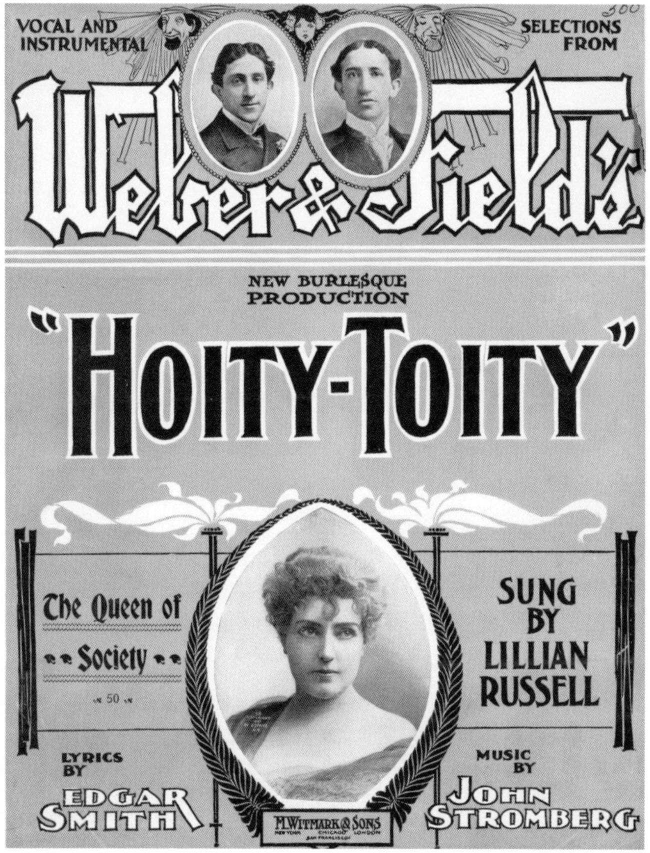

FIGURE 59. Sheet music cover for "The Queen of Society" introduced by Lillian Russell in the Weber and Fields revue *Hoity-Toity.* (Publisher: M. Witmark & Sons, New York, Chicago, London, 1901. Music Division, the New York Public Library for the Performing Arts, Astor, Lenox, and Tilden Foundations.)

The comedy team of Joe Weber and Lew Fields produced and starred in their own shows that were premiered in their own music hall. In their shows, they played low burlesque "Dutch" characters with thick Yiddish accents. Their humor was broad but never vulgar. Even with the requisite line of chorus girls it was their goal to keep the shows family friendly.

The two comedians inaugurated their acting partnership as young men on New York's East Side. In 1884, they joined the Miner's Bowery Theatre Company where they developed their own brand of rowdy humor and created their Dutch characters. Two years later, they took over the management of the Imperial Music Hall on Broadway and changed its name to the Weber and Fields Music Hall. There they presented a series of shows that were a combination of burlesque, meaning satire, and vaudeville with titles such as *Hurly Burly, Whirl-I-Gig, Fiddle-Dee-Dee, Twirly Whirly,* and *Whoop-de-Doo.* One act of their two-act shows was often

FIGURE 60. With box office receipts of $56,000 at the end of its initial New York run in 1884, *A Bunch of Keys or, The Hotel* was Charles H. Hoyt's first musical farce hit. The show was still going strong twenty years later, in 1904, when it played the Tibbits Opera House and the Ramsdell Theatre. In the play, one of three Keys sisters has been bequeathed a backwater hotel. Which one? Whichever sibling is deemed to be the homeliest. (Publisher: U.S. Printing Co, New York, ca. 1899. Retrieved from the Library of Congress.)

a series of skits that satirized current Broadway plays; *The Girl and the Judge* was presented as *The Curl and the Judge*, and *Madame Du Barry* was *Madame Du Hurry*. The other act consisted of star performers doing songs, dances, or specialties. Lillian Russell and Fay Templeton were among the regulars who appeared in a number of the Weber and Fields shows in New York City, but they were not part of the *Hoity-Toity* touring company and, for that matter, neither were Weber and Fields.

The first act of *Hoity-Toity* may have been inspired by the title of the 1892 British Music Hall song "The Man Who Broke the Bank in Monte Carlo." The action takes place in that international playground and involves three New York delicatessen owners who have cornered the market on sauerkraut and have come to Monte Carlo to try their luck at gambling. In order to underwrite their adventure, they convince the wealthy, albeit not-too-savvy, Philip Sauerbraten to open a bank with his own money, and they then proceed to bamboozle him out of his fortune. Intertwined with that plot is another that involves an American billionaire who has come to Monte Carlo in search of wealthy husbands for his six marriageable daughters who are traveling with him.

The following year, 1905, *Hoity-Toity* played the Ramsdell Theatre a second time. Sandwiched between its two showings in Manistee it was seen in Coldwater, and a year later it was in Red Jacket.

"I Love a Musical Comedy Show"

Oh, My Dear!, lyrics by P. G. Wodehouse, music by Jean Schwartz, 1918

**Happy Hooligan*, the cartoon musical advertised as "The Queerest, Quaintest of All Comedy Creations," provided Ramsdell patrons with two opportunities to enjoy the show in 1904. There was a traditional evening performance and a special matinee for ladies and children. *Happy Hooligan* was not the only cartoon musical to play at the Ramsdell Theatre.

Between 1904 and 1917 **Buster Brown*, **Mutt and Jeff*, and **Bringing Up Father* all made a stop in Manistee as well as many non-cartoon-inspired musicals: **The Wizard of Oz* with a "Large Company, Mostly Girls, Brilliantly Gowned," **The Isle of Spice*, *Madame Sherry*, *The Red Mill*, and **The Cat and the Fiddle*.

In 1906, *Hooligan in New York* was on the bill of attractions in Manistee. One might reasonably assume from the title that it was a sequel to the earlier *Happy Hooligan* musical based on the happy-go-lucky cartoon character. But one would be mistaken. *Hooligan in New York* was set in an opium den in New York's Chinatown "where wretched victims of the drug inhale the poppy fumes."

When the 1904–5 season opened on August 1, the first event was Charles H. Hoyt's very popular play *A Texas Steer* featuring the Texas Steer Quartette. Hoyt was represented again that season by the musical farce comedy *A Bunch of Keys*.

The following year, another Hoyt farce, *A Hole in the Ground*, made its way to Manistee with a cast of twenty—"Mostly Girls."

"Stouthearted Men"

The New Moon, lyrics by Oscar Hammerstein II, music by Sigmund Romberg, 1928

In addition to the shows that featured "mostly girls," there were some productions that featured male stars. A few men who were not new to the touring circuits but were new to Manistee audiences made appearances in the fall of 1904 playing their signature roles. The first two to appear were Thomas Jefferson as Rip Van Winkle and Ben Hendricks as Ole Olson. A third new face in an old play was Porter J. White in *Faust*. White returned the next year in *Trilby*, and the *Manistee Daily News* couldn't have been more delighted:

> After a surfeit of musical farces it will be a relief to turn to a really strong and fascinating play like "Trilby" which will be seen at the theatre tonight. "Trilby" will be presented by that splendid player Porter J. White.

The year ended on an up note when on December 26 the internationally known acrobats the Donazettas flew into the Ramsdell Theatre in their spectacular and breath-taking production of **The Span of Life*.

The first major attraction of 1905 took place on January 24 with a presentation of the play concerning absinthe addiction, **A Hidden Crime*, a heavy subject matter that was balanced by the inclusion of "Plenty of Specialties" performed between the acts.

In May 1905, twelve years before the United States entered World War I, the Milwaukee German Theatre Company was at the Ramsdell Theatre with a prophetic political satire that promised to be "A great laugh provoker"—*The German Eagle vs. Star Spangled Banner*.

"Brush Up Your Shakespeare"

Kiss Me, Kate, lyrics and music by Cole Porter, 1948

If the press and, perhaps, the public desired to see drama of a higher stature on the bill, they must have been ecstatic with

FIGURE 61. *The Sleeping Beauty and the Beast*, a musical extravaganza, opened on Broadway in November 1901 where it played 241 performances. After the show closed in May 1902, it headed out on a national tour arriving in Manistee just in time for Christmas. (Publisher: M. Witmark and Sons New York, 1901. Music Division, the New York Public Library Digital Collections.)

the booking of five plays by Shakespeare at different times during the 1905 season: *Hamlet*, *Richard III*, *Twelfth Night*, *The Merchant of Venice*, and *Othello*.

Othello, starring William Owen as Iago and J. W. McConnell as Othello, was of particular note. The most arresting element of that production was Owen's innovative interpretation of Iago:

> Mr. Owen's conception of Iago is the more interesting in that he has left tradition behind. . . . Heretofore the actors playing the part have been content if they have suggested his villainy . . . the scowls, the crossed arms, the sneers, the growling voice. But what becomes of the fact that every character in the play calls him "honest" and that except at the very end he deceives even his wife? (*Manistee Daily News*, August 6, 1905)

The article commented that Owen took on the task "to set in motion a double train of impressions, one for the audience to understand the character's true nature and one for the benefit of the other characters in the play." William Owen was seen in Manistee two years later in *Romeo and Juliet*.

The year ended with a special holiday production of "The Famous London Drury Lane Christmas Extravaganza, *The Sleeping Beauty and the Beast*" that featured the famous Louvre Seminary Girls Band from France. The advertisement assured prospective audience members that it was "Positively the most Gigantic and Gorgeous Spectacular production ever offered in Manistee."

"Every Day Is Ladies Day with Me"

The Red Mill, lyrics by Henry Blossom, music by Victor Herbert, 1906

Each week for a ten-week period in 1907, the *Manistee Daily News* ran a two-column photo of a Broadway leading lady with a short biography. The women selected included Maude Adams, Ethel Barrymore, Mrs. Patrick Campbell, and Julia Marlowe, to name four of the ten. None of them ever performed at the Ramsdell Theatre, but it is an indication that there was an interest in the ladies of the theatre on the part of the citizens of Manistee. Consequently, when *Roselle Knott and Eva Tanguay came to town, it was a major event.

In the spring of 1906, the Ramsdell Theatre presented what it called the "Star Attraction of the Season," the romantic historical drama *When Knighthood Was in Flower* starring Roselle Knott as Mary Tudor. At the Ramsdell Theatre in January 1907, Eva Tanguay, the eccentric stage personality, rang in the New Year in the musical *A Good Fellow*. As most of her career was in vaudeville, she proclaimed herself to be "the girl who made vaudeville famous."

FIGURE 62. This family photo of the famous vaudevillians the Four Cohans was taken in 1888 when George M. Cohan (at his mother's knee) was just ten years old. Three years later they were touring the country in *Peck's Bad Boy* with "Georgie" playing the mischievous Henry Peck. (Photographer unknown. Billy Rose Theatre Division, the New York Public Library Digital Collections.)

"Boys Will Be Boys"

The Beauty Spot, lyrics by Joseph W. Herbert, music by Reginald De Koven, 1909

Peck's Bad Boy was in Manistee for two performances on two consecutive evenings in 1907. The advertisement boasted that the show included "16 Musical Numbers with Girls Who Know How to Sing" and that it was "Not a Moving Picture but a Merry-Go-Round of Fun." The show's management called it "A 21-Year Triumph." Indeed, it had been around for a while. It opened in 1884 and toured continuously for more than two decades.

Charles Felton Pidgin, author of the *Quincy Adams Sawyer* novel, adapted the play from a series of newspaper stories called "The Bad Boy Sketches" by George Wilbur Peck who was first the mayor of Milwaukee and then the governor of Wisconsin. Before he was a politician, he was a newspaperman who wrote a series of short stories about a young prankster. The sketches were the basis for the play, and later they evolved into a series of six *Peck's Bad Boy* novels. Although the character of young Henry Peck has some traits in common with Buster Brown and the Katzenjammer Kids, his pranks were less in the spirit of "fun and games" and much more physical.

In 1891, the popular vaudevillians the Four Cohans took a

hiatus from vaudeville to venture into the world of legitimate theatre with a yearlong tour of *Peck's Bad Boy* with young George M. Cohan in the title role.

In 1907 Cohan recalled some of his character's actions in the play:

> The audiences liked the climax of the third act, for it was then that I scared my mother into hysterics, pushed my father into a washtub full of suds, threw a scuttle of coal into a policeman's face and tumbled the hired girl out of the window. (David Collins, "George M. Cohan in America's Theater")

The advertisement for the play confessed that it was "without plot, but with a purpose—to make people laugh." The critics confirmed that the play had no plot but that the humor was "irresistible." The bad boy comedy, even without the Cohans, was warmly welcomed in Manistee and many times in Red Jacket and Coldwater.

While the play was based on the sketches and is therefore episodic with no real through-line, the two film versions of *Peck's Bad Boy*, 1921 and 1934, are more closely based on the first novel, *Peck's Bad Boy and His Pa*, which does have a plot.

Missing in Action

By the time the Ramsdell Theatre opened there were fewer major stage personalities on tour to towns in rural areas. Four hit shows came to town without the stars that made them famous. In 1907 "George M. Cohan's Greatest Success," *Little Johnny Jones*, brought with it a company of seventy-five, but none of them was George himself. In 1908 "Walker Whiteside's Greatest Comedy Success," *We Are King*, was performed without Walker Whiteside. In 1909, when *A Good Fellow* returned to Manistee, the role made famous by Eva Tanguay was played by Dainty Alice Williams, and **Peg o' My Heart* showed up in 1915 but its original star Laurette Taylor did not.

By 1907 *Humpty Dumpty* was no longer considered a major attraction, but it lingered on and apparently did have its fans. Whether or not those fans remembered or knew of George L. Fox, the man who had originally created the pantomime and played The Clown, is doubtful. But on October 14, 1907, a revised version of the show titled *Saville's Twentieth Century Humpty Dumpty* was on the Ramsdell's bill.

"Father and Son"

Modest Suzanne, lyrics by Harry B. Smith and Robert B. Smith, music by Jean Gilbert, 1912

Local theatergoers had the opportunity to see Joseph Jefferson in his iconic role of Rip Van Winkle that he played continually for forty years in his over seventy-year career. He performed that American classic at Manistee's Grand Opera House (aka the Scandinavian Opera House) years before it burned down.

Joseph "Joe" Jefferson (1829–1905) was part of a multi-generational acting dynasty that began in 1728. He made his theater debut at the age of four when he was carried onto the stage by Thomas D. Rice (aka Jim Crow), and then spent his early years acting with his parents and siblings as they toured the country. When, in 1865, he appeared in *Rip Van Winkle* in London, his performance was so highly acclaimed that he played the drowsy reprobate in two Broadway productions and on tour for the rest of his career.

Three sons of Joseph Jefferson carried on the family tradition. William and Joseph Jr. took the leading roles in Richard Sheridan's *The Rivals*. Earlier, when members of the Jefferson family first toured in *The Rivals*, it featured father Joseph as Bob Acres with his son Joseph Jr. as Sir Lucius O' Trigger. However, when the elder Jefferson fell ill, his son William assumed his father's role and became a permanent replacement. Based on the following review of William's performance from the *Pittsburg Times*, he was able to fill his father's shoes—literally:

> He shows his father in every movement, off the stage as well as on, the clothes he wears in the play are those his father wore, and not even the shoes required alteration. The fit is perfect.

Joseph Jr. and William toured in *The Rivals* for years, and the show played in many of Michigan's playhouses including the Tibbits Opera House and the Calumet Theatre.

Thomas Jefferson (1856–1932), a third son of Joseph, assumed the role of Rip Van Winkle after his father retired from the stage. Like his father, he toured the play throughout the country with stops in Red Jacket, Coldwater, and Manistee. In 1905, he starred in a Broadway revival of the sixty-year-old drama.

FIGURE 63. "A splendid scenic revival of the greatest of American dramas." This poster for *Rip Van Winkle*, featuring Thomas Jefferson, depicts the scene in which Gretchen expels Rip from their cottage and sends him out into the storm, 1905. (Artist unknown. The University of Wisconsin Digital Collections.)

He eventually moved into films, appearing in more than fifty of them between 1913 and 1932. He played Professor Potter in three silent Tarzan films and the title role in two movie versions of *Rip Van Winkle*, 1914 and 1921. In 1931 he appeared in the film version of *Ten Nights in a Bar Room*.

"Daddy's Sweetheart"

Princess April, lyrics and music by Monte Carlo and Alma Sanders, 1924

On October 4, 1904, the *Manistee Daily News* published an article announcing the Ramsdell Theatre's upcoming production of *Rip Van Winkle* starring Thomas Jefferson with his daughter Loretta Jefferson in the role of Rip's daughter, Meenie. The newspaper pointed out that Miss Jefferson was the fifth generation Jefferson to appear on the stage, but the first Jefferson female to do so. Her father had not encouraged her to pursue an acting career, but when he saw her in "a little amateur playlet" he was so impressed that he offered her the opportunity to join his company for its annual tour.

"Forever and a Day"

Speak Easy, lyrics by Irving Bibo, music by John Philip Sousa, 1927

At the time the century turned, it seemed as if two plays that had premiered fifty years before had the staying power to always find an audience. Beginning in 1909 and continuing for a period of six years, these very familiar titles were seen on the Ramsdell season schedule: *Ten Nights in a Bar Room* and, of course, *Uncle Tom's Cabin*. The first of four *Uncle Tom's Cabin* productions presented at the Manistee theater was billed as "Stetson's Original Mammoth '*Uncle Tom's Cabin*'" and featured "a stereoptical recreation of the men who freed the slaves—a tribute to Lincoln, Grant, Sheridan, Sherman, and Douglass."

A Changing of the Guard

In 1909 Ramsdell leased the theater to the Chicago-based Western Theater Association (WTA). That theatrical booking organization was attempting to create a circuit in Michigan's northwestern region and, to that end, had made similar arrangements with the opera houses in Cadillac and Traverse City. The WTA booked shows for the Manistee venue until 1912.

One of the plays booked into the opera house during the WTA's tenure was the controversial *Paid in Full*. According to the show's manager it was "A Play that all Women Should See!" Newspapers ran a novelized version of the play in five installments; each installment consisted of one to two full pages of text.

The play deals with the issues that arise when ambition goes awry and, in this situation, leads to the exploitation of a woman. A young man, Joe Brooks, is envious of the promotions a coworker receives while he seems unable to move up the business ladder. In an attempt to advance his own career he tries to coerce his wife into prostituting herself with someone who could help him in his quest for success. The wife must choose between her love for and obligation to her husband and her own self-respect. She makes her decision in a dramatic moment in the play—she leaves her husband.

Paid in Full opened at New York City's Astor Theatre on February 25, 1908, and it ran there for two seasons that according to the press release upset all theatrical precedent. It was in Coldwater in 1909 and then, the following year, traveled north to Red Jacket twice. It played in Manistee in 1911, 1912, and 1913.

> The enormous numbers of persons that have crowded to the play, so vast indeed as to demand five companies to get it all over this country, stamp "Paid in Full" as the dramatic wonder of this generation and unmistakably declare it the most alluring stage entertainment the theatre in this country ever has known. (*Coldwater Daily Reporter*, September 15, 1909)

"Stock Report"

Put It in Writing, lyrics by Fred Ebb, music by Norman L. Martin, 1963

A total of thirteen stock companies took up residence at the Ramsdell Theatre over an eight-year period, 1903 through 1910. The Ideal Stock Company, the last to be booked into the playhouse, was there the week of November 21, 1910. No longer were stock companies relying on nineteenth-century favorites to entice an audience. The plays in repertory now consisted primarily of melodramas, musical comedies, and Western sagas.

Vaudeville became an integral part of the stock company's program. The Carl W. Cook Stock Company offered Ramsdell audiences a collection of new plays and "5 Big Vaudeville Acts Headed by the Great Arnolda," and the Williams Stock Company had "New Up-to-Date Plays Together with Advanced Vaudeville Between Acts."

Something for Everyone

There was brawn, a few beasts, and a little magic on the Ramsdell Theatre stage in those early days. The last attraction of the 1904–5 season was a lecture-demonstration by Bert Jennings, a bodybuilder who was professionally known as Treloar.

The *Manistee Daily News* was impressed and stated in their review that Treloar was physically everything a man could ever hope to be. After the demonstration, Mr. Jennings delivered an instructional talk on how to develop physical perfection. Two dramatic sketches, several musical selections, and a bayonet drill by the Light Guard rounded out the program.

Unlike the facilities in Coldwater and Red Jacket, there is no indication that the Ramsdell Theatre hosted wrestling or boxing matches—at least not in the flesh. It did on occasion screen moving pictures of major bouts of national interest. In 1907 it offered original Jack O'Brien versus Tommy Burns fight motion pictures, and three years later it presented the "Great Championship Fight" between James J. Jeffries and Jack Johnson that had been photographed at ringside in Reno, Nevada, on the Fourth of July.

There was magic in the air at the Ramsdell Theatre in 1903 when the Great Nicholi Company presented "The World's Greatest Magicians Exploiting a New Series of Weird and Startling Illusions." Madam Gertrude, promoted as "the world's greatest seeress," took over the playhouse for five days in 1909. Ticket holders were instructed to "Bring Your Questions and Have Them Answered."

The next year, 1910, Sciro and Cook's Big Hypnotic Show

was at the theater. The highlight of the show took place when Professor Sciro awakened a man from a nonstop piano-playing hypnotic state that had been induced by the professor ten hours earlier. Seven years later, the Great Griffith did Sciro one better:

> A subject will be put to sleep at seven o'clock Saturday in Bradford Furniture Store Window and will remain in a cataleptic state until Monday night at which time he will be taken to the Ramsdell theatre and awakened. The hypnotic condition is induced over the long distance phone by Griffith from Manitowoc, Wisconsin. (*Manistee News Advocat*e, September 24, 1917)

Almost as magical as Sciro and Griffith were Professor E. K. Crocker's "Educated Horses" that appeared on stage unharnessed and performed for more than two hours. Everything was controlled by word of command. The program for the event indicated, "This entertainment receives the patronage and approbation of clergymen, lawyers, physicians, scientists, and has received the endorsement of humane societies."

Every Ramsdell Theatre season included many musical events but far fewer lectures than were offered at the Tibbits Opera House or the Calumet Theatre. There may be two reasons that account for the dearth of speakers behind a lectern at the Manistee theater. First, the facility was conceived as an entertainment venue comparable to Broadway playhouses in New York City. Based on T. J. Ramsdell's initial statements as reported by his daughter, he envisioned plays, not lectures, on the stage of his theater. Second, there were several other venues in Manistee that played host to orators: Union Hall, service club halls, and several churches.

However, there were exceptions; a few solo speakers were heard at the Ramsdell Theatre. At the theater on March 15, 1910, Henry George Jr. delivered a lecture of note titled "The World's Progress Toward Social Justice." The *Manistee Daily News* called it "A Great Lecture By a Great Lecturer."

"Music in the Air"

A Hero Is Born, lyrics by Agnes Morgan, music by Lehman Engel, 1937

Lectures may have been few in number at the Ramsdell Theatre, but music events were plentiful. The first, in 1904, was a concert by the Kilties that the press described as "Canada's Greatest Concert Band, They Sing . . . They Play . . . They Dance. With bandsmen, pipers, singers, and native dancers of exceptional merit the program offered by the Kilties is one without comparison in this field of amusement."

The Mozart Club, a local organization that sponsored concerts with local, regional, national, and international musicians, presented its first annual May Music Festival at the Ramsdell Theatre in 1905. The same year, the Mozart Club booked the Ernest Gamble Concert and Recital Party that consisted of a singer, violinist, and pianist. The trio's prospectus stated, "Every member of this party of artists is chosen for his individual merit and for his value to the program as a whole. There is no star." The article in the *Manistee Daily News* at the time of the concert focused only on Mr. Gamble and created the impression that indeed he was the star:

> It may be truthfully said that no American singer has ever attained a more enviable position then Mr. Gamble. Today . . . the best musicians in Europe, as well as in our own country, unite in placing him at the very head of American bassos.

Other concerts under the auspices of the Mozart Club included the second annual May Festival in 1906 that featured four solo singers with a chorus of fifty, followed by the third May Festival in 1907. In 1908, it presented a joint concert involving Rudolph Ganz, "the Eminent Swiss Pianist," and Max Bedix, "America's Greatest Violinist," that the press predicted would "without a doubt be the finest recital given in Manistee."

The diverse slate of events sponsored by other local organizations included the Le Brun Grand Opera Company, performing *Martha* and *Il Trovatore*; the Beulah Buck Quartet; the Old Home Singers, a quintet of three women and two men singing old love songs and ballads; the Romanian Orchestra; the Musical Guardsman, "A Singing Orchestra"; and a lecture by ex-governor Edward W. Hoch of Kansas.

Among the international artists that performed in Manistee were Swedish dancers from Stockholm who presented their native dances dressed in provincial costumes and Axel Skovgaard, "the World's Famous Danish Violinist," whose concert was sponsored by the Danish Brotherhood.

"Homemade Happiness"

The Clinging Vine, lyrics by Zelda Sears, music by Harold A. Levey, 1922

The Ramsdell Theatre provided a space for many locally generated attractions. There were operettas, plays, concerts, and minstrel shows all performed by hometown talent. In 1904, Ward Baker's Orchestra gave three concerts. Mr. Baker was a local violin and piano teacher who encouraged folks to "come and help elevate the taste for good music in Manistee."

The war drama *Under the Stars and Stripes* with local talent and a grand chorus was presented in 1906 as a benefit for Company M. The next year, the Ladies Glee Club gave a benefit concert under the direction of Miss Birdelia Belle Conat that featured Miss Minnie Wheeler Reynolds, contralto from Grand Rapids.

In addition to the many productions of comic operas, especially those by Gilbert and Sullivan, there was an original musical revue titled *King Jollity* produced by the Knights of Pythias.

The newspaper reported that the opening night of *King Jollity* attracted the largest house of the season and that the performance was of professional quality. It went on to itemize the pros and cons of the production:

> Mr. Roy Nickerson in the leading role was splendid. Miss Ruth Ramsdell sang sweetly and danced gracefully. . . . The evening was remarkably like a professional performance. Occasionally there was a lack of "snap" to conversational portions and lack of proper facial expressions among the chorus, but these faults were minor ones. (*Manistee Daily News*, February 8, 1906)

The reviewer went on to say that it was to be hoped that the problem with the colored light manipulation that failed at most critical points opening night would be solved.

Amateur minstrel shows produced by service clubs took place with some regularity. In 1904 the Knights of Columbus performed songs and skits while wearing blackface, and four years later a show was mounted called the Big Elks Minstrels. The Traverse City Minstrel Company performed in 1912 under the auspices of the Manistee Area Fraternal Order of Eagles.

The Elks were at it again with another presentation by the Big Elks Minstrels in 1917. This time they brought in a professional director, Phil Lyon, who traveled the country putting together minstrel shows for local organizations using local talent. For this production, the Elks paid a sizeable royalty to use a sketch created by Lew Fields (of Weber and Fields) from his 1913 Broadway show *All Aboard*.

There were also some novelty attractions at the theater. In 1909, the *Boy Circus* took the stage featuring local youths performing as acrobats, clowns, trick riders, and jungle beasts. The variation on that theme took place in 1917: the *High School Circus* with Swedish drills, Hindu acrobatics and gymnastics, and an elephant created by four students in one costume. Beginning in 1921, the opera house was the venue for Manistee High School class plays.

The Beginning of the End

The first week in April 1917, President Woodrow Wilson announced that the United States would enter World War I. That same week, a new entry in the *Bringing Up Father* cartoon musical comedy franchise arrived in Manistee. The day after the performance the newspaper gave the show a positive review that came to a very prophetic conclusion:

> "Bringing Up Father in Politics" served as an excellent vehicle for . . . detracting attention temporarily from the gloom spread by the imminence of war. The theater was profusely decorated with the Stars and Stripes, while a large national flag hung suspended from the dome of the auditorium adding a fitting patriotic touch to what probably will be the last professional show staged in the Ramsdell for a long time. (*Manistee News Advocate*, April 7, 1917)

Although the prediction was prophetic, it was not immediate. The announcement that the Ramsdell Theatre would be closed for the duration of the war did not come until fourteen months later. In the interim it was, for a while, business as usual, and booked attractions continued to grace the Ramsdell stage.

The 1917–18 season opened with the Milton Schuster Musical Comedy Company. It was in residence for four nights and presented a different musical each evening. As a special attraction, at the conclusion of one night's performance, there was a chorus girl specialty competition. The company was so well received that it was held over for an extra night. It no sooner left town than *The Million Dollar Doll* took over the theater. The show required a special ramp to be built that projected out from the stage into the audience so that the doll, supported by "The Greatest Dancing Chorus on Tour," could be well exhibited.

Later that year, Lyman H. Howe and his Travel Festival showed moving pictures of exotic places and current events including "Uncle Sam's Warships in Action."

— HEADLINE —

Ramsdell Will Remain Closed for Rest of War

On July 1, 1918, John Stronach Jr., who had been the Ramsdell Theatre's manager since 1914, announced that due to the government's transportation regulations, very few professional touring productions were traveling to towns in rural areas. Therefore, "the Ramsdell theatre has been closed, and will remain in its state of darkness for the duration of the war." He then assured the citizens of Manistee that "with the conclusion of the war the theater will be re-decorated and reopened with its former high standard of attractions."

Too Many Cooks Spoil the Broth

Although the reason given for the closing of the Ramsdell Theatre was the dearth of available touring productions, another factor was that it had been dealing with strong competition for some time—not only as a venue for legitimate theatre, but also as a venue for motion pictures.

Three months after the Ramsdell Theatre opened in 1903, it announced that "Great Moving Pictures" would be shown at the playhouse. Unfortunately, they were not the only movie show in town. By 1907, there were several small venues in Manistee that presented motion pictures, some with vaudeville or other attractions. In the summer of 1909, the Ramsdell confronted the competition head on:

— HEADLINE —

Ramsdell Theatre Home of Vaudeville and Motion Pictures

There were five theaters that showed moving pictures in Manistee by 1912: the Bijou, the New Electric Theatre, the Scenic Theatre, the New Gem, and the Royal Theatre that advertised "Advanced Vaudeville, High Class Motion Pictures, and Illustrated Songs."

The competition for ticket buyers between the Ramsdell, primarily a venue for live entertainment, and the five movie theaters was not subtle. On May 5, 1910, the play *St. Elmo* was at the Ramsdell Theatre, and down the street and around the corner, the New Electric Theater was showing *St. Elmo*, the moving picture, at the same time. The Lyric Theater screened the film version of *Damaged Goods* in April 1917 starring Richard Bennett, the popular actor who had originated the leading role on Broadway. The advertisement explained, "This is a remarkable picture version of the sensational problem play that has startled the world." As there was no "R" rating for films in those days, the producers came up with their own policy: "Children Admitted Only When Accompanied by Elderly Person or Parent." A month later, a stock company was in residence at the Ramsdell with the live stage version of **Damaged Goods*. The newspaper informed its readers, "This will be the first time that the dramatic version has been seen in the city."

Also competing for audiences was the Orchard Beach Theatre that was built in 1899. An impressive wide veranda with Corinthian columns surrounded the building on three sides; inside there were seven hundred seats, a well-equipped stage, and ample dressing rooms. Ostensibly the Orchard Beach Theatre was a summer operation active only when the Ramsdell Theatre was dark. In fact, there was a time when John Stronach Jr. managed the Ramsdell Theatre during the fall to spring theatre season and the Orchard Beach Theatre in the summer. Although the theater was an open-air performance space, it could be shuttered, which made it possible to be used in inclement weather. Consequently, there were events that took place at the Orchard Beach facility in the spring and fall that appear to have been in conflict with events at the Ramsdell.

"As the Years Roll By"

Her Regiment, lyrics by William Le Baron, music by Victor Herbert, 1917

In 1904, there were fifty-three live-theatre touring productions presented at the Ramsdell Theatre. Twelve years later, in 1916, the year before the playhouse closed its doors for a three-year hiatus, only eleven professional live-theatre productions made their way to Manistee.

As promised by Stronach, the Ramsdell Theatre reopened in 1920, two years after the war, but without having been redecorated and on a limited basis. Its glory days as a venue for professional theatre productions had passed. There were only three productions presented that year: one with amateur actors put on by the local Women's League and two professional touring productions. Every year from 1921 to 1926, one to three professional productions could be seen at the playhouse. During that last five-year period, some of the better-known plays performed by professional companies included **Abie's Irish Rose*, George Kelly's *The Show-Off*, and Victor Herbert's operetta *Sweethearts*.

In 1927, there were five touring productions at the Manistee playhouse. The next year there was no live theatre in the theater, and there wasn't another show until the Kiwanis produced one in 1937 with local talent. In 1938, that service organization presented another local talent show and imported a production by the Radio Theatre Guild of Chicago. In 1939, the Manistee Civic Players moved in and made it their home.

Currently, the Ramsdell Regional Center for the Arts presents a full season consisting of children's shows; concerts by singers, musicians, orchestras, and dance companies; as well as lectures, workshops, educational programs, and the digitally broadcast operas that are "Live from the Met."

PLATE 1. Tibbits Opera House Stage and Auditorium, 2017. The colorful stripe on the stage-right side of the proscenium that extends from the stage to the dome is a representation of the original colors of the proscenium, boxes, auditorium walls, and ceiling. Restoration plans include replicating that color palette on the interior of the opera house. (Photograph by Dennis James Photography, Coldwater, Michigan. Courtesy of the Tibbits Opera Foundation and Arts Council.)

PLATE 2. Tibbits Opera House Boxes and Auditorium, 2017. (Photograph by Dennis James Photography, Coldwater, Michigan. Courtesy of the Tibbits Opera Foundation and Arts Council.)

PLATE 3. Tibbits Opera House Lobby, 2017. The mural was designed and painted by Disney animator Alfred Parke in 1964. (Photograph by Dennis James Photography, Coldwater, Michigan. Courtesy of the Tibbits Opera Foundation and Arts Council.)

PLATE 4. Calumet Theatre Cornice with Gold Leaf Plaster Relief, 2017. (Photograph by Laura Miller, courtesy of the Calumet Theatre.)

PLATE 5. Calumet Theatre Auditorium, 2008. (Photograph by Bill Fink, courtesy of the Calumet Theatre.)

PLATE 6. Calumet Theatre Proscenium Arch with Paintings of Five Muses, 2008. (Photograph by Bill Fink, courtesy of the Calumet Theatre.)

PLATE 7. Calumet Theatre Proscenium Panel–Painting Muse, 2017. (Photograph by Laura Miller, courtesy of the Calumet Theatre.)

PLATE 8. Calumet Theatre Proscenium Panel–Drama Muse, 2017. (Photograph by Laura Miller, courtesy of the Calumet Theatre.)

PLATE 9. Calumet Theatre Proscenium Panel–Music Muse, 2017. (Photograph by Laura Miller, courtesy of the Calumet Theatre.)

PLATE 10. Calumet Theatre Proscenium Panel–Poetry Muse, 2017. (Photograph by Laura Miller, courtesy of the Calumet Theatre.)

PLATE 11. Calumet Theatre Proscenium Panel–Sculpture Muse, 2017. (Photograph by Laura Miller, courtesy of the Calumet Theatre.)

PLATE 12. Ramsdell Theatre Auditorium and Proscenium, date unknown.
(Photograph courtesy of the Ramsdell Regional Center for the Arts.)

PLATE 13. Ramsdell Theatre Auditorium Dome with Venus, Cherubs, and Doves, designed and painted by Frederic Winthrop Ramsdell, date unknown. (Photograph courtesy of the Manistee County Historical Museum.)

PLATE 14. Ramsdell Theatre Show Drop, "A Grove Near Athens," designed and painted by Walter Burridge. (Photograph by Beverly Wilkens, Old Hippie Productions, Manistee, Michigan, 2017.)

PLATE 15. Ramsdell Theatre Auditorium, date unknown. (Photograph courtesy of the Ramsdell Regional Center for the Arts.)

Extra-Added Attractions!

FIGURE 64. From the moment Thomas D. "Daddy" Rice applied burnt cork to his face and danced his famous "Jim Crow Jump" in the 1830s, minstrel shows provided family-friendly entertainment to Americans, 1836. (Artist unknown. Jerome Robbins Dance Division, The New York Public Library for the Performing Arts, Astor, Lenox, and Tilden Foundations.)

Minstrel Shows, Vaudeville, and Moving Pictures

> Edwin Booth did his first acting in black face. Edwin Forrest was a minstrel long before he thought of playing "Virginius" and "Othello." Burnt cork played a large part in the early life of Joseph Jefferson. Of the noted actors now before the public who started in this branch of the profession are Francis Wilson (the first president of Actors' Equity), Edward Harrigan, Chauncey Olcott, Otis Skinner. —*Coldwater Daily Reporter*, August 5, 1910

The Evolution of Minstrelsy

What was introduced in 1832 by one blackface entertainer dancing a jig, Thomas D. Rice (aka Jim Crow), had expanded by 1843 into four blackface entertainers, Dan Emmett and the Virginia Minstrels, playing instruments, singing songs, and telling jokes, and by 1846, thanks to Christy's Minstrels, had evolved into the first indigenous form of American entertainment—the minstrel show.

> Among the many musical and theatrical entertainments offered to the multitude of our pleasure seekers, none appeal more to the average audience, nor is welcomed with greater enthusiasm by both old and young than a first class minstrel show. (*Coldwater Daily Reporter*, September 5, 1905)

Traditionally, when the curtain went up, the minstrels marched onto the stage singing and playing instruments performing what was called the "walkaround." After the opening number, the Interlocutor would say, "Gentlemen, be seated," and the company sat down on chairs arranged in a semicircle facing the audience. The Interlocutor, who was the only performer not in blackface, was dressed in formal attire; the other minstrel men, whose faces were covered with burnt cork makeup, wore outlandish costumes that often consisted of colorful swallowtail coats and striped trousers.

FIGURE 65. On March 4, 1881, by special invitation from the White House, the Haverly United Mastodon Minstrels, one of the most prestigious minstrel companies at the time, marched in President James A. Garfield's inauguration parade in Washington D.C. Also participating in the parade was John Philip Sousa and his band. (Publisher unknown. Retrieved from the Library of Congress.)

The Interlocutor was positioned in the center of the semicircle, and on the far stage right end was Mr. Tambo with his tambourine; opposite him, on the far stage left end was Mr. Bones with two animal bones, two pieces of wood, or a clapper. Once the company was seated, the jokes began:

INTERLOCUTOR: Gentlemen, be seated! Well, Mr. Bones, how are you feeling this evening?

BONES: Very well, Mr. Interlocutor, and how are you—how are all your folks?

INTERLOCUTOR: We're all well, excepting my brother. You see, a team of horses ran away with him, and he's been laid up since.

BONES: That's a very strange coincidence, same thing happened to my brother.

INTERLOCUTOR: You don't say.

BONES: The only difference is, it was my brother who ran away with the team of horses; he's been laid up ever since, but they'll let him out next month.

Two of the most successful and influential pre–Civil War minstrel companies were Christy's Minstrels and Bryant's Minstrels. Beginning in 1846, Christy's Minstrels performed on Broadway for eight consecutive years and introduced many of Stephen Foster's songs including "Old Folks at Home." Bryant's Minstrels were also based in New York. After the Virginia Minstrels disbanded, Dan Emmett went to work for the Bryant brothers as a musician and songwriter. He is credited with being the composer of "Dixie" that was introduced by the Bryant's Minstrels in 1858. Both of these companies seldom toured, and when they did, it was to major metropolitan theatrical centers. However, before movies trumped live entertainment, there were many well-known touring minstrel companies that did perform at opera houses located in Michigan's rural areas including Haverly's United Mastodon Minstrels.

At Michigan opera houses, minstrel shows were among the earliest attractions. The first documented professional production at the Adrian Union Hall in 1867 was Lloyd's Minstrels and Brass Band. It turned out to be a disappointing event—at least for the performers. While they were on stage the last night of their engagement, William Alvin Lloyd, the leader of Lloyd's Minstrels, absconded with the box office receipts, leaving his minstrels stranded.

The predecessor of the Calumet Theatre, the upper-floor Red Jacket Opera House, opened in 1887 with a performance by the Beach and Bowers Minstrels. After the Red Jacket Opera House's position as the area's major performance venue was usurped by the Calumet Theatre, thirty minstrel productions played the new facility during its first nineteen years of operation.

The first minstrelsy production to be presented at the Tibbits Opera House was by the New Orleans Minstrels in January 1883, just four months after the playhouse opened. From then until 1919, seventy minstrel shows were performed there.

In December 1903, three months after *A Chinese Honeymoon* had left Manistee, the Alabama Minstrels were singing and dancing on the Ramsdell Theatre stage.

"A Wand'ring Minstrel I"

The Mikado, lyrics by W. S. Gilbert, music by Arthur Sullivan, 1885

Two of the most celebrated post–Civil War touring companies, Al G. Field Greater Minstrels and John W. Vogel's Big City Minstrels, played at the Tibbits Opera House and the Calumet Theatre several times. Only Al G. Field's company made it to the Ramsdell Theatre.

Al G. Field Greater Minstrels originated in Marion, Ohio, in 1886. The company was immediately successful and quickly became one of the top touring minstrel troupes in America. Originally, the Field Minstrels featured "Ethiopian delineators"—white men performing in blackface. By 1898 Field was promoting a company of "real Negro minstrels"—white men performing in blackface.

After fifty years of minstrelsy, the semicircle, song-and-dance format of the shows had become very predictable. Audiences wanted something different:

> The public are continually demanding something new. Minstrelsy has followed a beaten path for a number of years and, whilst it is the most popular of all American amusements, the people demand some changes. (*Coldwater Republican*, August 24, 1889)

Al G. Field answered the call. The changes he initiated involved abandoning the traditional semicircular arrangement and, instead, when the curtain went up on one of his shows the audience discovered a military encampment on stage. The first part began with a military drill in place of the walkaround, minstrel songs, banter, and jokes. To reinforce the military idea, the end men, Mr. Tambo and Mr. Bones, were played as comic servants to the officers. It was a step from traditional minstrelsy toward musical comedy.

Field branched out to become a producer-director of a company that was not his own as was reported in the *Coldwater Daily Reporter* on June 26, 1907:

> Arrangements have been completed whereby the coming theatrical season in Coldwater will be opened on Aug. 3 when Al. G. Field will present Donnelly & Hatfield's Greater Minstrels. It is an all white organization that has

FIGURE 66. The Al G. Field Greater Minstrels' "The Show You Know" poster and calendar has a blank space for text to be added containing information pertaining to the city, place, and date of their performances. (Publisher: Courier Company, Buffalo, ca. 1905. Retrieved from the Library of Congress.)

made an enviable reputation throughout the states and Canada.

Later in the summer, the newspaper published an update reporting that Field was in Europe to engage specialty artists for Donnelly & Hatfield's Greater Minstrels. On August 3, the day it played the Tibbits Opera House, the *Coldwater Daily Reporter* announced that the Donnelly & Hatfield All White Magnificent Minstrels under the personal direction of Al G. Field would open with the "old time semi-circle of black and white face comedians." The company went on to play the Ramsdell Theatre the next week.

Three years later, Field was back on tour with his own troupe, and the Coldwater press exclaimed that they were the biggest and best minstrel company that had ever played the opera house.

> Now on its twenty-fourth annual tour, the Field Minstrel Company is stronger than ever. . . . Never before in the history of the Tibbits opera house has Coldwater offered a similar attraction to equal A. G. Field's. Many out of town automobile parties are being arranged to see Al G. Field's Minstrels next week. (*Coldwater Daily Reporter*, April 12, 1910)

In his article "The Younger Generation in Minstrelsy and Reminiscences of the Past" that appeared in the March 27, 1915, issue of the *New York Clipper*, Frank Dumont wrote that when producers Klaw and Erlanger of the Syndicate were asked to name the best touring theatrical group in the country, the response was "Al G. Field Greater Minstrels."

John W. Vogel's Big City Minstrels flourished from its very start and came to be looked upon as one of the foremost minstrel companies in America. It continued to tour and present its shows long after its predecessors had left the stage. As the last man standing, Vogel, referred to as "the Minstrel King," made a fortune in the minstrelsy business. His company played at various Michigan opera houses including the Tibbits Opera House and the Calumet Theatre.

> Manager Vogel's offerings in the past have been as good, if not better, than anything of the kind seen hereabouts; his performances having been conspicuously popular because of the many innovations introduced. (*Coldwater Daily Reporter*, May 6, 1903)

Certainly Vogel's 1905 production was innovative. When the curtain went up the audience saw the spacious and elegant lobby of a Chicago hotel. The Interlocutor served as the desk clerk, and the end men (Tambo and Bones) and other comedians assumed the duties of the porters, elevator men, and bellboys. The *Coldwater Daily Reporter* proclaimed, "'Tis a novel idea well presented."

The specialty acts secured for this production included Count DeRobeo, comedy trick cyclist, and Carlosa and Silverton, artists on the high wire. Previously, both acts had performed for a season at London's Hippodrome.

When Vogel's company appeared at the Tibbits Opera House in 1907, the newspaper exclaimed that

> John W. Vogel's fifty all white big city minstrels have reached the highest summit of perfection, towering above all similar attractions, a monument to the march of progressive minstrel enterprises. The public's wants have been carefully considered by Manager Vogel who has acquired recognition for the advancement and further development of minstrelsy. (*Coldwater Daily Reporter*, May 7, 1907)

Perhaps the most innovative and ambitious production presented by John W. Vogel's All White Big Minstrels was titled "Japland or The Garden of the Mikado," advertised as an "Operatic Minstrel Farce-Comedy" with a "Geisha Girl Chorus and Double Symphony Orchestra."

The press was ecstatic and shared its excitement with its readers:

> The offering is a novelty because of its absolute newness of idea and construction, containing a bit or two from every form of stage creation, opera, farce and minstrelsy predominating. The fact that a girl chorus of twenty is carried will be welcome news to the followers of minstrelsy . . . many theatre-goers want to see and hear the girls, they of trim forms and beautiful voices together with their ability to cavort, pirouette and dance. (*Coldwater Daily Reporter*, September 5, 1916)

"Black Boys / White Boys"

Hair, lyrics by James Rado and Gerome Ragni, music by Galt MacDermot, 1967

After the Civil War black entertainers formed their own companies and began to tour the North. Both the Sunny

FIGURE 67. In 1872, Charles Callender acquired the Original Georgia Minstrels, and as Callender's Famous Georgia Minstrels, the troupe performed in Europe and throughout the United States including Coldwater and Red Jacket. (Lithograph: O. V. Schubert, Cleveland, ca. 1876. Retrieved from the Library of Congress.)

South Company that was billed as "America's Greatest of All Colored Shows, Kings of Koontown Komedy" and Thomas P. Kelly's All Star Colored Minstrels, "The Swellest Minstrel Show That Ever Left Dixie," were popular attractions in Michigan.

When in 1865, Charles Barney Hicks, an entertainer and manager, formed his all-black company, the Georgia Minstrels (aka the Original Georgia Minstrels), he claimed that the audience would experience "genuine Africans depicting plantation life." According to Washington Cooke in his study "A History of the Croswell Opera House," when the Georgia Minstrels performed at the Adrian Union Hall on December 23, 1869, the *Adrian Daily Times and Expositor* suggested that they "go back to plowing cotton and leave minstrelsy to white men with burnt cork."

Over the years the gentlemen from Georgia perfected their act and became one of the most popular and successful black troupes on the minstrel touring circuit and one of the first companies to take the uniquely American form of entertainment abroad.

"I Wants to Be an Actor Lady"

In Dahomey, lyrics by Vincent Bryan, music by Harry Von Tilzer, 1903

In addition to black and white minstrel men, there were also minstrel ladies. In November 1889, Duncan Clark's Lady Minstrels and New Arabian Nights performed at the Tibbits Opera House. The local newspaper declared it to be "the vilest show that ever appeared in Coldwater." It opened with eight scantily dressed females sitting on stage. The local reviewer was not favorably impressed; he reported that the singing was "insipid," the march "horribly executed," and he hoped that "this city will be spared the infliction of another like exhibition."

Before the show left town, one of the female minstrels, Miss Adelle Carlton, brought suit against Duncan Clark, the manager of the company. She testified that the minstrel ladies were paid only $3.00 a week plus expenses to appear on stage, and fines assessed by an "unscrupulous, hard-hearted manager" sometimes reduced that amount. The all-male jury brought in a verdict for the plaintiff for $80 and costs. Mr. Clark, who could or would not pay the fine, was sent to jail.

"End of the Line"

The Real Life Story of Johnny De Facto, lyrics and music by Douglas Post, 1989

The blackface tradition died a slow death. Elements of the traditional minstrel show were absorbed by musical comedy on stage and screen. In the 1920s, on Broadway and in the movies, Al Jolson, wearing his signature blackface makeup, got down on one knee to perform his sentimental "mammy songs." Judy Garland and Mickey Rooney, also in blackface, ended two of their three 1930s "Backyard Musical" films, *Babes in Arms* and *Babes on Broadway*, with a high-stepping minstrel number.

As late as the 1940s, fraternal service organizations raised money for their good works when local doctors, lawyers, and businessmen applied dark makeup to their faces, donned clownish costumes, sat in a semicircle, and performed minstrel songs before an audience of town folk.

"The Two-a-Day"

Parade, lyrics and music by Jerry Herman, 1960

Opera house audiences supported many forms of entertainment in the early part of the twentieth century, but when it came to variety shows, minstrelsy had the edge over vaudeville. However, vaudeville was definitely in evidence in season programming after 1900. Some programs involved only a few specialties that played back-to-back to create one act that was attached to a two- or three-act scripted entertainment. Later, it was not uncommon for an evening's entertainment to consist of both a motion picture and a program consisting of a wildly disparate collection of vaudeville acts.

The Dvorak Davidson Stock Company was in residence at the Tibbits Opera House from May 29 to June 3, 1905, and offered

> a splendid program of vaudeville . . . consisting of ballads, songs and dances, moving pictures, monologues, character impersonations, sketches, illustrated songs, etc. Among the vaudeville features are, the funniest of comedians, Jack C. LeRoy; the ladies' and children's favorite, Baby Louise; the dancing marvel, Al. Fox; the Sherwood Sextette; the little magnet, Lena Devine; Harry Gadsby in illustrated songs and Prof. Leighton's moving pictures, as good as any and better than many. (*Coldwater Daily Reporter*, May 26, 1905)

A large two-column advertisement appeared in the *Manistee Daily News* in 1909 announcing that on Thursday night, June 10, a new program of vaudeville and moving pictures would be presented four nights a week—Thursday through Sunday—at the Ramsdell Theatre. "Regular theatrical engagements will be booked from time to time for the early part of the week."

The newspaper's review that was published on June 11

heralded the success of the new endeavor. The reviewer wrote laudatory comments about many of the acts including one billed as Tops and Topsy that consisted of a mime and his "wonderful little dog, quite the cleverest that has ever been exhibited here."

From the review, it is obvious that the vaudeville portion of the evening was more successful than the screening of the motion picture: "A little trouble was had with the machine, but Mr. Bingham will soon have it running smoothly."

In Coldwater, both Manager Jackson at the Tibbits Opera House and the *Coldwater Daily Reporter* were very aggressive in their attempt to attract first-class vaudeville companies to their town and to attract the local citizens to the shows. On April 1, 1908, the newspaper reported that John Jackson had become a member of the Western Vaudeville Association. The press expressed the hope that his involvement would bring the finest acts from the circuit to the local stage at the close of the regular theatre season. The plan was successful in attracting an appropriate vaudeville company but was apparently less successful in attracting an audience. When the Allor, Barrington, and Swan Company performed in Coldwater, it was the opinion of the press that they deserved better crowds.

> Coldwater audiences are certainly uneducated to first class vaudeville. . . . There are 7,000 people in Coldwater and yet only about six hundred in all have attended the performances. That leaves 6,400 men, women and children in our fair city that are missing a mighty good thing at extraordinarily low prices. (*Coldwater Daily Reporter*, May 13, 1909)

Two years later, a new elaborate plan was initiated to encourage attendance at vaudeville shows. The Tossell Vaudeville Tours, a booking and management organization, was formed for the purpose of bringing small cities high-class vaudeville. A six-city circuit was created that included four towns in Indiana and two in Michigan: Grand Haven and Coldwater. Every week the parent company, the Theatre Booking Corporation, sent out the Tossell Vaudeville Show from Chicago that consisted of five acts and a motion picture. The program played one night a week in each city but each week presented a different motion picture and set of acts. Tossell Vaudeville Tours Road Show Number One played in Coldwater on Saturday night, October 21, 1911, and the press proclaimed that it was "high class."

> What is "high class vaudeville?" The term itself conveys the impression it's being of the very best quality. But the phrase "high class vaudeville" is misused to represent a class of entertainment consisting of acts that are far from being up to the standard. . . . Then came "advanced vaudeville," followed by . . . "polite vaudeville," and now come(s) "high class, advanced, polite vaudeville." (*Coldwater Daily Reporter*, October 4, 1911)

In 1915, the question as to whether or not Coldwater was interested in vaudeville was once again an issue. In a headline, the newspaper inquired, "Does Coldwater Want Vaudeville?"

> The Western Association has sent out from Chicago a company of vaudeville talent . . . if the proper interest

is manifested these people will remain here, putting on two or three new programs every week with matinees on Saturdays. (*Coldwater Daily Reporter*, May 13, 1915)

The plan involved a company of players that would be in residence for seven weeks. Monday through Saturday they presented "tabloid" versions of well-known plays. The Western Theatre Association promised, "No long, drawn out, tiresome plays will be offered—only the most gripping scenes of the plays will be depicted." The program, which changed every Thursday, also included original revues featuring the latest songs and dances along with moving pictures.

In the fall of 1919, shortly after Vanes took control of the Tibbits Opera House, the following announcement appeared in the *Coldwater Daily Reporter*:

> Owing to the request of so many of our patrons to see vaudeville occasionally in connection with pictures, we have contracted with one of the best booking agencies to supply us with such acts as will be approved by our patrons beginning Monday night, October 13th. (D. R. Vanes, Owner and Manager, Tibbits Theater, October 9, 1919)

FIGURE 68. "Klaw and Erlanger's Advanced Vaudeville." In addition to sending theatre productions out on their circuit, Klaw and Erlanger (aka the Syndicate) also covered the country with vaudeville shows. (Publisher unknown, 1907. Retrieved from the Library of Congress.)

"A Man of the World"

Dr. Deluxe, lyrics by Otto Harbach, music by Karl Hoschna, 1911

For a different kind of evening's entertainment there was Lyman H. Howe and his Travel Festival. Frequently seen at all three venues featured here, the popular travelogues were presented once or twice a season.

In 1907 Howe's Travel Festival was on its twenty-fifth semiannual tour with a program titled "The World Revealed." Indeed, Howe did reveal the world, for over the next ten years among the locations photographed and presented

FIGURE 69. The image projected on the screen in this "Lyman H. Howe's New Marvels in Moving Pictures" poster is of an infantry attack during the Spanish-American War. The poster includes an insert with a portrait of Howe in the upper left corner. (Publisher: Courier Litho Co., Buffalo, N.Y., ca. 1898. Retrieved from the Library of Congress.)

were Alaska, Algeria, Antarctica, China, Coney Island, Egypt, Italy, Japan, Norway, and Russia, to name a few. The titles of the filmed segments revealed their subject matter: "The Funeral of King Edward," "The Eruption of Mt. Etna," "Carnival at Nice," "Ride Up the Eiffel Tower," "Through Austria by Rail," "Hunting from an Aeroplane," and "Other Subjects—Many Very Humorous."

The presentations were promoted as being supremely real depictions of world tours and the only moving pictures with sound. Howe's views of exotic locations, exciting activities, and current events were not the only draw to his Travel Festival; the film segments were interspersed with comedy, music, and song. In other words—VAUDEVILLE!

If You Can't Beat 'Em, Sell Popcorn

It was only a matter of time before motion pictures began infiltrating opera house programming. By the end of the first decade of the twentieth century, small, intimate movie houses that specialized in showing motion pictures began springing up, followed by large, luxurious movie palaces. Those opera houses that were still standing and still relying on their diminishing live-theatre programming found it difficult, if not impossible, to compete with the public's new favorite form of entertainment. Many of them became official or unofficial movie theaters themselves.

"Three Cans of Film"

Diversions, lyrics by Steven Vinaver, music by Buster Davis, 1958

The Birth of a Nation and *A Daughter of the Gods* were two controversial motion pictures seen at the Tibbits Opera House and both the Calumet and Ramsdell Theatres. *Cleopatra*, another film that raised eyebrows, did not travel north of US 12 and was not screened in Manistee or Calumet, only at southern Michigan opera houses.

Perhaps the most significant motion-picture event to take place at all three venues prior to their commitment to becoming full-time movie theaters was the screening of D. W. Griffith's 1915 iconic film, *The Birth of a Nation*. The film was based on the 1905 novel by Thomas F. Dixon titled *The Clansman*. Dixon immediately adapted his novel into a play with the same title. The drama made a national tour playing at many Michigan opera houses.

Ten years later, the film *The Birth of a Nation*, which took eight months to complete at a cost of over $100,000 and involved thousands of actors, technicians, and horses, also toured the country. It was advertised in the *Coldwater Daily Reporter* as "The Most Stupendous Dramatic Narrative Ever Unfolded on Any Stage in the World." The film arrived with a twenty-piece orchestra and a crew of ten. It was screened twice a day at the Tibbits Opera House on December 22 and 23, 1915, the year it was released. The newspaper recommended, "Not a man, woman or child within reasonable distance of Coldwater should overlook this opportunity to see the great historical American epic." The film was replayed several times at the Tibbits Opera House over the next three years.

The first of two engagements of *The Birth of a Nation* at the Calumet Theatre took place on January 30 and 31 and February 1, 1916. The announcement of the film's arrival included the information that

> a splendid symphony orchestra of sixteen pieces, in addition to several vocalists, accompanies the production and all the huge apparatus, manned by a small army of electricians, machinists, etc. are carried by the company, which is one of the largest traveling organizations on the road today. (*Calumet News*, November 6, 1915)

FIGURE 70. Annette Kellerman (also spelled Kellermann) in the nude scene from *A Daughter of the Gods*. In addition to her other accomplishments, Kellerman was a health and fitness advocate who attempted to swim the English Channel three times and is responsible for popularizing synchronized swimming. (Publisher: Bain News Service, 1915. Retrieved from the Library of Congress.)

On March 21, 1916, the film was back to celebrate the sixteenth anniversary of the opening of the Calumet Theatre. It played a week, the longest engagement of a single attraction at that theater up to that time. On June 16, 1916, there were two more screenings of the epic drama in Red Jacket.

FIGURE 71. Theda Bara in *Cleopatra*, 1917. The early screen siren Theda Bara is generally considered to be the cinema's first sex symbol and was marketed as "the Vamp." As the Egyptian queen, she wore fifty elaborate and extremely revealing costumes. Three scenes in which her naval was exposed were cut from the film when it was presented in Chicago. (Billy Rose Theatre Division, the New York Public Library for the Performing Arts, Astor, Lenox, and Tilden Foundations.)

The Birth of a Nation was shown twice in Manistee, in 1916 and again the next year.

A Daughter of the Gods, released in 1916, featured Annette Kellerman, the Australian swimmer who predated Esther Williams as an aquatic movie star. She was famous for having discarded the bathing costume that consisted of blouse, skirt, and bloomers in favor of the one-piece, form-revealing bathing suit that she introduced.

In *A Daughter of the Gods*, Miss Kellerman became the first performer to be filmed underwater and the first actress to appear on screen completely nude.

When it came to movies that were box office bonanzas, the 1917–18 season was filled with them. At the Tibbits Opera House there were showings of both *A Daughter of the Gods* and *The Birth of a Nation* as well as three films featuring superstar Theda Bara: *Under Two Flags*, *Salome*, and *Cleopatra*. According to the producing company, Fox Film Corporation, *Cleopatra* was one of the period's most expensive films, costing an estimated $500,000. The studio also boasted that the movie consisted of one thousand scenes, a cast of thirty thousand humans, three thousand horses, and a production crew of two thousand. It was shown accompanied by a full orchestra. Movies were here to stay!

Good-bye Sarah Bernhardt! Hello Theda Bara!

EPILOGUE

The Denouement

Years ago, theatre folk were known to say that motion pictures tolled the death knell for vaudeville. Motion pictures also took their toll on touring theatre productions. Once motion pictures caught the attention of audiences, the touring companies found that even their spectacular effects could not compare with what people were seeing on the silver screen. Consequently, fewer professional theatre groups toured the country. Some opera houses were forced to limit their offerings to regionally generated entertainment and civic events. Other opera houses closed or were left vacant, and some eventually burned down or were razed to make way for new buildings or parking lots under the "urban renewal" banner.

The Tibbits Opera House, the Calumet Theatre, and the Ramsdell Theatre all opened in a blaze of glory and enjoyed several years of renown presenting professional theatre productions as well as other events. All three fell on hard times as a venue for legitimate theatre with the advent of movies and the dearth of live-theatre booking options. But today, thanks to the efforts of concerned citizens, all three are open, active, and have a commitment to their communities as a home for local functions and as a venue for live entertainment—a commitment they have honored for over one hundred years.

Appendix I

NOW PLAYING!

FIGURE 72. Clockwise from top left are caricatures of Gumption Cute, Miss Ophelia, Uncle Tom, and Little Eva with Topsy in the middle. The poster states that they are "characters that will live forever." It just seemed like forever. In 1869, seventeen years after the novel had been adapted for the stage, a journalist writing for the *New York Times* revealed his fear that the public's interest in the play "would never wear out." The poster promoted Al W. Martin's Mammoth Production of *Uncle Tom's Cabin*. (Publisher: U. S. Printing Co., Cincinnati, U.S.A., ca. 1899. Retrieved from the Library of Congress.)

Particularly Popular Plays

In the early years of booking professional touring productions, Shakespeare's histories and tragedies, especially those featuring major stars, could be counted on to sell well; so could American tales (*Uncle Tom's Cabin, Rip Van Winkle*), melodramas (*East Lynne, The Streets of New York*), and anything that featured spectacular effects. Of the plays that were presented multiple times at theaters around the country during the Golden Age of American Opera Houses, those listed above were among the most often performed at Michigan opera houses. Finishing off the list were *Faust, Hazel Kirke*, and *Ten Nights in a Bar Room*.

"The Play's the Thing"

Hamlet, by William Shakespeare, ca. 1602

Uncle Tom's Cabin, based on the best-selling 1852 antislavery novel *Uncle Tom's Cabin; or, Life Among the Lowly*, by Harriet Beecher Stowe, enjoyed many dramatic adaptations due to the lax copyright laws at the time. The novel sold three hundred thousand copies in the first year of publication and was the second best-selling book of the nineteenth century, surpassed only by the Bible.

In spite of the enormous popularity of the novel, it is estimated that more people were introduced to the story by having seen it on stage rather than having read the book. In one adaptation or another, *Uncle Tom's Cabin* became the most produced play in America during the last half of the nineteenth century and was still being presented during the first two decades of the twentieth century. Over a twenty-year period, the drama was presented four times at the Ramsdell Theatre, thirteen times at the Calumet Theatre, and more than two dozen times at the Tibbits Opera House.

Prior to the Civil War, the book and play garnered support for the antislavery movement. In 1861, panic surrounding the Civil War created Uncle Tom mania in the North,

FIGURE 73. Another poster featuring "Eliza's Escape." (Publisher: Courier Litho Co., Buffalo, N.Y., 1899.) "Of all the plays that were played year after year at the Opera House, 'Uncle Tom's Cabin' was a perennial favorite. The touring company always paraded through town with the Bloodhounds the day of the performance. If the dogs seemed as though they would give Liza a good chase on the ice, we would make certain to go to the show." (Excerpt from reminiscences of *Uncle Tom's Cabin* at the Cheboygan Opera House from a letter written by Sophia Elliot Fultz, 1893–1969.)

which resulted in the simultaneous presentations of four different productions of the play in New York City. The most frequently produced stage version was by George L. Aiken, an actor/playwright. He adapted the novel into a six-act play in 1852, the same year the book was published. In the original production, he played the role of the runaway slave George Harris in blackface. In early productions of the play, all of the black characters were played by white actors.

Today, most people have at least a vague idea of the message of the play that concerns the plight of slaves prior to the Civil War. Eliza, a slave who has been separated from her husband, George, flees from her owner when she learns that he intends to sell her young son. When she reaches the icy Ohio River she says, "Better to sink beneath the cold water with my child locked in my arms than have him torn from me and sold into bondage." Pursued by bloodhounds and carrying her boy, she crosses the river moving from ice floe to ice floe. Eventually Eliza, her son, and her husband are reunited and escape to Canada and freedom.

In the meantime, Uncle Tom, who is being transported down river on a steamboat to a slave auction, saves a young white girl, Eva, from drowning. Her grateful father, Mr. Augustine St. Clare, buys Tom to be a companion to Eva.

On her deathbed, Little Eva, succumbing to consumption, begs her father to free his slaves. Once he agrees, Eva dies and, in most productions of the period, literally ascends to heaven. Before he is able to free his slaves, Eva's father is killed and Uncle Tom is sold to the evil Simon Legree. When Tom disobeys Legree's orders to flog another slave, he is beaten to death. With his last breath, he forgives his transgressors.

ACT VI, Scene vii

Gorgeous clouds, tinted with sunlight. Eva, robed in white, is discovered on the back of a milk-white dove, with expanded wings, as if just soaring upward. Her hands are extended in benediction over St. Clare and

Uncle Tom who are kneeling and gazing up to her. Expressive music. Slow Curtain.

The plot and relevance of the play accounted for much of its popularity; however, the special effects, such as Eliza crossing the ice and Little Eva ascending to heaven, provided additional selling points.

The story is harsh and tragic, but the proceedings are occasionally lightened by the antics and observations of a young black girl named Topsy. Although she is a secondary character in the drama, Topsy was so popular with audiences that the actress playing the role often received top billing.

To keep the audiences coming back to see the same play again and again, some later adaptations took liberties with the script and used it as a structure to support other forms of entertainment.

In 1909, the Stetson's Big Double Production of *Uncle Tom's Cabin* was on tour. It promoted "Grand Transformation Scenes and Mechanical Effects, Cotton Picking Scenes, Floats and Tableaux drawn by Shetland Ponies, Jubilee Singers, Cake Walkers, Buck Dancers, two Brass Bands," and "2 White and Colored Funny Topsys."

That production featured one prop that received special attention:

> Before the Civil War, there was hardly a plantation in the south but boasted a whipping post to which the owner's slaves were fastened while being punished with the cruel whip. To faithfully depict the actual scene . . . Manager Washburn uses in his production . . . a whipping post which was in service on the Red River plantation for many years prior to the Rebellion. (*Coldwater Daily Reporter*, December 1, 1909)

The story has inspired other forms of entertainments as well; in 1924 a musical with the title *Topsy and Eva* opened on Broadway.

Over twenty-five years later, another Broadway musical included a dance version of Eliza's flight across the river and Eva's ascension to heaven when Jerome Robbins created "The Small House of Uncle Thomas" ballet for *The King and I*.

FIGURE 74. "The *Uncle Tom's Cabin* play of today has taken on the characteristics of a minstrel performance in some ways and is a mixture of music and dancing with just enough of the text of the old play worked in to hold the piece together." *Coldwater Daily Reporter*, December 31, 1910. This illustration captures members of the cast of *Uncle Tom's Cabin* performing the fashionable cakewalk dance. (Publisher: U.S. Printing Co., Cincinnati, U.S.A., ca. 1898. Retrieved from the Library of Congress.)

FIGURE 75. A painting of Topsy and Eva inspired by Eva saying to Topsy, "I love you because you haven't had any father, or mother, or friends because you've been a poor abused child." (Artist: Louisa Corbaux. Printer/Publisher: Stannard and Dixon, London, ca. 1852. Retrieved from the Library of Congress.)

In addition to the many stage versions, *Uncle Tom's Cabin* was made into a movie several times during the silent film era, the last in 1927. Sixty years later, an *Uncle Tom's Cabin* made-for-television movie was broadcast starring Avery Brooks, Phylicia Rashad, and Samuel L. Jackson. There were also two Uncle Tom cartoons, one starring Mickey Mouse, the other starring Bugs Bunny.

East Lynne was based on a "sensation novel" written by British author Mrs. Henry (Ellen) Wood. It dealt with the consequences of jealousy, betrayal, and adultery. Shortly after it was published in 186l, several play adaptations by different playwrights were produced. The first one in this country opened in Brooklyn, New York, in 1863, and within two months there were two other versions playing across the river in Manhattan. Eventually, there were a total of nine stage adaptations of the novel. Clifton W. Tayleur wrote the most successful of these for actress Lucille Western who played the leading role in New York and on tour for a period of ten years.

As it toured the country, the drama received mixed reviews; critics did not agree about the quality of the material. While the *Savannah News* praised the play as "one of the most pathetic and emotional to be found in the modern drama," a reviewer in another town dismissed it as "sickly nonsense." Perhaps the range of opinions had to do with the fact that there were so many different stage adaptations being presented, probably not all of the same quality.

Regardless of the critical response from the press, the play became an enduring favorite with the public. *East Lynne*, performed in England and America for over forty years, was first presented at the Tibbits Opera House in 1884, the first of nineteen productions; at the Calumet Theatre in 1901, the first of four productions; and only once at the Ramsdell Theatre in 1909.

In the melodrama, Lady Isabel—who is married to a straight arrow, hard-working attorney, Archibald Carlyle—is convinced by the unscrupulous Sir Francis Levison that her husband is being unfaithful to her, which is untrue. Unfortunately, Lady Isabel believes the worst and, in a vulnerable and jealous state of mind, is persuaded by the dastardly Levison to leave her husband, abandon her children, and run away with him. He has promised to marry her once she is free, but instead, he leaves her destitute with their child who was born out of wedlock.

Her illegitimate child dies, and she returns to East Lynne, the Carlyle family home, disguised as a governess, to care for her own children that she had deserted. At the death of one of her charges, who is actually her son, she collapses and dies in her forgiving former husband's arms.

In addition to Lucille Western and Ada Gray, both of whom made a career of playing Isabel Vane, other notable actresses who took a turn at portraying the tragic heroine include Laura Keene, Helena Modjeska, and Ida Van Cortland. After it ceased to be a star vehicle, it was taken over by stock companies. For a while it proved to be such a surefire moneymaker that whenever a stock company needed an influx of revenue, *East Lynne* was pulled out, dusted off, and put on the stage one more time. Eventually, however, *East Lynne* was produced so frequently that audiences became weary of it. In 1905, the Orchard Beach Theater in Manistee announced that the Marquette Stock Company would be presenting six performances of *East Lynne*. However, the theatrical dinosaur was replaced with the comedy *Nance Oldfield* after only four performances. Apparently, there were few theatre enthusiasts who were interested in seeing Lady Isabel's sad saga played out on the stage again.

There were three silent film adaptations of *East Lynne* released in 1913, 1916, and 1925. The 1916 version starred Theda Bara and was placed in a contemporary setting. The 1931 "talkie" was nominated for the Best Picture Academy Award. Also in 1931 there was a British film titled *East Lynne on the Western Front*, a comedy about bored World War I soldiers who stage a burlesque of the play to entertain themselves. *East Lynne* has been produced as a made-for-television movie twice, once in England in 1976 and an American version in 1982.

Rip Van Winkle first appeared as a short story in *The Sketch-Book* by Washington Irving. According to the

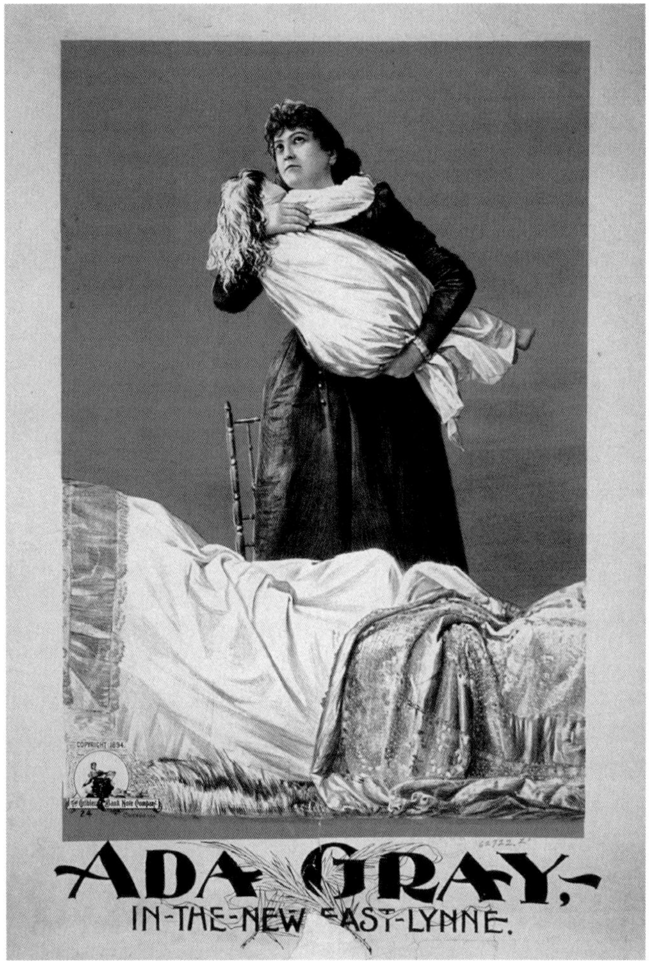

FIGURE 76. "Ada Gray in the new *East Lynne*," the play that made her famous. The poster depicts the heart-rending scene in which Lady Isabel's child dies in her arms. "Dead! Dead! And never called me mother." (Publisher: Gribler Bank Note Company, Chicago, ca. 1894. Retrieved from the Library of Congress.)

introduction to *Rip Van Winkle, as Played by Joseph Jefferson*, the actor was so intrigued by the original story and the character when he read it in 1859 that he decided to create a dramatization as a vehicle for himself. His adaptation was first performed in Washington, D.C., to a less than enthusiastic audience. In his words,

FIGURE 77. "Joseph Jefferson as Rip Van Winkle (before the sleep of 20 years)" is the title of this illustration. *The Oxford Companion to the American Theatre*, ed. Bordman and Hischak, states that Jefferson was "the most popular and respected American comedian of the nineteenth century." From Storms, *The Players Blue Book*, 1901: "Mr. Jefferson enjoys the distinction of being the richest player in the world, his wealth being estimated at more than two millions." Today in Chicago, not unlike Broadway's Tony Awards, the Joseph Jefferson Awards are bestowed on theatre artists in recognition of their achievements. (Publisher: Lemercier & Cie, Paris, ca. 1890. Retrieved from the Library of Congress Prints and Photographs Division.)

> the play was acted with a result that was to me, both satisfactory and disappointing. I was quite sure that the character was what I had been seeking, and I was equally satisfied that the play was not.

Five years later, when Jefferson was performing in London, he met with the well-established playwright Dion Boucicault who agreed to rewrite the drama for him. The Boucicault adaptation with Jefferson's performance in it was so successful that the actor played Rip Van Winkle at home and abroad for the next forty years.

The published version of the script is attributed to Washington Irving, Dion Boucicault, and Joseph Jefferson. Jefferson said, "It will thus be seen that the play is by no means the work of one mind, but . . . has been often molded, and by many hands."

The play, like the original story, takes place in New York's Catskill Mountain region. In the first act, all of the major characters are introduced: Rip Van Winkle, a charming ne'er-do-well who has sold much of his property to support his drinking habit; Gretchen, his long-suffering wife; Derreck Von Beekman, a greedy, conniving villager; Meenie, Rip and Gretchen's young daughter; and Hendrick, Meenie's devoted friend.

The plot is initiated when Derreck, who believes he has purchased most of Rip's property, receives a letter stating that unless he can produce a proper bill of sale, the real estate remains in Rip Van Winkle's possession. Derreck offers to extend Rip a loan to pay his debt at the tavern but, knowing that Rip can't read, gives him a bill of sale for the property to sign telling him that it is the loan agreement. Rip, who is suspicious, has young Hendrick read the document to him and uncovers Derreck's deception.

Before he is able to confront Derreck with his discovery, Rip becomes embroiled in an altercation with his wife. They argue about his drinking and the fact that he is indolent and does not provide for his family. The second act ends with her turning him out of their cottage into a raging storm.

FIGURE 78. Photographs of "The Original *Hazel Kirke* Company" adorn this poster from 1880. When the play opened in New York City, it made a star of the leading lady, Effie Ellsler (*center*), who also played the role on tour across the country. She eventually created her own *Hazel Kirke* Company. (Photography Collection, the Miriam and Ira D. Wallach Division of Art, Prints, and Photographs, the New York Public Library, Astor, Lenox, and Tilden Foundations.)

At this point the play changes from a domestic comedy-drama to a fantasy. Jefferson wrote, "The fairy element in the play seems to be attached to it as the fairy element in *A Midsummer Night's Dream*."

After leaving his home on that dark and stormy night, Rip wends his way into the mountains. There he meets a small demon that leads him to the ghosts of seventeenth-century explorer Henry Hudson and his crew. They invite Rip to drink with them, which he does. The drink puts him to sleep for twenty years.

Rip awakens in Act IV, a disoriented old man with long white hair and beard. He finds his way back to the village where no one recognizes him, and he discovers that his wife, who believed that he was dead, has married Derreck, who abuses her. His daughter, now a young woman, is engaged to her childhood friend, Hendrick, a sailor, who may be lost at sea.

By the end of the play, Rip's identity is revealed, he produces the paper that proves he still owns his property, Derreck's villainy is exposed, Hendrick returns from the sea in time to rescue Meenie from an unwanted arranged marriage, and Rip and Gretchen are reconciled.

Rip Van Winkle was seen in Coldwater first in 1885 followed by many more productions with various actors in the leading role, among them, Joseph Jefferson's son Thomas in 1901 and again in 1902. The play was also presented in Red Jacket and Manistee starring Thomas Jefferson.

Hazel Kirke by Steele MacKaye was almost as popular and ubiquitous as *East Lynne*. Within a few years of its 1880 New York City opening it had been performed an estimated two thousand times by multiple touring companies roaming the country. It was produced continually for a period of thirty years, and by the middle of the first decade of the twentieth century it had been seen everywhere in the United States and in England, Australia, and Japan as well.

Hazel Kirke, originally advertised as a "domestic comedy drama," is generally considered to be a melodrama. However, what makes it unique for its period and genre is that it is a melodrama with no traditional villain.

The play begins with the miller, Dunston Kirke, who is the domineering patriarch of the family, in conflict with his strong-willed daughter Hazel. He is trying to persuade her to marry an elderly neighbor to whom Kirke is in debt. Hazel defies her father and elopes with an English nobleman, Arthur Carringford. Unfortunately, her new mother-in-law, Lady Carringford, dislikes her; she had hoped that her son would marry a woman with money or title—not a miller's daughter.

To complicate matters, Hazel is led to believe that her husband perpetrated a sham wedding, that she is not legally married, and that she is now dishonored. She returns home, but her father, described by another character as "the pig-headedest old hard heart I ever knew," disowns her. Homeless and hopeless, she tries to drown herself in the river that runs by the mill. At the last minute, Carringford arrives, professes his love, and tells her that in fact, they are legally married. Father Kirke, now blind, sees the errors of his ways. All is forgiven.

One of the many *Hazel Kirke* touring companies arrived in Michigan in the spring of 1883 and played at the Tibbits Opera House for the first of many times. Another company performed at the Ramsdell Theatre in 1907. Eventually, like *East Lynne*, the play became a staple for stock companies and was performed in repertory at theaters everywhere. In 1905, the Edison Manufacturing Company made a thirteen-minute film version of the play titled *The Miller's Daughter*. Another short version with the original title, *Hazel Kirke*, was made in 1912; and finally, in 1916 a film was released that also had the original title and was based on the complete original script.

An opera version of *Hazel Kirke*, commissioned by the Lake George Opera Festival and composed by Mark Houston, premiered in 1987, almost a century after Steele MacKaye had written and first produced his play.

Ten Nights in a Bar Room, based on the 1854 bestseller *Ten Nights in a Bar Room and What I Saw There* by Timothy Shay Arthur, was the most produced temperance melodrama of all time. Although the plot was thought to be sensational with its depiction of what was considered to be immoral behavior, the clergy endorsed it, as it was the first novel to advocate prohibition. It was the third best-selling book of the second half of the nineteenth century following the Bible and *Uncle Tom's Cabin*.

With an abbreviated title, *Ten Nights in a Bar Room*, a play was adapted from the novel in 1858 by William W. Pratt. It opened at New York's National Theatre where it played seven performances. The melodrama was never especially popular with city dwellers, but on the rural circuits it was the second most produced play after *Uncle Tom's Cabin*. It was seen at the Ramsdell Theatre in 1910, at the Calumet Theatre in 1904 and 1911, and multiple times over a period of many years at the Tibbits Opera House.

The plot presents a contrasting parallel between Joe Morgan, a drunkard who by the end of the play redeems himself, and Frank Slade, a sober young man who by the end of the play has descended into perpetual drunkenness. Morgan, a former mill owner who was swindled out of his property and is now destitute, spends all of his time at the local tavern in a state of inebriation.

His young daughter, Mary, begs him to come home. Six years after the play's premiere the heart-rending song "Come Home, Father" was interpolated into the melodrama, and from that point on, Mary's entreaty was musical. Today, the song is best known by the opening line of the lyric, "Father, Dear Father Come Home with Me Now." Little Mary sings the song three times. Her first plea:

Father, Dear father, come home with me now!
The clock in the steeple strikes one;
You promis'd, dear father, that you would come home,
As soon as your day's work was done.
Our fire has gone out—our house is all dark
And mother's been watching since tea;
With poor brother Benny so sick in her arms,
And no one to help her but me.

But her plea falls on drunken, deaf ears.

She returns every hour to sing another verse that contains increasingly dire news: Benny is at death's door and calling for you, and by verse three, Benny is dead.

The real villain in *Ten Nights in a Bar Room* is not the drunkard Joe Morgan, but the greedy tavern owner, Simon Slade. He is the man who cheated Morgan out of the mill he owned, and then sold it to buy the tavern as it was a more lucrative endeavor that required less manual labor. He is happy to sell liquor to anyone, including Morgan, as long as the drinker has the money to pay for it.

When Morgan, in a drunken rage, attacks Simon Slade for his past transgressions, Slade attempts to ward off the attack by throwing a glass at him. He misses his mark, and instead, the glass strikes Mary in the head. On her deathbed, little Mary begs her father to abstain from alcohol. Once he agrees she dies and, like Little Eva, ascends to heaven. Although the audience did not witness the ascension, it could be assumed that she was in heaven as for the rest of the play Mary is referred to as the "angel child."

In the meantime, the son of the tavern owner, Frank

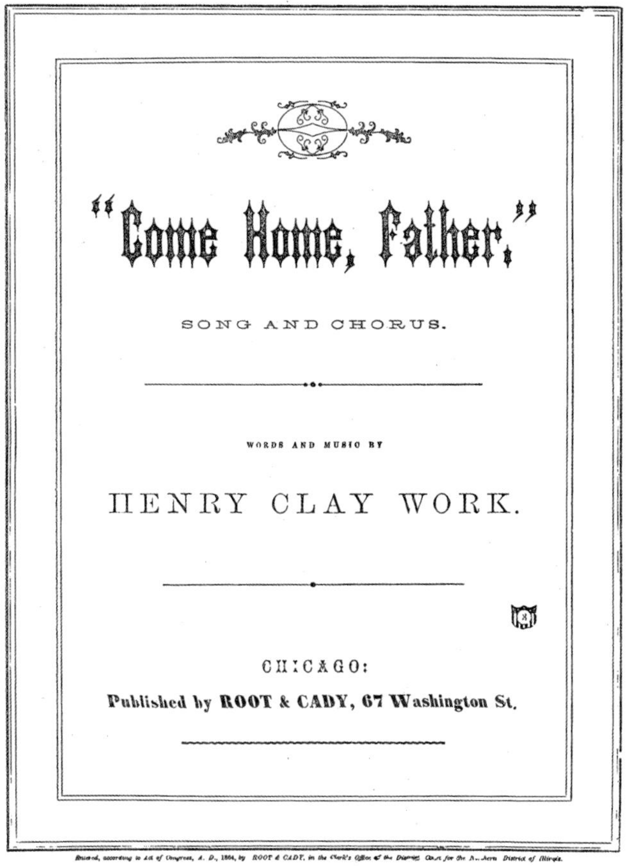

FIGURE 79. The sheet music cover for "Come Home, Father" composed by Henry Clay Work. Although thought to be incredibly maudlin by today's standards, in its time the song became an anthem for the temperance movement and was regularly sung at temperance meetings as if it were a hymn. (Publisher: Root & Cady, Chicago, Ill., 1864. The David M. Rubenstein Rare Book & Manuscript Library, Duke University.)

Slade, who begins the play as a responsible young man described by his father as "a son worth having," has fallen victim to drink. In the final moments of the drama, Frank kills his father, Simon Slade, in a drunken rage by hitting him over the head with a bottle of whisky. The play ends with a plea to the audience for prohibition.

ACT V, Scene vi

SWITCHEL: Who'll jine my cause? Will you?—or you?
You will?—'nuff sed; we'll put her through.
I'll raise my standard—spread it bold and high:
Down with rummies—"root, hog, or die!" (Curtain)

Between 1910 and 1931, four film versions of the story were released. The first three were silent; the last was a talkie. After prohibition was repealed in 1933, the play continued to be produced but was most often presented as a parody or burlesque of nineteenth-century melodramas.

Faust was first seen in Coldwater in 1893, the first of twelve productions to be presented at the Tibbits Opera House. There were seven productions of the play in Red Jacket and one in Manistee. Although the version of the tale by Johann Wolfgang von Goethe was the one most often seen on the stage during this period, there are other plays that tell the story of Faust and Mephistopheles including *Doctor Faustus* by Christopher Marlowe and *The Power of Satan or, Faust and Marguerite*, a nineteenth-century version of the sell-your-soul-to-the-devil tale. In London during the Victorian era, *Faust up to Date* was an extremely popular musical burlesque of the famous drama, and in 1897 *Faust* made a quick appearance on Broadway in what must have been a rather unusual variation of the traditional story titled *Very Little Faust and Much Marguerite.*

Most people are familiar with the basic plot of the play. Faust, who is dissatisfied with life, is dazzled when Mephistopheles conjures up a group of spirits that convince him to accept an alternate lifestyle. The devil then makes Faust an offer he can't refuse—Mephistopheles will serve Faust on earth and guide him to a state of transcendence. If he is successful, Faust will serve the devil in Hades for eternity. Faust accepts the devil's deal, and their adventure begins.

One day, Faust sees Marguerite, and the attraction is immediate. Through the chicanery of Mephistopheles that involves an irresistible casket of jewels, Faust is successful in seducing the innocent young maiden. Disaster follows: Marguerite gives birth to a baby that she drowns; she is imprisoned for her crimes; and she goes mad. In the end, Faust attempts to rescue her from prison, but she refuses to join him and cries out, "God of Judgment! To you I give myself!" Mephistopheles leads Faust away as an ethereal voice from above assures Marguerite and the audience that "She is saved!"

In the prelude of the play that involves three characters identified as the director, the dramatist, and the comedian, the director demands that the production employ trapdoors, elaborate scenery, spectacular stars, rocky cliffs, fire, and water. It is apparent from the advertisements and newspaper articles promoting the play that the producers took these suggestions to heart, as in most productions of the period, the text was overpowered by technology. Producers correctly assumed that rather than Goethe's script, which included philosophical debates and long monologues, their prospective audiences would be more readily enticed by the promise of a circle of fire, an electric cross, an electric skull, and the electric sword duel.

"The Devil Is a Man You Know"

The World's My Oyster, lyrics and music by Lorenzo Fuller and Carley Mills, 1956

In the many productions of *Faust* presented during this period, the star role was not Faust but Mephistopheles. The two actors most frequently seen at Michigan opera houses as the devil were Porter J. White and Lewis Morrison.

Porter J. White was the producer and leading actor of his own touring company that played primarily in rural towns. It was in 1893 at the Tibbits Opera House that he was first seen as Mephistopheles in Michigan. He went on to play that role in Red Jacket as well. In 1905, he traded one devil in for another. He took on the persona of "the arch-fiend hypnotist" Svengali in a dramatization of George du Maurier's novel *Trilby* that he played in both Red Jacket and Coldwater. He guaranteed that $1,000 would be given to charity if he did not appear as the great Svengali at any scheduled performance.

Lewis Morrison was born in Jamaica of English, Spanish, African, and Jewish heritage. He launched his stage career first in New Orleans and then in San Francisco. He eventually moved to New York City where he achieved stardom in 1889 when he portrayed Mephistopheles in a Broadway production of *Faust*. He formed his own company and played that role in this country and abroad for fifteen years. Of the venues featured here, he was first seen in his signature role in Coldwater in 1895 and later in Red Jacket.

FIGURE 80. "Morrison's Original Production of *Faust*." Before launching his acting career, Lewis Morrison was the first black Jewish officer to serve in the Confederate Army during the Civil War. (Publisher: Liebler & Maass Lith., New York, ca. 1896. Retrieved from the Library of Congress.)

The Streets of New York, written by Irish-born playwright-actor-manager Dion Boucicault, was originally titled *The Poor of New York* based on the French play *Les Pauvres de Paris*. Today the melodrama is most often produced as *The Streets of New York*. Among the many other plays for which Boucicault was responsible are *London Assurance*, *The Octoroon*, and the dramatization of Washington Irving's *Rip Van Winkle* for Joseph Jefferson.

The New York premiere of *The Poor of New York* took place in December 1857 and was an immediate hit. Boucicault sent it out on tour in this country and produced it internationally, changing the locale and title from New York to the name of the city where the drama was playing. The success of the play may be attributed to several factors: it was timely as it revolved around the financial panic of 1857; it included spectacular stage technology that was the current theatrical rage; and it was an excellent example of the popular melodrama genre replete with dastardly deeds and a cast of characters that included a handsome hero, an innocent ingénue, a defenseless widow, and three cold-hearted villains, one of them a woman.

The story is propelled by the greedy machinations of banker Gideon Bloodgood, who is in desperate straits. He has spent a fortune on his spoiled daughter, Alida, and has paid another fortune in blackmail money to his clerk, Badger, who has threatened to reveal that the banker has embezzled funds from the accounts of his clients. Bloodgood also is aware of the imminent collapse of his bank.

As ill fortune would have it, honest Captain Fairweather enters Bloodgood's bank where he deposits his life savings. He then learns of the impending collapse of the institution and demands the return of his money. When Bloodgood refuses, Fairweather dies of a heart attack. The captain's death and the banker's denial of Fairweather's deposit leave the widow, Mrs. Fairweather, and her two grown children, Lucy and Paul, destitute.

During the next four acts, the audience learns that handsome Mark Livingston, who was born into a socially prominent family but who has fallen on hard times, is in love with Lucy Fairweather. However, he is engaged to Alida Bloodgood as she has convinced her father to give him a loan to pay his debts in exchange for his hand in marriage. Although she has a secret lover, Alida desires to marry Livingston, as he is her ticket to enter high society.

In the meantime, Badger, the bank clerk, has come into the possession of the receipt that proves Fairweather did indeed deposit his life savings with Bloodgood. This time, rather than blackmailing his employer, Badger undergoes a change of character from villain to avenger and decides to reveal Bloodgood's treachery. In an attempt to foil Badger, Bloodgood sets fire to the tenement where Badger lives with the hope that the receipt and Badger will go up in flames. As a typical melodrama coincidence would have it, the tenement is the same building in which the Fairweathers reside. And, as typical melodrama luck would have it, Badger enters the burning two-story tenement just as it collapses, narrowly escaping with the incendiary document in hand.

ACT V, Scene ii

> The house is gradually enveloped in fire . . . the interior is seen in flames. . . . The shutters of the garret fall away and discover Badger in the upper floor . . . a loud crash is

heard, Badger disappears as if falling with the inside of the building. . . . Badger drags himself from the ruins.

Before the final curtain falls, Bloodgood's treachery is exposed, the Fairweathers' funds are restored, and Mark and Lucy are reunited. There is an epilogue delivered by Mrs. Fairweather who addresses the audience:

> when you leave this place, as you return to your homes, should you see some poor creatures, extend your hands to them, and the blessings that will follow you on your way will be the most grateful tribute you can pay to the POOR OF NEW YORK.

Patrons of the Tibbits Opera House first saw the melodrama in 1886; several more productions of the play occurred there in the following years. The play had passed its peak popularity by 1900 and was not seen at either the Calumet or Ramsdell Theatres at that time. However, in 1965 it was produced as part of the Keweenaw Playhouse summer season at the Calumet Theatre.

FIGURE 81. Assorted street people loiter on *The Streets of New York*. The melodrama, with olios performed between the acts, was produced as part of the 1965 Keweenaw Playhouse (Calumet Theatre) summer season. The majority of the Equity company was from New York; however, the young woman on stage right, Lucinda Mitchell, was a teenager from Houghton, Michigan, who later became a member of the Martha Graham Dance Company and performed with that troupe nationally, internationally, and on Broadway. (Photographer: James D. Cromie. Photograph courtesy of the Calumet Theatre Archives.)

Ethnic Plays and Personalities

"The International Rag"

All Aboard, lyrics and music by Irving Berlin, 1913

During the Golden Age of American Opera Houses, ethnic stereotypes were fodder for light, usually tuneful, entertainment. In addition to the parody of African Americans in minstrel shows, there were caricatures of Scandinavians, Germans, and the Irish. Audiences of the period found these ethnic stereotypes entertaining for they sang, they danced, and they were often overtly sentimental: they longed for home, loved their mothers, and were always a step ahead of or a step behind everybody else.

"Ireland, Land of My Dreams"

The Voice of McConnell, lyrics and music by George M. Cohan, 1918

Plays about the Irish and Irish Americans as well as performances by Irish entertainers were very popular in the last quarter of the nineteenth century. Pat Rooney, "the Great Irish Comedian," performed in Michigan several times throughout the years, as did Walter Lawrence, "Ireland's Greatest Singing Comedian," and there were performances by the Irish Minstrels as well.

William J. Scanlan (1856–98), the actor-singer-songwriter, was the most celebrated Irish tenor of his time. He first appeared on the Tibbits Opera House stage in *Friend and Foe* in 1884. The advertisement for the show promised that he would "sing 10 of his own songs," and the review published in the *Courier* praised his performance:

FIGURE 82. "Scanlan is not an Irish buffoon, but a careful and artistic delineator of true Irish character. His voice is wonderfully pleasing whether in his most passionate speeches or bursts of Irish wit, and certainly captivating in his songs." *Coldwater Republican*, May 9, 1884. (Publisher: Strobridge Litho Co., Cincinnati, N.Y., and London, ca. 1890. Retrieved from the Library of Congress.)

> W. J. Scanlan played to a large audience . . . and succeeded as usual capturing them en masse with his beautiful songs and acting. . . . Mr. Scanlan can always count upon good business whenever he visits our city.

And, visit he did! Later the same year, he introduced the play *The Irish Minstrel* to his Michigan fans. He was a regular visitor to Coldwater every year until 1889; sometimes he made two visits in one season.

Scanlan was born into an Irish family in Springfield, Massachusetts. He began his career performing in vaudeville, but later, and for most of his professional life, he starred in Celtic romances filled with songs that he composed himself.

The play for which he was best known, *Shane-na-lawn*, opened in New York in 1885. The score included some songs for which he was already famous, such as "Peek-a-Boo," as well as some that he composed especially for the show, such as "Remember, Boy, You're Irish." Both songs generated healthy sheet music sales.

For the final encore in *Shane-na-lawn*, Scanlan sang his song "Beautiful Rose," and as he took his bow he always tossed a rose to a female audience member. An article that was published in the *Louisville Courier-Journal* in May 1885 related an incident concerning this tradition: "the rose dropped into the hands of a pretty heiress and the next day she sent the minstrel a beautiful red sash adorned with a heart of diamonds."

The play *Mavourneen*, an Irish romance, opened in New York on September 14, 1891, starring William J. Scanlan, but because of health issues brought about by syphilis, he was forced to leave the show. When *Mavourneen* opened at the Walnut Street Theatre in Philadelphia, the first stop on its tour, Chauncey Olcott played the leading role. The reviewer was not disappointed: "the manager would have had much trouble to procure a comedian who could portray the character better than Olcott." After the Philadelphia run, the show traveled across the country.

Chauncey Olcott (1860–1932), the Irish American

FIGURE 83. "Chauncey Olcott in the Great Play *Mavourneen*." When the Irish tenor took over the leading role from the ailing William J. Scanlan, his performance propelled him to stardom and a twenty-five-year career. As a songwriter, Olcott was the co-lyricist of over a dozen iconic Irish ballads including "Mother Machree" and "When Irish Eyes are Smiling." (Publisher: Strobridge Litho. Co., Cincinnati, N. Y., ca. 1895. Retrieved from the Library of Congress.)

actor-singer-songwriter, was named Chancellor John Olcott at birth. His mother was born in Ireland and immigrated to this country with her family as a child. As a youngster, he received musical training in his hometown at the Buffalo Academy of Music, and at the age of nineteen began his professional career with a minstrel company in Chicago. He then returned to Buffalo to appear with the well-known Haverly's United Mastodon Minstrels. His beautiful lyric tenor voice prompted professional colleagues to encourage him to move on from minstrelsy and pursue a career as an Irish ballad singer in plays and operettas. He followed that advice and made his New York debut in the 1886 production of *Pepita* starring Lillian Russell. However, after fourteen years in show business, it was his performance in *Mavourneen* that made him an "overnight sensation."

> The principal part . . . is impersonated by Chauncey Olcott, a former operatic tenor and clever actor. He has an excellent voice, and he sings the sweet Irish melodies with feeling and magnetic charm . . . the longer he sang the more imperative was the demand for him to continue. (*Detroit Free Press*, February 27, 1894)

Irish plays featuring Irish tenors who typically sang about their "darlin' colleen," their silver-haired mother, and their beloved Emerald Isle remained popular into the twentieth century. After *Mavourneen*, Olcott appeared in a string of other Irish-themed romantic musical plays with such titles as *The Irish Artist*, *The Isle o' Dreams*, and *Minstrel of Clare*.

In September 1912, he brought *Macushla*, a musical about horseracing, to Red Jacket. The local reviewer proclaimed, "The attraction was one of the most notable of the year." He made his last appearance on the New York stage in the 1925 all-star revival of *The Rivals* after which he retired to Monte Carlo.

Today, Chauncey Olcott may not be remembered as a performer as much as he is as a songwriter; many of his

FIGURE 84. One of Chauncey Olcott's last appearances on Broadway was in *The Voice of McConnell* in 1918. The book, music, and lyrics were written especially for him by George M. Cohan. (Publisher: Strobridge Litho. Co., Cincinnati, N. Y.: From a photograph by Butler, Brooklyn, New York, ca. 1900. Retrieved from the Library of Congress.)

lyrics are still heard, especially around March 17. For "My Wild Irish Rose," which he traditionally sang as an encore, he is credited as the sole lyricist and composer. More often, however, he collaborated with George Graff Jr. on the lyrics that they set to the music of composer Ernest R. Ball.

"The Irish Have a Great Day Tonight"

Eileen, lyrics by Henry Blossom, music by Victor Herbert, 1917

Among the many plays about folks from the Emerald Isle that were seen at Michigan opera houses were *The Irish Detective, The Irish Statesman, The Irish Boarder, The Irish Pawnbrokers,* and *The Irish Hero.*

Finnigan's Ball was the most popular and, therefore, the most frequently produced comedy about Irish Americans. It played at both the Tibbits Opera House and the Calumet Theatre. The Finnigan plays were the obvious successors to the innovative Harrigan and Hart productions of the 1870s and 1880s. In 1873 Edward Harrigan and Tony Hart introduced their vaudeville sketch called *The Mulligan Guard* at the Academy of Music in Chicago. The act was so successful that within two months they were performing it at Tony Pastor's Variety House in New York. They then added a story line that related the adventures of an Irish immigrant family, and what had been a sketch evolved into a full-length domestic comedy titled *The Mulligan Guard Picnic.* The production included original songs and specialty acts that were integrated into the action of the play merging vaudeville with musical comedy. The success of the show

FIGURE 85. "The Famous Originals, Murray and Mack," are presented on this poster in the personas of Connor Casey and Timothy Finnigan, respectively. With *Finnigan's Ball,* they made the transition from the two-a-day to legitimate theatre. (Publisher: U.S. Lithograph Co. Cincinnati, New York, ca. 1905. Retrieved from the Library of Congress.)

spawned eight sequels and inspired many imitators—the Finnigan comedy series was one of them.

In the early 1890s, Charles A. Murray and Ollie Mack, a well-established vaudeville comedy team, began to perform in this series of plays with songs that chronicled the shenanigans of two Irish American pals, Connor Casey and Timothy Finnigan. The plot of *Finnigan's Ball* involves an elaborate prank orchestrated by Connor Casey (Murray) at the expense of his pal Timothy Finnigan (Mack). A letter is ostensibly written by Finnigan but actually forged by Casey who sends it to an attractive actress suggesting a rendezvous. Comic complications ensue, the prank backfires, and it is Casey who is hoisted by his own petard when his wife believes that it is her husband who is involved with the other woman.

During the action of the play, there was a crowd-pleasing boxing match "burlesque" between Casey, the aggressor, and Finnigan, the passive "stooge." The first revival of the show in 1895 advertised completely new specialties and an updated script but assured prospective patrons that the "side-splitting boxing match" had been retained. The show was revised again in 1898.

Finnigan's Ball was so successful that it spawned several sequels including *Finnigan's Alley* and *Finnigan's 400*. All of the Finnigan shows had rather loose plots that allowed for the inclusion of specialty acts that could change from time to time without impacting on the story line. The shows were very popular on tour, but not so much in New York. Only one of the Finnigan comedies was presented there; *Finnigan's 400* opened on Broadway in 1899 where it played nine performances.

Following their Broadway bow, Murray and Mack went back on the road with *Finnigan's 400* and a new play that chronicled the continuing adventures of Finnigan and friends, *Finnigan's Courtship*. The advertisement for *Finnigan's Courtship* announced that it was "a new play, the funniest yet." However, a one-sentence newspaper review stated, "There are differences of opinion as to the merits of the performance."

FIGURE 86. For six years, *Peg o' My Heart* held the record for having the longest run of any nonmusical play on Broadway. (Publisher: Strobridge Lithographing Company Circus and Theatre Posters, 1913. The Public Library of Cincinnati and Hamilton County.)

After 1900, there were new plays centered around Irish

FIGURE 87. "Without a question *Ole Olson,* the new Swedish dialect play has been one of the greatest successes ever known to the American stage." *Courier,* December 12, 1891. (Publisher: Shober & Carqueville, Chicago, 1890. Retrieved from the Library of Congress.)

colleens: *My Rosie O'Grady, The Daughter of Mother Machree,* and *Peg o' My Heart,* to name a few.

Peg o' My Heart is a sentimental comedy about a poor Irish girl who is sent to England with her mongrel pup to live with her highbrow British relatives. By the time the play ends, she has charmed her new family, inherited a fortune, and found love—an early twentieth-century *Annie.*

The play opened on Broadway in 1912, where it racked up over six hundred consecutive performances and made a star of the leading lady, Laurette Taylor, whose husband, J. Hartley Manners, wrote the comedy. Taylor played Peg on an extensive tour, and in 1921 revived it on Broadway where it ran for nearly seven hundred performances. The next year, she starred in a silent film version of the play. Thirty years later, Taylor scored big on Broadway again as Amanda in the original production of Tennessee Williams's *The Glass Menagerie.*

Peg o' My Heart was so popular that the year after it closed in New York, there were more than a half dozen companies touring the country. In 1914 one of those touring productions played Red Jacket. Unfortunately, it was not the one featuring Laurette Taylor; it starred Florence Martin. In 1915 another touring production, this one featuring Dorothy Mackaye as Peg, played Coldwater and Manistee. Although she wasn't there in person, Laurette Taylor was not altogether ignored as the advertisement reminded patrons that they were about to see the play that was "Laurette Taylor's Perpetual New York Triumph," albeit without Laurette.

> The cast is said to be fully up to the one in New York which was headed by Laurette Taylor. Dorothy Mackaye, a talented young Irish-American actress will play the title role. (*Coldwater Daily Reporter,* March 13, 1915)

"It's a Big, Wide, Wonderful World"

All in Fun, lyrics and music by John Rox, 1940

The Irish were not the only ethnic folk seen on the stages of Michigan's opera houses. Ben Hendricks, "America's Foremost Dialect Comedian," represented another country in his play that was simply called *Ole Olson,* "The First and Best Scandinavian Comedy." It was presented at the Tibbits Opera House in 1891.

The next year, Hendricks appeared in *A Letter from Ole Olson's Sisters,* and three years later he introduced audiences to *The New Ole Olson*. An extra attraction of that production was the participation of the National Swedish Lady Quartette. Ben Hendricks performed as Ole Olson several times in all three of the playhouses discussed here. After his first appearance in Red Jacket in 1900, Hendricks returned six more times, five of them as Ole Olson; however, in 1904, the show in which he toured was called *Erick of Sweden*.

"The Yodeler"

Pepper Mill, lyrics by John Latouche and Erika Munn, music by Magnus Henning, 1937

Bavarian born Al H. "Metz" Wilson, billed as "the Ambassador of German Dialect," played in many Michigan opera houses including the Tibbits Opera House and the Ramsdell Theatre, but he was particularly welcome at the Calumet Theatre where he was such a hit that he and his fans enjoyed an eleven-show "Metz" marathon that began in 1901 and did not end until 1917.

"Metz" vehicles seen at the Calumet Theatre and elsewhere include *The German Gypsy*; *A German Prince*; *It Happened in Potsdam*; and *Metz in the Alps, a Story of Picturesque Switzerland*.

Not only was Wilson an accomplished singer of ballads, he was also a renowned yodeler. In the song-filled play *The Watch on the Rhine*, he introduced "In Tyrol," a yodeling song that he had written with Sidney R. Ellis. According to the *St. Louis Democrat*, "There is no yodeler living to-day who is as good as 'Metz' Wilson. For expression, found notes and triple trills he has no equal."

FIGURE 88. After years of performing in comic operas and vaudeville, Al H. Wilson became a star when he appeared for the first time as his alter ego "Metz" in *The Watch on the Rhine*. (Publisher: U.S. Printing Co, Cincinnati, New York, ca. 1900. Retrieved from the Library of Congress.)

As World War I raged on, he played down his German heritage; the advertisement for *As Years Roll On* in 1916 announced that he would sing "American songs," and he changed the location of his plays from the Alps to Ireland. His last appearance at the Calumet Theatre was in *My Killarney Rose*.

FIGURE 89. In the opinion of the *St. Louis Democrat*, *Metz in the Alps* was "the best vehicle Mr. Wilson has ever had . . . it contains so nice a blending of humor and pathos and sentiment that it touches the heart very closely. But above all, it gives Mr. Wilson ample opportunity to sing—he has the most abundantly musical voice before the public to-day." (Publisher: U. S. Lithograph Co. Cincinnati, New York, ca. 1906. Retrieved from the Library of Congress.)

New Plays for a New Century

"Twentieth Century Rag"

The Whirl of the World, lyrics by Harold Atteridge, music by Sigmund Rombert, 1914

Although still produced, *East Lynne*, *Hazel Kirke*, *Rip Van Winkle*, and *The Streets of New York*, four of the most popular plays of the last quarter of the previous century, began to disappear from opera house season schedules after 1900. However, like "Ole Man River," *Uncle Tom's Cabin* just kept "rollin' along" year after year.

In contrast to the tried-and-true warhorses and Shakespearean classics, early in the new century touring companies presented new plays that introduced elements of dramatic realism. Spectacle, however, never went out of fashion!

The Span of Life, by Sutton Vane and featuring "The World's Most Famous Acrobats, the Donazettas," made the first of many Michigan appearances in 1901. Subsequently, it was seen in Coldwater, Red Jacket, and Manistee. The script for the melodrama includes pages ripped from the *Kit, the Arkansas Traveler* and the *Uncle Tom's Cabin* playbooks. The villain, a slave hunter, kidnaps a woman and her child. They escape to the mountains but are pursued by the villain and his gang. In the mountains, the mother and child reach a chasm that has them trapped between certain capture and certain death. But wait! The Donazettas come to the rescue. The acrobats interlock their bodies high above the stage to create "The Human Bridge" over which the heroine and offspring flee to safety.

When the show played at the Weston Opera House in Colorado, the reviewer for the *Leadville Herald Democrat* reported that the scene "attracted more than usual attention" and that in addition to forming "the living bridge from which the title of the play is derived," the famous Donazettas performed "a number of their excellent acrobatic feats."

Attached to this play is a story that may be apocryphal but is worth the telling. To create the illusion of a river under the human bridge, a trough of water was placed on the stage floor in front of scenic elements painted to resemble rocks. A mattress was hidden from audience view behind the two-dimensional painted rocks that was there to be a cushion should the heroine fall during her flight across the elevated bodies. That much may be true, but allegedly, at one performance she did fall from the human bridge, creating a loud "thud" when she hit the mattress. Moments later, the actress emerged from behind the scenery seemingly intact, unhurt, and obviously dry. The audience's initial gasp of horror quickly turned into a burst of laughter when someone in the balcony called out, "Good heavens! The river must be frozen!"

"Old Friends"

Hip! Hip! Hooray, lyrics by Sam Erlich, music by Gus Edwards, 1907

A new century with old friends in new plays! Murray and Mack were back but this time not in a Finnigan comedy. In 1901, they toured as brand new characters in a brand new show, *Shooting the Chutes*. The newspaper explained:

> Murray and Mack are old-time favorites, and their engagement here should prove the most successful of their career as they bring with them this season a new farce that has replaced their successes of former years. (*Copper Country Evening News*, March 11, 1901)

All good things must come to an end, as did the partnership of Murray and Mack. Sometime during the first decade of the new century, they decided to go their separate ways, and their separate ways brought both of them back to Red Jacket, but not together at the same time. First, on March 25, 1912, Ollie Mack arrived, not as Finnigan but as Casey Jones in a show of the same name. The *Daily Mining Gazette* predicted success for Mr. Mack and his new endeavor: "an enthusiastic reception will, no doubt, be accorded this old favorite in a new play." But in the opinion of the reviewer the show did not live up to its promise:

> He (Ollie Mack) has considerable reputation . . . as an "Irish" comedian, though his impersonation looks no more like an Irishman than it does like anything else that is human. The farce is absolutely without merit. (*Daily Mining Gazette*, March 26, 1912)

Two months later, on May 6, 1912, Charles A. Murray was in Red Jacket with his new show, *Alma, Where Do You Live?* The play had premiered in Paris; it was then translated into German and presented in Berlin before coming to New York. The *Calumet News* provided prospective patrons with the play's history in this country:

> This is the brilliant German-French comedy which ran for a season at Phillip's German Theater on the East Side of New York and was then done in English by Joe Weber at his own Music Hall and ran there all last year.

Although Mr. Murray was not in the cast at Weber's

Music Hall in 1910, he did star in the touring production two years later. The actor and the French farce met with greater success than did Mr. Mack and *Casey Jones*:

> The comedy is on the traditional French order, with flashes of lingerie, and references to forbidden joys and bits of business that suggests things. But it is all very funny. Charles A. Murray was the principal producer of the laughs. . . . he brought to it a wealth of experience as a comedian and illuminated the part with bits of facial expression, exhibitions of agility and dexterity, and vocal and dancing ability of a high order. (*Daily Mining Gazette*, May 8, 1912)

Murray went on to have a very prolific film career; he appeared in 283 films between 1912 and 1938. Among others, he was in the Max Sennett Keystone Cop movies, and in 1925 he took on the title role in a silent film version of *The Wizard of Oz*.

"(There'll Be) a Hot Time in the Old Town (Tonight)"

Lyrics by Joseph Hayden, music by Theodore M. Metz, 1896

During the first decades of the twentieth century, entertainment by black performers evolved from minstrelsy and vaudeville to book musicals. It all started with Bob Cole (1868–1911) who got his start working as a performer in and writer for a touring vaudeville show, the Black Patti Troubadours, billed as "the greatest colored show on earth." In collaboration with a fellow actor-writer, Billy Johnson, they wrote and starred in *A Trip to Coontown* that opened in 1891. It is considered to be the first full-length musical comedy to have been written, produced, and performed by African Americans. After its New York run, the show went on tour playing in opera houses across the country—Michigan included.

The success of *A Trip to Coontown* was the incentive for the creation of several other all-black plays with music that found their way to Michigan: *Derby Day in Coon Town*, and *A Hot Time in Coon Town*, among others. White audiences customarily attended these all-black musicals as well as minstrel shows with black performers and, in the 1920s, various revues presented at speakeasies, the Cotton Club, for example. When black entertainers were cast in otherwise all-white productions, they primarily were used for "specialties" and seldom interacted with the white actors. The theatre's journey from nineteenth-century racial segregation to twenty-first-century blind casting progressed slowly and on a rocky road.

The play presented at the Tibbits Opera House on September 9, 1905, was *A Romance of Coon Hollow* by C. E. Callahan billed as a "Tennessee Comedy." A week before the performance, the *Coldwater Daily Reporter* informed its readers about the show, stating that it was "a story of life, love, and jealousy in the Tennessee Hills" featuring "darkey male and female plantation dancers," from which the reader might have inferred that *A Romance of Coon Hollow* had an all-black cast. When the journalist discovered that the cast consisted of both black and white performers, under the headline, "An Error Corrected," the following explanation was published:

FIGURE 90. Bob Cole and J. Rosamond Johnson dressed in formal attire for their vaudeville act that contained no hint of minstrelsy and was a major factor in expanding opportunities for and perceptions of black entertainers. (Photographer unknown, ca. 1900. Billy Rose Theatre Division, the New York Public Library Digital Collections.)

Misled by the name and by the fact that it is a southern play, an impression prevails that "A Romance of Coon Hollow" is a negro show. This is a great mistake as the entire cast is composed of well known white artists of standing and the colored buck dancers and jubilee singers are simply introduced in their plantation scenes to illustrate negro life in the south but have no relation to the story of the drama. (*Coldwater Daily Reporter*, September 6, 1905)

"When the Colored Regiment Goes Off to War"

Ruggles of Red Gap, lyrics by Harold Atteridge, music by Sigmund Romberg, 1915

Back in 1897, Bob Cole broke new ground with *A Trip to Coontown*, and he did it again ten years later with *The Shoo-Fly Regiment*. After *A Trip to Coontown* closed, Bob Cole and Billy Johnson dissolved their partnership. Bob Cole then began collaborating with two other Johnsons, J. Rosamond Johnson and James Weldon Johnson who were brothers but who were not related to Billy.

The three of them wrote over two hundred songs; many were interpolated into Broadway shows. "Under the Bamboo Tree," their greatest success, sold over four hundred thousand copies of sheet music after it was introduced in the 1904 musical comedy *Sally in Our Alley*. Forty years later, in 1944, Judy Garland and Margaret O'Brien performed the song in the film *Meet Me in St. Louis*.

Eventually, Cole and J. Rosamond Johnson formed a vaudeville act. They did not sing songs about the good old days on the plantation, they did not play the tambourine or the bones, they wore no brightly colored costumes, and they told no "Why did the chicken cross the road" jokes. Instead, Johnson played several classical pieces on the piano, and Cole sang a few German songs. They then performed songs that they had written.

In 1906, Cole and the two Johnson brothers created *The Shoo-Fly Regiment*. The program credited composing duties to J. Rosamond Johnson with lyrics by his brother, James Weldon Johnson. Other sources indicate that in addition to writing the book and starring in the show, Bob Cole also collaborated on the music and lyrics. *The Shoo-Fly Regiment* moved the black musical even farther away from minstrelsy than had Cole's earlier effort. A year before its Broadway opening in 1907 the musical was on tour and played in Coldwater.

The central character in the plot is a recent college graduate who postpones his wedding plans and his dream of becoming a teacher to do his patriotic duty and fight in the Philippine–American War with a regiment that had been recruited from his alma mater. The work is notable for its lack of ethnic caricature and in that the romantic scenes were played with genuine tenderness instead of the burlesqued displays of affection between African Americans previously seen on the stage.

On December 27, 1906, the day it played at the Tibbits Opera House, the *Coldwater Daily Reporter* announced,

> The first real American negro play with original music will be presented at the opera house tonight by those eminent composers and famous colored comedians, Cole & Johnson. . . . It is far different from anything ever offered to the public by the negro on the stage, creating a new thought in the field of dramatic possibilities.

"Together at Last"

Pardon My English, lyrics by Ira Gershwin, music by George Gershwin, 1933

The first step toward racially integrated casting is credited to Harrigan and Hart. According to Cecil Smith in his book *Musical Comedy in America*, published in 1950, "Harrigan and Hart were the first major producers to employ Negro performers."

FIGURE 91. *The Mulligan Guard Ball*, ca. 1879, was the second in the Harrigan and Hart plays-with-songs series and one of the first to feature a racially integrated cast. The plays concerned the day-to-day life of an Irish American family living in an ethnically diverse lower Manhattan neighborhood and, with comedy, dealt with contemporary issues. (Photographer unknown. Billy Rose Theatre Division, the New York Public Library Digital Collections.)

For the 1879 production of Harrigan and Hart's *The Mulligan Guard Ball*, Edward Harrigan employed black actors to portray members of the Skidmore Guard, a black militia that in the play, was in competition with the Irish militia, the Mulligan Guard. Harrigan continued hiring black performers for the duration of the Mulligan Guard series that culminated with *Cordelia's Aspirations* in 1883 in which the black performers played members of a touring *Uncle Tom's Cabin* company.

In the Mulligan shows, there was a contradiction in theatrical styles that apparently was accepted by the audience. Whereas black performers portrayed the majority of black characters, Tony Hart played the role of Rebecca, the Mulligan's maid, in drag and in blackface makeup.

Harrigan and Hart's initial racially integrated casting turned out to be an isolated incident. Over twenty-five years later when Florenz Ziegfeld hired the popular African American comedian Bert Williams to perform in the *Ziegfeld Follies of 1910*, several white cast members took an "it's him or me" stand. Ziegfeld held his ground and metaphorically opened the exit door by announcing that he was prepared to replace anyone in the cast except Bert Williams.

"Something New, Something Different"

Harrigan 'n Hart, lyrics by Peter Walker, music by Max Showalter, 1985

After 1900, three dramatic genres emerged that caught theatergoers' attention. They all had their antecedents in the late nineteenth century, but after that century turned they came into their own: the sagebrush sagas; the "girl" shows, many of which were musicals; and the social issue dramas.

Go West, Young Man

phrase originated with John Babsone Lane Soule, 1851,
often attributed to writer Horace Greeley, 1865

At the end of the nineteenth century and into the first decade of the twentieth, plays set in what at the time was the not-so-Old West were particularly popular with audiences east of the Mississippi River. All of the Western dramas mentioned below were presented at one, two, or all three of the Michigan opera houses featured here. Plays set in the West became so profitable that playwrights often used "cowboy" in the title to make it absolutely clear that what was being offered was a sagebrush saga: *The Cowboy Preacher*, *The Cowboy Foreman*, and *The Cowboy and the Sheriff*, for example.

There were those plays with specific state titles that indicated where the drama would unfold such as *Arizona* and *Colorado*. Augustus Thomas, who was noted for being one of the first playwrights to set his dramas in the American West, wrote both plays. *Arizona*, considered to be Mr. Thomas's best effort, opened on Broadway in 1900 with scenery by Walter Burridge (responsible for the *Wizard of Oz* and the Ramsdell Theatre's stock scenery).

The titles of other Western plays implied that the exploits of legendary Western heroes and desperados would be recounted in the drama. Their names were used as the title of the show: *Jesse James*, *Billy the Kid*, *The Younger Brothers*, as well as *Daniel Boone on the Trail*, with Chief Young Buffalo, "a tribe of Genuine Sioux Indians and a den of ferocious wolves that are kept behind a heavy screen to protect the audience."

As Told in the Hills was advertised as a Western melodrama,

> Depicting Life Among Indians, Cowboys, Scouts, Emigrants, and Tenderfoots featuring Princess Wah-Ta-Waso, a full-blooded Iroquois Indian maid, granddaughter of Chief Red Jacket. (*Coldwater Daily Reporter*, August 15, 1907)

The advertisement for the play went on to indicate that there would be "a number of clever specialties introduced by members of the cast who have established reputation in vaudeville."

The Girl of the Golden West was written by impresario David Belasco who also produced and directed the original 1905 Broadway production. The play inspired a Puccini opera and, in 1938, a popular film with America's favorite singing sweethearts, Jeanette MacDonald and Nelson Eddy.

Another popular cowboy drama was *The Texas Cattle King* that brought with it the Original Cowboy Band. According to the managers, *The Texas Cattle King* was different from other plays of that genre:

> In presenting to the public . . . "The Texas Cattle King" we wish to assure them that this production is devoid of the sensational clap-trap and blood and thunder which has characterized so many western plays and we endeavor to portray in a faithful manner scenes and incidents characteristic of western life. The company carries an original cowboy band costumed in the full dress of the cowboy as he is seen on the plains of the great west. (Brownlee & Reed, Managers, the Texas Cattle King Company, January 17, 1910)

When *The Texas Cattle King* was performed in Coldwater, the company offered a "special matinee performance" that was explained in the press:

> As a recreation for the school children it will be a rare opportunity, and for the older people who do not find it convenient to come out in the evening it has its advantage. . . . A special courtesy has been extended to the children of State School and the inmates of the county infirmary. (*Coldwater Daily Reporter*, January 17, 1910)

FIGURE 92. "*Arizona*, America's Greatest Play," was one of the most produced Western dramas of the early twentieth century. In 1900 it played 140 performances on Broadway, toured extensively, was revived in New York in 1913, and was adapted for the screen several times—first in 1913, then in 1918 starring Douglas Fairbanks, and in 1931 with John Wayne. (Publisher: U.S. Lithograph Co., Cincinnati, New York, ca. 1907. Retrieved from the Library of Congress.)

A Texas Steer, written by Charles H. Hoyt, was the Western play most often presented at all of the opera houses in Michigan. It was particularly appreciated in Red Jacket where it played at the Calumet Theatre six times in as many years. Unlike many other Western plays *A Texas Steer* is not about cows, cowboys, rustlers, or guns. It is a domestic,

FIGURE 93. "Clyde Fitch's greatest comedy, 'Girls.'" Mr. Fitch's *Girls* got around. They opened on Broadway in March 1908, and by the following January a touring company was on the stage of the Tibbits Opera House. They were back on Broadway in February 1909, and in May they returned to Michigan, this time to appear at the Calumet Theatre. (Publisher: Dana T. Bennett Co., New York, ca. 1910. Retrieved from the Library of Congress.)

situation comedy about folks from Red Dog, Texas. The story concerns the misadventures of a wealthy Texan who is manipulated by his wife and daughter to run for Congress fueled by their desire to live in the nation's capital. A silent film version of the play was released in 1927 starring Will Rogers and Douglas Fairbanks Jr.

"Girls! Girls! Girls!"

The Merry Widow, lyrics by Adrian Ross, music by Franz Lehar, 1907

Ubiquitous in the new century were plays about girls. Perhaps this fascination can be attributed to the phenomenal success of a London import, *A Gaiety Girl*, that opened in New York on September 18, 1894. In his authoritative book, *American Musical Theatre*, Gerald Bordman calls *A Gaiety Girl* "one of the most important musicals in the history of the American Musical Theatre." He based his opinion on the fact that it "dealt not with royalty or unworldly figures but with more or less everyday men and women in more or less everyday difficulties." Whether producers realized the significance of *A Gaiety Girl* is unknown, but what they did realize was that shows with the word "girl" in the title would sell tickets, and perhaps, a show that advertised many girls in the cast would put more seats in the seats.

To fan the fire of interest in these shows, advertisements

highlighted the ladies of the chorus. *Uncle Sam's Belles* was playing the circuit in 1917. It was "The Whirly Girlie Show with Bevies of Bewildering Broadway Blonde and Brunette Beauties, Dozens of Dainty Dimpled Dresden Doll Divinities, 40 People, Mostly Girls." If that was more information than was wanted by the reader, the advertisement for another show cut to the chase by simply asking and answering the question, "Girls? Yes! Plenty!"

The title of Clyde Fitch's 1908 comedy left nothing to the imagination—it was simply *Girls.*

Fitch was one of the most produced Broadway playwrights at the turn of the century. Between 1887 and 1912, fifty-one plays by Fitch premiered on New York stages, and adding the revivals of some of them, his name was up in lights sixty-eight times on the Great White Way. In New York, his plays were star magnets: Maude Adams (*The Masked Ball*), Ethel Barrymore (*Captain Jinks of the Horse Marines*), Richard Mansfield (*Beau Brummell*), and Otis Skinner (*His Grace de Grammont*).

"A Girl for Every Day of the Week"

Head Over Heels, lyrics by Edgar Allen Woolf, music by Jerome Kern, 1918

Other girl plays revolved around the trials and tribulations, often romantic, of working girls or the girl next door, for example, *The Telephone Girl*, *The Sewing Machine Girl*, and *The Girl from Home*, "A Gripping Heart Story with a Thousand Laughs."

Between 1910 and 1919, there were more than thirty-five plays, mostly musicals, with the word "girl" in the title presented at the Tibbits Opera House, twenty-two at the Calumet Theatre, and eighteen at the Ramsdell Theatre. Some sample titles include *The Girl from Milwaukee* with "Rich Comedy, Beautiful Costumes and a Bevy of Dazzling Girly Girls," *The Girl He Couldn't Buy*—perhaps because she was *The Girl Who Had Everything*, and *A Girl of the Underworld* that asks the question, "Does a Man Love a Woman Like a Woman Loves a Man?"

In addition to the girls in gorgeous gowns and the girls in dire straits were the social issue girl dramas. There were two that played in Michigan in 1917: *One Girl's Experience*, "a melodrama telling the story of the dangers that beset poor girls who work for their livelihood," and *The Girl Without a Chance*, "The Truth About the White Slave Traffic." The advertisements for both of these shows emphatically notified prospective theatergoers, "Not a Moving Picture!"

"Danger Ahead"

Blue Eyes, lyrics by Zeke Meyers, music by I. B. Kornblum, 1926

Actress Mary Shaw, who introduced Ibsen's *Ghosts* to American audiences, brought that show featuring members of the original Broadway cast to Michigan opera houses in 1903. Two other social issue dramas that did not gain the classic status of the Ibsen play were *A Hidden Crime* and *Damaged Goods.*

A Hidden Crime deals with the impact of absinthe addiction on the addict's loved ones. Although not as popular, like *Ten Nights in a Bar Room* it sought to draw attention to the dangers of alcohol abuse. Several days prior to the play's

February 3, 1905, opening at the Tibbits Opera House, the *Coldwater Daily Reporter* predicted the audience's reaction to the drama:

> The janitors who clean up the opera house after each performance will be using mops this week instead of dust brooms. The reason . . . is that the crying interest of "A Hidden Crime" is such that the tears of feminine sympathy flood the house. It is a shame to use a mop on such precious drops.

Two days before the opening a synopsis of the play appeared in print:

> The author, Mr. John P. Lockney, has created several characters heretofore unknown to the stage. Chief among these is an aged millionaire who is a slave to absinthe. . . . In "A Hidden Crime" the absinthe fiend struggles manfully to rid himself of this debasing habit but is led on by a treacherous relative who hopes to benefit financially by his death. The comedy element is said to be of an unusually hilarious nature. (*Coldwater Daily Reporter*, February 1, 1905)

The day after the opening, the newspaper posted its review predicting that the play "will undoubtedly some day be regarded as a classic . . . the moral lesson taught will make a lasting impression."

Damaged Goods was promoted as "The Play Which Strips The Veil of Secrecy From The Most Vital Sex Problem Today."

> The play is a serious and powerful arraignment of a subject which has been subdued not only by the medical fraternity, the clergy and the orators, but also by the lay public in general. (*Coldwater Daily Reporter*, March 2, 1915)

Not unlike Ibsen's *Ghosts*, the play *Damaged Goods*, by Eugene Brieux, concerns the impact of venereal disease on what is perceived to be a respectable family. The major difference between the two plays is that *Damaged Goods* is much more didactic than *Ghosts*. Brieux makes the argument that by keeping silent or ignoring the condition it continues to spread. The solution, he says, is to overcome the stigma of the sexually transmitted disease, to talk about it candidly, and thereby to educate and inform others.

In a piece titled *The Social Significance of the Modern Drama* written in 1914 by Emma Goldman, she enthusiastically endorsed the work:

> Brieux is among the few who treated the question in a frank manner showing that the most dangerous phase of venereal disease is ignorance and fear, and that if treated openly and intelligently, it is perfectly curable. Brieux also emphasizes the importance of kindness and consideration for those who contract the affliction. . . . Therein lies the superiority of "Damaged Goods" to most scientific treatises.

Damaged Goods opened on Broadway in 1913 produced by and starring popular matinee idol Richard Bennett. Bennett, who was an established stage and screen actor, is credited for getting an English-language version of Brieux's play on the stage. Because of the subject matter, he met with some resistance, but he prevailed. He also produced and starred in the 1914 film version. There was a New York City revival of the play in 1937.

In the play, George Dupont, from a wealthy family, learns that he has contracted syphilis. His doctor assures him that with patience and time he can be cured but advises that he postpone his wedding to protect his soon-to-be wife and any future offspring. George refuses to put off the marriage; it is his fear of exposure followed by the inevitable public shame that keeps him silent.

In the subsequent acts, time has passed, George has married, and his wife has given birth to a child that has congenital syphilis. The child in turn transmits the disease to the unsuspecting wet nurse. In the last scene of the play, the doctor who is the voice of reason makes a case for "complete social and economic change, which alone can free us from the scourge of syphilis and other social plagues."

The play had the distinction of being the first, and perhaps only, theatrical entertainment brought from Broadway to Washington, D.C., for one performance only. The purpose of the special performance was to afford members of Congress and other officials the opportunity to consider its fitness for presentation to the general public.

Damaged Goods toured the country for almost half a dozen years. It was presented in Michigan opera houses from 1912 until 1915.

Twin Beds, by Margaret Mayo and Salisbury Field, was another adult-themed attraction that made the rounds of Michigan opera houses. However, this play did not deal with serious social issues; it was a bedroom farce. It premiered on Broadway in 1914 where it played 441 performances, and a year later, one of several touring productions opened the 1915 Calumet Theatre season. It was advertised as "the Ben Hur of Comedy . . . a hundred critics in a hundred cities have unanimously decreed it is the best farce in years." It also played Manistee in 1915 and Coldwater in 1918 and returned to Red Jacket in 1923. There were film adaptations of the play released in 1920, 1929, and 1942.

The plot concerns a newlywed husband, Harry Hawkins, who is looking forward to spending some quiet, romantic evenings with his young wife, Blanche. His hopes are dashed as they are constantly interrupted by two of the bride's still amorous admirers and their suspicious spouses. One of the couples lives in the apartment one floor above the Hawkins, and the other couple lives in the apartment one floor below. At the end of Act I, Harry decides that in order to avoid future unwanted visits from Blanche's former beaux and their wives, he and his bride will move to a different apartment building.

In Act II, the couple is ensconced in their new apartment only to discover that in order to remove their husbands from temptation, the wives of Blanche's two admirers made the same decision and have unwittingly moved into the same apartment building—one floor above and one floor below the Hawkins. Then, due to innocent circumstances on the part of one admirer and not-so-innocent intentions on the part of the other, the two men end up in Blanche's bedroom. The possible discovery of the interlopers by Harry and the two men's wives generates a great deal of hiding in closets and under beds and climbing in and out of windows—in

FIGURE 94. "This is not a social call, Mrs. Hawkins. I've merely come to ask you one single question. Do these belong to you?" Mrs. Larkin (Laura Singer) confronts Blanche Hawkins (Minnie Gordon Gaster) after finding Blanche's silk stockings in Mr. Larkin's hat to the horror of Norah, the maid (Isabelle Hagen), in the Keweenaw Playhouse (Calumet Theatre) 1966 production of *Twin Beds*. (Photographer unknown. Courtesy of the Calumet Theatre Archives.)

other words, all the activities that go into creating a fast-paced bedroom farce.

Forty-three years later, still amusing but no longer thought to be particularly naughty, *Twin Beds* was produced as part of the 1966 professional theatre season at the Calumet Theatre that was renamed the Keweenaw Playhouse every summer for approximately ten years.

"Clean Up Your Own Backyard"

Walk Down Mah Street!, lyrics by Patricia Taylor Curtis, music by Norman Curtis, 1968

Perhaps as a reaction to the for-mature-audiences-only fare, managers thought it prudent to compensate by presenting family-friendly, "clean" entertainment. To make the point, they included the virtues of their offerings in their advertisements, for example: "A Clean Bright Comedy," "A Strictly Clean Musical Comedy," "An Absolutely Clean Musical Comedy," and, in a slightly more subtle vein, "A Mile of Smiles Without a Blush."

"The Family Brawl"

Dr. Deluxe, lyrics by Otto Harbach, music by Karl Hoschna, 1911

Abie's Irish Rose was one from the "there's no accounting for taste" category. Although it received unfavorable reviews when it opened on Broadway in 1922, and was allegedly reviled by many theatre professionals, the comedy by Anne Nichols was adored by the public. It ran for five and a half years, breaking the previous longest-run-of-a-Broadway-play record. It generated two Broadway revivals, two film versions, and a radio show, and it held the record as having the longest running tour until that record was broken by the *Hello, Dolly!* tour in the 1960s.

The domestic comedy made one stop in Red Jacket to do two performances of the play in 1924 and was presented at the Ramsdell Theatre in Manistee two years later. The play deals with the troubles that ensue when the son of an Orthodox Jew elopes with the daughter of a devout Irish Catholic. The feud escalates between the couple's two fathers when the newlyweds announce that a baby is on the way. The major question becomes in what culture and religion will the expected grandchild be raised? The dispute is resolved when the young wife gives birth to twins.

The Musicals

"Sing for Your Supper"

The Boys from Syracuse, lyrics by Lorenz Hart, music by Richard Rodgers, 1938

Looking at the list of events that were booked for any given season at an opera house is like looking at the list of dishes available on a buffet table. There was something for every taste, and altogether the individual offerings made a well-balanced meal. Placed between the meat and potatoes (melodramas, comedies, and plays by Shakespeare) were the side dishes (lectures, concerts, and athletic events), and then there were the sweet desserts (the MUSICALS!). They may have been sweet, but did they have substance? About as much as meringue. However, some of them were significant: some because they were groundbreaking or because of their scores or because of their choreography, but few because of their librettos. The musical theatre pieces that were originally produced between 1866 (*The Black Crook*) and 1919 (*Irene*) are seldom revived today, and when they are their books are often significantly altered.

The following pages consist of synopses and production histories of four of the musicals that were among the most often seen at the opera houses as well as a shipload of musical comedies that were set on an island. There is also a quick nod to the works by Victor Herbert and George M. Cohan, as well as to the innovative early shows of Jerome Kern and Irving Berlin. The last section is devoted to the series of enormously popular musicals that were based on cartoon characters.

The Black Crook premiered at Niblo's Garden Theatre located in lower Manhattan, a complex that consisted of a garden park, coffee shop, concert hall, and a 3,200-seat theater. The musical extravaganza opened on September 12,

FIGURE 95. This poster is from the first of eight New York City revivals of *The Black Crook*. It illustrates the villain, Hertzog, confronting the hero, Rudolphe (*lower left*); the Arch Fiend directing Hertzog to Hell (*center*); and Stalacta, Queen of the Fairies, dressed for combat (*lower right*). (Publisher: H.A. Thomas Lith. Studio, N.Y., ca. 1879. Retrieved from the Library of Congress.)

1866; the curtain went up at 7:45 p.m. and came down at 1:15 a.m. During that five-hour-plus period, the audience experienced the most sumptuous and sensational spectacle that had ever been presented on the American stage. It became one of the most popular and financially successful productions of the nineteenth century, playing an unprecedented 474 consecutive performances over a sixteen-month period and grossing $660,000 on its initial run.

The ingredients for *The Black Crook* consisted of one part German melodrama and one part French Romantic ballet. The producers had a libretto originally intended for a German-style opera and a cast that included a French ballet troupe. They put them together, added music, and produced the entire thing in the then popular production style, the extravaganza, that consisted of song, dance, fantasy, lavish costumes and scenery, as well as spectacular special effects.

What resulted was a work that some theatre historians have dubbed "the first American musical," claiming that it was the first musical entertainment to attract a cultural cross-section of society as musicals do today. For the highbrow there was the ballet, for the lowbrow there was the burlesque humor, and for everyone there was the spectacle.

Other theatre scholars have rejected the "first American musical" designation:

> nothing about 'The Black Crook' justifies its position as the precursor of our modern musical stage; all its forms and conventions derive from a long tradition, established well before 1866. (Julian Mates, *America's Musical Stage*, 1987)

Inspired by a production of the opera *Der Freischutz*, Charles M. Barras wrote *The Black Crook* to be an opera libretto. For the script he "borrowed" themes, characters, and plot elements from *Der Freischutz* as well as from Goethe's *Faust*, the French fantasy *Undine*, and other established works. The result was a hackneyed melodrama with stilted, pretentious dialogue. However, when the show was produced, the script was significantly enhanced by stunning scenery, spectacular special effects, and girls in pink tights.

The story takes place in Germany's Harz Mountains in the early seventeenth century. An aging sorcerer, Hertzog, the Black Crook, is described in the script as "a hideous deformity, with leaden complexion, humped back, knotted limbs, crooked body, and lame." He has made a pact with the Arch Fiend, the devil, to avoid death by delivering to him one soul a year.

FIGURE 96. The Kiralfy Brothers' revival of *The Black Crook* at Niblo's Garden Theater took place sixteen years after its premiere. This poster depicts the final confrontation between Count Wolfenstein with his army of mortal men (*stage right*) and Rudolphe backed by Stalacta and her Amazon fairy entourage (*stage left*). Amina has fainted center stage. (Publisher: Forbes Co., Boston, ca. 1882. Retrieved from the Library of Congress.)

Rudolphe, the hero, is a starving artist in love with Amina, a rural beauty. They plan to wed as soon as Rudolphe has accrued enough wealth to support a wife. The lecherous Count Wolfenstein, who has taken a fancy to Amina, exercises his feudal authority to announce that he, rather than Rudolphe, will marry the maiden. To eliminate his competition, the count has Rudolphe locked in his castle's dungeon.

In the meantime, Hertzog, who had planned to use Rudolphe to fulfill his yearly obligation to the Arch Fiend, helps him escape. He convinces the young artist to venture into the forest where he will find a cave laden with gold and gems that will provide him with the means to marry Amina. In reality, Hertzog has arranged that when Rudolphe reaches the cave, rather than finding a treasure he will meet his death.

As Rudolphe travels through the forest searching for the cave, he encounters a dove that is being threatened by a serpent. He kills the predator and saves the dove that is really Stalacta, the Queen of the Fairies, who had been transformed by the Arch Fiend into "a poor, weak, fluttering bird." Stalacta warns Rudolphe of Hertzog's treachery and rewards him for saving her from the serpent with gifts of gems and gold.

The drama ends with a climactic battle between Rudolphe, who is supported by Stalacta and her fairy entourage all dressed as Amazons, and Count Wolfenstein backed by his army of mortal men. In the end, Wolfenstein is killed, Rudolphe and Amina are free to marry, and the Black Crook is carted off to Hades by the Arch Fiend.

Amid all of the drama and dazzle there was some broad comedy provided by Count Wolfenstein's bumbling steward, Von Puffengruntz, and his wife. She beats him over the head with a broom; his wig pops off and flies away.

The critics dismissed the book: the *New York Tribune* called it "rubbish," and the *New York Times* agreed, but they were unanimous in their praise of the physical production. The *New York Tribune* proclaimed that it consisted of "some of the most perfect and admirable pieces of scenery that have ever been exhibited upon the stage." It was declared to be "a triumph of form over content."

The budget for the production was the largest ever spent

on such a venture. According to the *New York Times*, it cost $50,000 to mount the show. In order to facilitate the transformation scenes, the producers spent over $25,000 to have the stage house completely rebuilt.

ACT V, Scenes vii and viii

> Subterranean gallery of emerald and crystal stalactites. Music. Grand procession of amphibia and gnomes bearing in their arms and on their head salvers, shells, and quaint vases filled with gold and jewels. They are followed by amazons in armor, led by STALACTA . . . the scene breaks away to . . . an elaborate mechanical and scenical construction of the Realms of STALACTA, occupying the entire stage. This scene must be of gradually-developing and culminating beauty, introducing during its various transformations, the entire host of fairies, sprites, water nymphs, amphibia, gnomes, etc., bearing treasure that STALACTA presents to RUDOLPHE, AMINA, GREPPO, and CARLINE. Calcium lights, brilliant fires, and slow curtain.

In addition to the scenery and special effects, the other major draw to the production was the ballet or, for some, the ballet dancers. As the dancers in *The Black Crook* played fairies, nymphs, and Amazons, they wore character-appropriate costumes that consisted of corsets and tights with very short skirts. Never before on the respectable American stage had so much of the female form been revealed.

The ballerinas, their choreography, and their costumes proved to be very controversial. The *New York Times* raved, "New York has never enjoyed the presence of so beautiful . . . graceful and thoroughly captivating a *corps de ballet* as the one herein introduced." On the other hand, in a letter to the editor of a New York newspaper, one outraged clergyman stated, "the attitudes were exceedingly indelicate . . . ladies dancing so as to make their undergarments spring up, exposing the figure beneath from the waist to the toe."

The score for *The Black Crook* was a pastiche. Thomas Baker, credited as the music director and composer, wrote much of the ballet music. However, he primarily interpolated into the musical mix preexisting pieces from many different sources.

The only song praised by the critics was "You Naughty, Naughty Men," with lyrics by Theodore Kennick and music by George Bickwell. The *New York Times* critic noted that the enthusiastic audience response to the number elicited an encore. "You Naughty, Naughty Men" was introduced in the show by the soubrette, a village maid named Carline. In the song, she describes the underhanded tricks men employ when trying to take advantage of a woman during their courtship. She complains that when "you naughty, naughty men" finally marry a woman,

> *You take us from our mothers,*
> *our sisters and our brothers,*
> *when you get us, flirt with others,*
> *Oh, you naughty, naughty men.*

When *The Black Crook* opened, the reviews were decidedly mixed. One critic simply condemned it: "Nothing in any other Christian country, or in modern times, has approached this indecent and demoralizing exhibition." Other critics praised it: "No similar exhibition has been made on an American stage that we remember. Certainly none where such a combination of youth, grace, and beauty was found . . . decidedly the event of this spectacular age."

Between 1868 and 1900, the show was revived in New York eight times; the last major revival took place in 1929 with future choreographer Agnes de Mille (*Rodeo, Oklahoma!*) in the role of Stalacta. It was on tour throughout the country for more than twenty-five years. Wherever *The Black Crook* played, people were offended, shocked, outraged, and bought thousands of dollars' worth of tickets.

A Trip to Chinatown, with a book by Charles H. Hoyt, music by Percy Gaunt, and lyrics by both of them, was one of the most produced plays of the late nineteenth century. Hoyt's comedies contained a number of songs, and although the songs were not always well integrated into the plot, his shows are considered an early form of musical comedy.

In addition to the songs, *A Trip to Chinatown* consisted of dances, gags, and a fairly simple plot. Two young men, Rashleigh Gay and Wilder Daly, and their sisters, Tony and Flirt, respectively, want to attend a masquerade ball. Rashleigh and Tony fear that their Uncle Ben, a wealthy merchant who is their guardian, will not permit them to embark on such a wild escapade. Consequently, they tell him that they are going to take a tour of Chinatown chaperoned by a charming widow, Mrs. Guyer. She is not a widow who is given to serious mourning; in fact it was she who suggested the Chinatown subterfuge. Rashleigh, who is smitten with her, states, "The widow's more fun than any girl I know."

Uncle Ben intercepts a letter to Rashleigh from Mrs. Guyer that he mistakenly believes was intended for him.

FIGURE 97. Charles H. Hoyt was one of the most prolific and popular American playwrights in the last two decades of the nineteenth century. Over a fourteen-year period he wrote seventeen Broadway hits including *A Bunch of Keys, A Texas Steer,* and *A Trip to Chinatown.* Theatre historians have referred to him as the "Father of American Farce." (Publisher: U.S. Printing Co. Cincinnati, New York, ca. 1899. Retrieved from the Library of Congress.)

In the note, she suggests that they meet at a fashionable restaurant before the ball. As he is fascinated by the widow and encouraged by her invitation, he decides to pursue the possibilities. He arrives at the establishment unaware that his wards and Mrs. Guyer are in the next room. While waiting for her arrival, Uncle Ben becomes intoxicated, and when

FIGURE 98. *A Trip to Chinatown* poster, 1891. The show's 635 performances on Broadway set a record as the longest running Broadway musical, which it held for twenty-eight years. In 1926, a silent film version of the play was released. (The University of Wisconsin Digital Collections)

he is given the bill for his drinks, he discovers that he has left his wallet at home. A brawl ensues.

The next day, Mrs. Guyer convinces Uncle Ben that she sent the note to him on purpose as she had a bet with his wards that she could lure him into an indiscretion. All ends well, but contrary to what the title suggests, no one ever takes . . . A Trip to Chinatown!

If this all seems somewhat familiar it is because a number of the plot points and characters in the show bear some similarity to those in Thornton Wilder's *The Matchmaker* and the musical *Hello, Dolly!* Unlike those two shows, in *A Trip to Chinatown* several of the characters have names that are indicative of their personalities or positions. There is the all-knowing waiter, Noah Heap; a hypochondriac, Welland Strong; and a much put upon servant, Slavin Payne.

Three of the songs in the show enjoyed great popularity. Two of them, "The Bowery" and "Rueben, Rueben," were by Hoyt and Gaunt. However, the most enduring hit was "After the Ball," by Charles K. Harris. It had been written for a minstrel show that was playing in Milwaukee when *A Trip to Chinatown* was there on tour prior to its New York opening. The leading singer in the Hoyt and Guant show, J. Aldrich Libbey, billed as "the Peerless Baritone," heard the song and insisted that it be interpolated into the play so that he could sing it. Hoyt and Guant resisted the intrusion of a song by another songwriter into their score, but Mr. Libbey, who was accused of having the temperament of a grand opera singer, could sing whatever he wanted.

Following a tour of almost twelve months, *A Trip to Chinatown* opened in New York in 1891, where it set the record as Broadway's longest running musical comedy. It held on to that distinction for twenty-eight years until *Irene* came along. The show was so successful that a second production opened in New York while the first one was still playing.

The Wizard of Oz, the original musical adaptation of L. Frank Baum's classic tale *The Wonderful Wizard of Oz*, opened on Broadway thirty-six years before Judy Garland sang "Over the Rainbow" for the first time and seventy-two years before the curtain went up on the updated version, *The Wiz*. With the abbreviated title of *The Wizard of Oz*, the show opened on Broadway in 1903, where it played for ten months then closed but returned the next year for an additional seven-month run.

Baum wrote the book and lyrics for the show; the original score was by Paul Tietjens. They offered the project to Julian P. Mitchell, the prominent director of the original productions of *A Trip to Chinatown* and *Babes in Toyland* as well as several editions of the *Ziegfeld Follies*. Mitchell believed that to be successful a musical required spectacle and humor, more than was evident in Baum's original treatment of *The Wizard of Oz*. He engaged Glen MacDonough to add new scenes and topical jokes to the libretto. During his career, MacDonough provided the book and/or lyrics for operettas by Franz Lehar, Reginald De Koven, and Victor Herbert, among others.

True to the novel and the 1939 film, this version opens with Dorothy living on a farm in Kansas, but instead of her little dog Toto, Mitchell and MacDonough gave her a pet cow, Imogene.

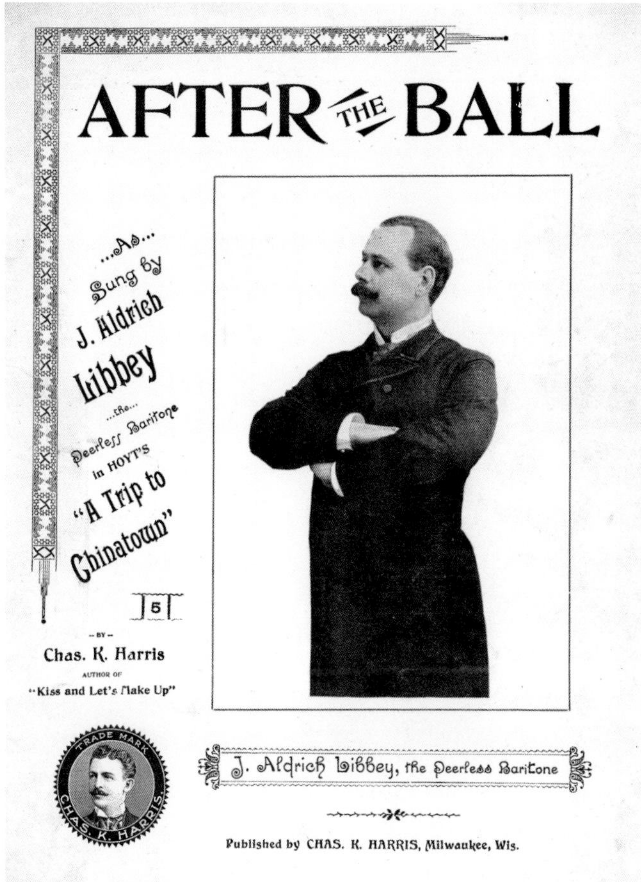

FIGURE 99. In 1900, if a song sold fifty thousand copies of sheet music it was considered a hit, and if it sold one hundred thousand copies it was a megahit. "After the Ball" sold five million copies of sheet music. The song was sung on Broadway again in 1927 when Jerome Kern and Oscar Hammerstein II interpolated it into the score of *Show Boat*. (Publisher: Chas. K. Harris, Milwaukee, WI., 1892. Music Division, the New York Public Library Digital Collections.)

ACT I, Scenes i and ii

Descriptive Tableaux showing DOROTHY and her pet cow IMOGENE. At the rise of the curtain FARM HANDS and SERVANT GIRLS are discovered performing their various duties. Suddenly an OLD FARMER points to the approaching cyclone. Everyone frantically rushes off stage. The cyclone effect is worked upon the gauze. The lights go down. "Transformation" music is heard. The lights go up on the Blue Munchkin Country in the Land of Oz. CHORUS OF MUNCHKINS discovered all dressed in blue and dancing about a Maypole. Their festivities are interrupted by the entrance of the WICKED WITCH who chases them about the stage. Someone calls her attention to the approaching cyclone. All rush about wildly. Lights gradually go out. When they go up again, a house similar to the farmhouse of the Kansas Scene is discovered crushed to the ground.

The Wicked Witch is squashed when the house lands on top of her. Dorothy and Imogene enter intact. The Good

FIGURE 100. This poster for the Broadway premiere of *The Wizard of Oz* features a range of characters in their motley attire in front of the requisite comic opera chorus girls. (Publisher: U.S. Lithograph Co, Cincinnati and New York, 1903. Retrieved from the Library of Congress.)

Witch rewards Dorothy for ridding the land of the Wicked Witch with a pair of magic slippers and a wish-granting ring.

When Dorothy expresses her desire to return home, the Good Witch encourages her to seek the advice of the mighty Wizard of Oz. So that she will have a companion on her journey, Dorothy uses her wish ring to bring a scarecrow to life who explains that he has no brain. He sings, “Alas for the Man Without Brains.”

Before getting very far down the road, they encounter a tin woodman that tells them that the Wicked Witch stole his heart. With the hope that the Wizard of Oz will be able to restore their missing parts, the Scarecrow and Tin Woodman join forces with Dorothy in her quest to find the all-powerful wizard. In this version, the Cowardly Lion is a minor character and does not become a member of Dorothy’s entourage. Why would she need a lion when she already has a cow?

Soon the story varies from the more familiar film version and introduces a second plot line. It involves deposed King Pastoria II, the former monarch of Oz, who is leading a revolution to overthrow the Wizard and regain the throne.

Of special interest to Michiganders—Pastoria reveals to the chorus that he once was a motorman in Michigan, where the girls were particularly sociable. He then breaks into a song titled “In Michigan.”

In Michigan, in Michigan,
I would that I were rich again.
A ticket I’d buy, and away I’d fly
To the far-off fields of Michigan.
In Michigan, in Michigan,
my tent I’d like to pitch again.
I’ve a sweetheart true in Kalamazoo
And that’s what I’ve got in Michigan.

In the end, Pastoria is once more the king, the Wizard escapes in a hot air balloon, and Dorothy returns to Kansas.

The show featured spectacular scenery and breathtaking special effects created by Walter Wilcox Burridge who was responsible for the stock scenery at the Ramsdell Theatre. One of the production highlights created by the Burridge Studio was the cyclone effect at the top of the show, which garnered a great deal of praise from the press and became a "must-see" marketing tool.

While the original production was still playing in New York, the producer sent out several companies that were on tour for six years. One company made its way to Michigan in 1903 with two carloads of scenery, a cast of sixty-five, and a full orchestra. In December 1905, a different touring production of the Baum musical was the Tibbits Opera House's Christmas attraction. The local reviewer reported that the second production was not only bigger but also better than the first. The press proclaimed the stage adaptation of *The Wizard of Oz* to be "The Most Remarkable Success in Theatrical History."

Madame Sherry had a libretto by Otto Harbach that he adapted from a French farce. Harbach also wrote the lyrics for music composed by Karl Hoschna. The show opened in New York on August 30, 1910, and played 231 performances, and typical of so many musicals of the period, it had a plot that involved comic deception, mistaken identities, and romance. In this case, a dashing man-about-town, Edward Sherry, who owns the Sherry School of Aesthetic Dancing has convinced his very conservative Uncle Theophilus that he is a responsible married man with children. With this understanding, the uncle has agreed to underwrite his nephew's dance studio. In reality, it is his nephew's extravagant lifestyle that Uncle Theophilus is supporting. Edward is able to perpetuate this deception because his uncle, who is a wealthy amateur archeologist, took up residence in Greece years before where he is searching for Venus de Milo's missing arms.

The inevitable happens: Uncle Theophilus makes a completely unexpected appearance at his nephew's Manhattan establishment causing Edward to commandeer the participation of his Irish housekeeper, his young assistant dance instructor, and her royal Latin lover to impersonate his fictional wife and children.

Now, enter the ingénue, a recent graduate of a convent school, to whom Edward is soon attracted. But how does he let her know that he is interested and available while maintaining the pretense that he is a married man with children? Does it all work out in the end? Of course it does—this is a musical comedy!

One special attraction in the production was a specialty that was a cross between an apache dance and pas de deux of sorts called "The Danger Dance." The review referred to it as "the sensation of the evening."

The score was filled with popular songs and songs that became popular. In particular "Put Your Arms Around Me, Honey (Hold Me Tight)," a preexisting tune with lyrics by Junie McCree and music by Albert Von Tilzer, was interpolated into the show shortly after it opened.

Indigenous to the original score was "Every Little Movement (Has a Meaning All Its Own)" that became a hit with one of the period's largest sales of sheet music. The melody was used as if it were a leitmotif reoccurring throughout the show from time to time, and each time it had a meaning all its own. At the top of the show, the young dance instructor

FIGURE 101. The original production of *The Wizard of Oz* marked the legitimate theatre debut of David Montgomery and Fred A. Stone, a well-established and popular vaudeville team, who played the Tin Woodman and the Scarecrow, respectively. (Photographer: Windeatt, Chicago, 1903. Billy Rose Theatre Division, the New York Public Library for the Performing Arts, Astor, Lenox, and Tilden Foundations.)

FIGURE 102. "The Danger Dance is the latest terpsichorean musical comedy situation. The dance is a feature of *Madame Sherry*, . . . and is described as a novelty, where the male dancer is always on the ground and his fair partner mostly in the air whither he swings, pulls and tosses her, as he might a gay scarf. The woman . . . is said to wear a specially devised steel corset to protect her ribs from cracking in the clinches." *Coldwater Daily Reporter*, April 1, 1911 (Photographer: Hall, 1910. Museum of the City of New York.)

sings it to her pupils as an explanation of the dance steps she is demonstrating. Later, the song takes on a different nuance when she sings it while dancing with her lover. Altogether the song is heard four times in the first act, sung twice by the dance instructor, once by Uncle Theophilus, and once as the accompaniment to a dance. During this period it was not unheard of to reprise a song in a show, but to do it in a different context with a new meaning was a new concept.

> There is one innovation in "Madame Sherry" which theatergoers will doubtless greet with their approval; it's not a waltz; it's a polka . . . its strains are heard at the beginning of the first act and continue thereafter. The polka is called "Every Little Movement." . . . By the time the end of the first act was reached last night everybody in the house knew it. (*New York Times*, April 31, 1910)

There is a play on the song's lyrics in the third act that takes place on a yacht when Uncle Theophilus says, "Every little stateroom has a bathroom all its own."

Atypical of comic operas of the period, the show had only half a chorus: a dozen girls playing the daughters of millionaires who have come to the Sherry School to learn to dance, but no chorus boys. Girls! Girls! Girls!

The *New York Times* critic expressed the opinion that with its clever libretto and well-integrated songs, *Madame Sherry* raised the musical theatre bar. "The plot plays a much more important part than it usually does in an American musical comedy."

> No musical comedy in a dozen years has scored such a hit as "Madame Sherry." Its musical gems, especially "Every Little Movement Has a Meaning All its Own" have captivated the world, and it is sure to prove the distinct hit of many years when presented at the local opera house. (*Coldwater Daily Reporter*, April 3, 1911)

"The Island of Never-Mind-Where"

The Golden Moth, lyrics by P. G. Wodehouse, music by Ivor Novello, 1921

Where better to create a unique, fantastical atmosphere appropriate for the plot of a comic opera than on a mysterious island? *The Isle of Champagne* was set on an island where the intoxicating bubbly flowed freely, but there was no water to be found. After a New York run in 1892, the show toured the country for ten years, playing in Coldwater in 1897.

Early in the twentieth century there were several musicals with island settings including *The Isle of Bong Bong*. Two weeks prior to the performance at the Tibbits Opera House this inquiry appeared in a newspaper article: "Where is the Isle of Bong Bong?" Journalists subsequently reported that schoolchildren throughout the area were industriously studying their maps, atlases, and globes to locate the elusive isle.

The Isle of Spice, advertised as a "Highly Seasoned Musical Mixture," was a much sought after hit as indicated by the following:

> Negotiations have been going on for the last six months between the New York office and Manager Jackson,

who has been untiring in his efforts to secure it for an engagement in Coldwater and at last they have accepted his final offer. (*Coldwater Daily Reporter*, February 6, 1905)

Perhaps, because of the fact that *The Isle of Spice* was the recipient of what the local press called "the most extensive advertising campaign ever attempted for a theatrical engagement in Coldwater," it generated "the largest first day advance sale of any attraction ever offered on the local stage." The much-anticipated production arrived with the original scenery, costumes, and mechanical and electrical effects that were used on Broadway.

When two American sailors descend upon the Isle of Spice in a hot air balloon, King Bompopka, ruler of the fictional island, believes them to be messengers from the sun, and he honors them accordingly. Later, when he discovers that the sailors are merely mortal men who had wafted in from an American warship, he orders their execution. The boys are headed for a beheading, but just as the axe is poised to fall, their shipmates march in to save the day.

The Cat and the Fiddle, a 1907 extravaganza not to be confused with the 1934 Jerome Kern musical of the same name, had music by Clarence N. Sinn and book and lyrics by Lincoln J. Carter. In spite of the fact that it did not have "Isle" in the title, much of the action in *The Cat and the Fiddle* takes place on one just the same. The show opened on Broadway where it played just five performances. Although it was not a success there, it was very popular on its extensive national tour that reached the Midwest in 1911.

The plot borrowed elements from *The Wizard of Oz* with a nod to the story of Aladdin and his genie-filled lamp. In Carter's libretto, a young girl, Polly, is kidnapped from her Aunt Matilda's farm by demons and whisked away to the Isle of Eye to be the annual human sacrifice. Happily, a Genie and her Gigantic Cat are magically released from a jar just in time to rescue Polly.

The synopsis with demons, a kidnapping, and the threat of human sacrifice doesn't read like a comedy, but there must have been some lighter moments in it as it was advertised as "The Merriest of all Musical Extravaganzas," and the producers predicted that the show would generate "sixty laughs a minute."

In addition to some plot points, another similarity between *The Cat and the Fiddle* and *The Wizard of Oz* was the use of multiple settings, twenty in all, at a time when many comic operas and operettas limited themselves to one setting per act.

FIGURE 103. *The Isle of Spice* touring company required a special train of cars to transport the cast, crew, and scenery at a daily cost of over five hundred dollars, making it a very expensive attraction for the one-night-stand towns. The large cast included a chorus of "one hundred young and pretty women." Here are fourteen of them. Where are the other eighty-six and do they also wear polka dot bloomers? (*Manistee Daily News*, September 12, 1905)

FIGURE 104. As a young Irish cellist Victor Herbert began his professional career playing in orchestras in Austria and Germany. When New York City's Metropolitan Opera Company offered his wife, an opera singer, a contract in 1886, the couple immigrated to this country. Soon Maestro Herbert was conducting his own band and composing music rather than playing it—the rest is history. (Photographer: Harris & Ewing, 1905. Retrieved from the Library of Congress.)

"Opera, Comic Opera"

The Royal Vagabond, lyrics and music by George M. Cohan, 1919

Victor Herbert (1859–1924) composed a number of comic operas that played in Michigan including his classic *Babes in Toyland,* as well as *The Only Girl* and *Princess Pat.* Michiganders also saw three works he created for "America's Most Famous Comedian," Frank Daniels: *The Ameer, The Wizard of the Nile,* and *The Tattooed Man.*

The Tattooed Man opened on Broadway in 1907 and went out on tour arriving in Coldwater the following year. Like its Herbert and Daniels predecessors, it took place in an exotic locale. Daniels played Omar Khayyam Jr., the interim shah of Persia, who has an unusual birthmark. There is a decree that should someone else appear with the same birthmark both Omar and his counterpart will be executed. For revenge, a woman who had been spurned by Omar arranges for the birthmark to be tattooed on two other men. For the rest of the comic opera, Omar attempts to avoid his fate. When the show came to Michigan, Mr. Daniels came with it.

Another Herbert hit, *The Red Mill,* was making the rounds in Michigan in 1910 where it could be seen on several occasions in both Coldwater and Red Jacket and once in Manistee. With book and lyrics by Henry Blossom, it was created for the comedy team of David Montgomery and Fred A. Stone who had originated the roles of Dorothy's two traveling companions in *The Wizard of Oz* on Broadway seven years earlier. Unlike Frank Daniels who went out on tour in the shows written for him, when *The Red Mill* left New York, Messrs. Montgomery and Stone did not.

FIGURE 105. A poster for Victor Herbert's comic opera *The Ameer,* 1899, featuring the star, Frank Daniels (*center top*). Four years earlier, Daniels played the title role in Herbert's *The Wizard of the Nile,* their first collaboration. The composer went on to create three other vehicles for the comedian. Daniels retired from the stage in 1912 and for the next nine years worked in silent films. (Publisher: U.S. Printing Co. Cincinnati, New York, ca. 1899. Retrieved from the Library of Congress.)

In addition to the many performances of the works by Victor Herbert, other comic operas seen in the Wolverine state include almost everything by Gilbert and Sullivan; John Philip Sousa's most successful stage work, *El Capitan*; and Reginald De Koven's *Robin Hood*, the most celebrated American operetta of the nineteenth century.

"Musical Comedy Man"

George M!, Lyric and music revision by Mary Cohan, 1968, song adapted from "Musical Comedy Maid," *The Honeymooners*, lyrics and music by George M. Cohan, 1907

George M. Cohan (1878–1942) and Victor Herbert were more or less contemporaries, but they represented opposite sides of the musical theatre coin. Herbert was classically trained, grew up in a well-educated family, and performed in the concert halls of Europe and America. Cohan was more or less self-taught, born in a trunk, and grew up in vaudeville. But they both wrote Broadway hits filled with tunes that when sold as sheet music brought them considerable fame and fortune.

One of the most popular and prolific creators of plays and songs of the period, George M. Cohan was also a song-and-dance man known for his patriotic, flag-waving performances. He was well represented in Michigan by two of his musical hits, *Little Johnny Jones* and *Forty-Five Minutes from Broadway*. Not only did he write the books and compose the songs for both shows, he also directed them. *Little Johnny Jones*, his first full-length musical, opened in 1905. He played the title character on Broadway but relinquished the role to another actor when the show went on tour. The musical, which included such enduring songs as "Give My Regards to Broadway" and "The Yankee Doodle Boy," traveled throughout the Midwest between 1907 and 1909.

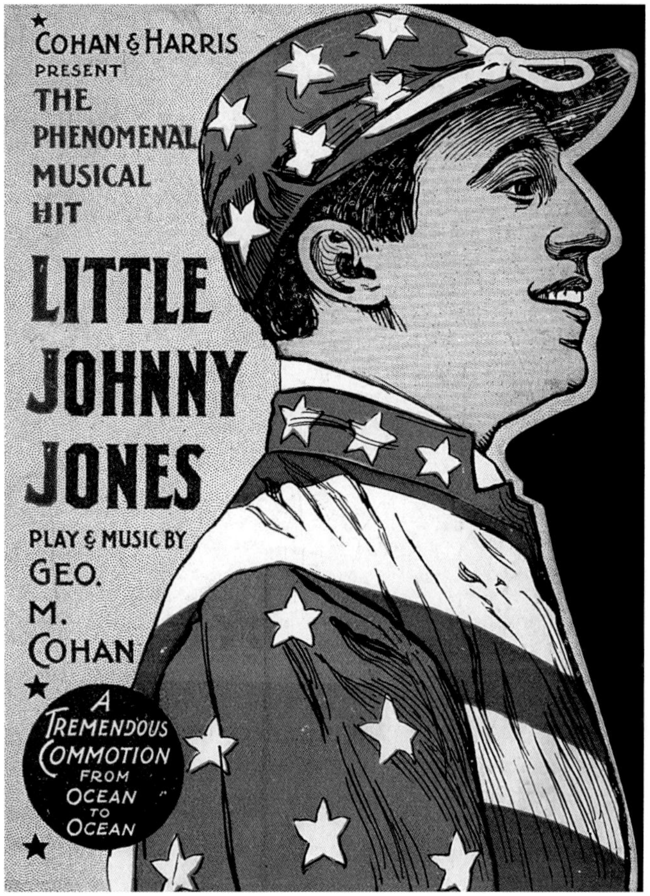

FIGURE 106. This promotional brochure for a touring production of George M. Cohan's *Little Johnny Jones* included a synopsis of the musical, a list of songs, and photographs from the production. (Publisher: Nyvall Press, New York, N.Y., 1907. Billy Rose Theatre Division, the New York Public Library for the Performing Arts, Astor, Lenox, and Tilden Foundations.)

Another Cohan hit, *Forty-Five Minutes from Broadway*, opened in New York in 1906 and toured from 1907 to 1914. It was the first show he wrote without a role for himself. He did, however, compose the songs and direct the production. The tune-filled play included the title song, as well as "Mary

FIGURE 107. Sergeant Irving Berlin is seen here dressed in his World War I uniform that he wore when he introduced the song "Oh, How I Hate to Get Up in the Morning" in his musical military review *Yip, Yip, Yaphank* in 1918. He reprised the song in his World War II musical military review, *This Is the Army*, in 1942. Berlin wrote the words and music for over one thousand songs including "White Christmas," "Easter Parade," and "God Bless America." Composer Jerome Kern once said, "Irving Berlin has no place in American music—he is American music." (Photographer: White Studio, 1918. Retrieved from the Library of Congress.)

(Is a Grand Old Name)" and "So Long, Mary." Both shows played in Red Jacket, Coldwater, and Manistee.

"Opera and Rag Time"

Bringing Up Father at the Seashore, lyricist unknown, music by Tom Grady, 1921

> Comic opera is almost extinct . . . musical comedy having taken its place. (A. D. Storms, *The Players Blue Book*, 1901)

During the first two decades of the twentieth century, there was a transition from the Golden Age of American Operetta to the birth of the Modern American Musical Comedy. Jerome Kern and Irving Berlin are credited for being instrumental in moving musical theater away from those Viennese-influenced operettas filled with lilting waltzes, military marches, enormous choruses, and story lines that often played like fairy tales. By contrast, the new American musical comedy had a fresh new sound, a modern setting, a smaller cast, and a contemporary plot and characters.

Between 1916 and 1917, audiences in Red Jacket and Coldwater experienced three of Jerome Kern's groundbreaking, up-to-date musicals: *Nobody Home*, *Very Good Eddie*, and *Oh, Boy!* Kern wrote them for New York's Princess Theatre, an intimate 299-seat playhouse. In addition to their catchy titles, they had catchy tunes with clever lyrics written in the current vernacular by P. G. Wodehouse and others.

At the same time they were enjoying the efforts of Jerome Kern, patrons of the Calumet Theatre were being introduced to twenty-six-year-old Irving Berlin's first Broadway show, *Stop, Look, Listen*, that had opened in New York in 1915. In 1917, Michigan playgoers had the opportunity to see Berlin's *Watch Your Step*, the first musical to incorporate into an original score the latest musical rage, RAGTIME! The show also introduced the first of several contrapuntal songs for which Berlin became famous, "(Won't You) Play a Simple Melody."

Thanks to Kern and Berlin, among others including George and Ira Gershwin, a contemporary, purely American sound infiltrated musical theatre scores and popular music. Say "hello" to "Alexander's Ragtime Band."

"See You in the Funny Papers"

Woman of the Year, lyrics by Fred Ebb, music by John Kander, 1981

In 1903, a musical opened in New York that was from a previously untapped source—the funny papers. Happy Hooligan stepped onto the Broadway stage that year; two years later Buster Brown followed him. Ever since that time, comic strips and comic books have served as rich fodder for what became known as cartoon musicals.

The Katzenjammer Kids was the first cartoon musical to go on tour. The show was based on a comic strip originally published in the Sunday supplement of the *New York Journal*, a Hearst publication, in 1897. Rudolph Dirks, a German immigrant, came up with the idea for the strip and created the characters. The story lines revolved around Hans and Fritz, two German brothers, who were constantly playing pranks on their long-suffering "Mama" and their befuddled father figure, "der Captain."

Hans, Fritz, Mama, and der Captain went on tour when the strip was adapted into a play with songs. It was advertised

FIGURE 108. The pranks perpetrated by Hans and Fritz in "The Katzenjammer Kids" comic strips invariably led to their being chased down and, in the last panel, paddled by Mama or der Captain. The brothers never learned their lesson, and their fans never tired of the familiar plot. The purpose of this newspaper cartoon that appeared in the January 17, 1916, issue of the *Coldwater Daily Reporter* was to promote the musical *The Katzenjammer Kids* that was soon to be presented at the Tibbits Opera House.

FIGURE 109. Every year that the musical went out on tour, it was simply advertised as *Happy Hooligan*, but it was never the same show as scenes and musical numbers were added and cut annually. The scene depicted here, titled "An Uprising in China," may have been new and selected for the poster to inform the audience that in this updated version of the show they could expect to see the happy hobo in previously unseen adventures. (Publisher: U.S. Lithograph Co., Cincinnati, New York, ca. 1904. Retrieved from the Library of Congress.)

as "A Smart Musical Show with Pretty Girls" and boasted that it was "Full of Pep and Ginger."

Court battles between Dirks and the Hearst organization over the rights to the comic strip resulted in Hearst retaining control of "The Katzenjammer Kids." Dirks was given permission to continue with the characters but with a new title. In 1914, he introduced "The Captain and the Kids" with very familiar characters in very familiar plots. Like its predecessor, "The Captain and the Kids" also generated a play with songs that toured the country, but it was never as popular or as frequently performed as *The Katzenjammer Kids* musical.

Happy Hooligan, another early cartoon character to tour the country, was a happy-go-lucky hobo who always remained optimistic despite his unrelenting misfortune. Created by cartoonist Frederick Burr Opper, Happy Hooligan was first seen in newspapers on March 11, 1900. His adventures ended only when failing eyesight rendered Opper unable to continue drawing the comic strip.

The cartoon character was the inspiration for two

FIGURE 110. Buster Brown's resolutions became so popular that they were used as newspaper advertisements. Once a week, beginning in October 1906, on the front page of the *Manistee Evening News* was a Buster Brown resolution that encouraged a visit to Frank's Store, a local haberdashery. In 1909 on the front page of the *Coldwater Daily Reporter* was the first in a similar series of advertisements for "Hilton, the Best Clothier and Shoe Man," featuring Buster, Tige, and their pals. (*Coldwater Daily Reporter*, April 14, 1909.)

musicals: one, titled *Happy Hooligan*, opened on Broadway in 1903, and the other, *Happy Hooligan's Trip Around the World*, opened in 1906; both had very short, less-than-three-week runs. Many touring companies of the original *Happy Hooligan* took to the road and played throughout the United States. Over the years several of those companies played several Michigan opera houses.

In April 1904, prior to a performance of the show at the Ramsdell Theatre, the *Manistee Daily News* published a story that concerned the *Happy Hooligan* touring companies. In the production there was a specialty number called "The Diamond Ballet" involving twenty chorus girls who swirled around the stage wearing black velvet gowns that were encrusted with rhinestones. The advertisement enticed the audience to attend the production by inviting them to "see the $10,000 feature of transcendent beauty, jeweled dresses."

Because the producers sent out multiple *Happy Hooligan* companies, many rhinestones were required to create many diamond costumes. That resulted in *Happy Hooligan* single-handedly depleting the available stock of the glittery gems for sale in this country. The stones were imported from Europe, and therefore, more were not immediately available. Allegedly, the price of rhinestones skyrocketed in America for approximately four months until the rhinestone coffers could be replenished.

Buster Brown was created and drawn by Richard F. Outcault and made his first appearance on May 4, 1902, in the *New York Herald*. After four years with the *Herald*, Outcault moved on to the Hearst organization where the strip was published until 1921.

In addition to playing pranks in comic strips, comic books, and eventually on stage, in the movies, and on the radio, Buster Brown also sold shoes. A sales executive with the Brown Shoe Company persuaded his employers to purchase the rights to the Buster Brown name. The shoe stores that carried Buster Brown shoes distributed Buster Brown comic books to their customers, and from time to time little men costumed as Buster would visit stores to promote sales.

The comic centered around a mischievous boy from an upper-class family who consistently played pranks on unsuspecting adults. The humor in *Buster Brown* was enhanced by the contrast created by a "bad boy" prankster dressed in "good boy" prissy attire. Buster's pranks invariably led to punishment, after which he would sum up the entire experience with a resolution.

In 1905, Buster Brown made his Broadway debut in a musical bearing his name. The show starred a twenty-three-year-old little person, Gabriel Weigel—stage name,

Master Gabriel—as Buster Brown. George Ali, an animal impersonator, played Tige, Buster's pet American pit bull terrier. Critics said that Ali as Tige stole the show. In 1924, Ali played Nana, the nursemaid dog, in the silent film version of *Peter Pan*.

The original songs for *Buster Brown* were composed by John W. Bratton with lyrics by Paul West and related to the plot or the characters such as "Boy the Woodshed and the Strap." However, it was an interpolated number that stopped the show, "Buster Brown's Bobby Burns Brigade." It was performed with military precision by twenty-four chorus girls in Scottish costumes doing what was described as the most intricate and difficult march ever done on the stage.

After the New York run, the musical went on tour where it was extremely popular wherever it played. It was presented at the Tibbits Opera House four times, and three times at both the Calumet and Ramsdell Theatres.

> "Buster Brown" has become an annual visitor to almost every town of any importance . . . there has not been in years a musical comedy that has equaled the success of "Buster Brown." It will make the old young and the young happy. (*Coldwater Daily Reporter*, October 13, 1908)

"More of the Same"

Ballroom, lyrics by Alan and Marilyn Bergman, music by Billy Goldenberg, 1978

Two of the early musicals based on newspaper comic strips evolved into franchises, *Mutt and Jeff* and *Bringing Up Father*. In each case, the plays were centered around the same characters but in a new and different predicament, often in a new and different locale, with each new edition having a title that was a variation of the original.

Mutt and Jeff and their misadventures were first depicted on the sport pages of the *San Francisco Chronicle* in 1907. Cartoonist Bud Fisher created the strip, but eventually Al Smith took over the drawing duties and turned out the comic for nearly fifty years. *Mutt and Jeff* was syndicated in 1908 at which time it went viral and remained in syndication until 1982.

One of the by-products of the cartoon was a series of plays with songs built around the two main characters. The first in the series of *Mutt and Jeff* musicals opened in 1911. It was so successful that the franchise produced eight more adventures:

- *Mutt and Jeff at the Races*
- *Mutt and Jeff in Mexico*
- *Mutt and Jeff in Panama*
- *Mutt and Jeff in Chinatown*
- *Mutt and Jeff in the Woolly West*
- *Mutt and Jeff in College*
- *Mutt and Jeff's Wedding*
- *Mutt and Jeff—Divorced.*

The producers knew that their audience base was not in New York and, consequently, geared the shows for the road where they were very well received. During the 1912–13 season there were six *Mutt and Jeff* companies on tour. Thereafter, many subsequent variations on the show made frequent stops in Coldwater, Red Jacket, and Manistee.

FIGURE 111. *Buster Is Coming!* The show was a frequent visitor to opera houses around the country, and like *Happy Hooligan*, although the title did not change from year to year the show did. Adjustments were made to the plot and new musical numbers were added to entice an audience back to see a show that they may have seen several times before. (Publisher: U.S. Lithograph Co, Cincinnati, New York, ca. 1907. Retrieved from the Library of Congress.)

FIGURE 112. Mutt and Jeff. Together they spent their time betting on horse races and creating get-rich-quick-schemes, usually unsuccessful at both. This is the front cover of a program for the Sandusky (Ohio) Theatre production of *Mutt and Jeff–Divorced*, 1920.

The shows' scores consisted of preexisting popular songs such as "Let Me Call You Sweetheart" and "Sail On Silv'ry Moon" along with songs that reflected the current ragtime craze, such as "The Barn-Yard Rag" and "Mr. Ragtime Whip-poorwill."

Bringing Up Father had an eighty-seven-year run in the newspapers—from 1913 until 2000. The characters and storyline were created by George McManus and centered on a nouveau-riche couple, Jiggs, an Irish immigrant who had won a million dollars in the Irish Sweepstakes, and his pretentious, social-climbing, wife, Maggie. The comedy often derived from the couple's conflicting priorities: Maggie wanted to break into high society whereas Jiggs preferred to spend his time with the lowlifes down at Dinty Moore's tavern.

Jiggs and Maggie first appeared on the Broadway stage in 1914 in a musical named after the source, *Bringing Up Father*. That same year, a touring version of the Broadway production was on the road. The first touring version was so well received that the producer, Gus Hill, created over a half dozen sequels including the following:

- *Bringing Up Father Abroad*
- *Bringing Up Father in Ireland*
- *Bringing Up Father on Broadway*
- *Bringing Up Father in Gay New York*
- *Bringing Up Father on Wall Street*
- *Bringing Up Father at Home*
- *Bringing Up Father at the Seashore*
- *Bringing Up Father in Politics*

Many of the songs in the *Bringing Up Father* shows reflected the heritage of the major characters, such as "That's the Irish in Her" and "I'm Looking for a Pair of Irish Eyes," and the score also included numbers that were integral to the plot: "They'll Never Bring Up Father 'Till They Tear Down Dinty Moore's."

After World War I, a new edition of the franchise *Bringing Up Father at Home* was on tour and arrived in Coldwater on May 5, 1919. Preexisting songs by various composers had been interpolated into the action of the play, but there was one original number sung by the entire company as the Act I finale, "We're All Back from Calling on the Kaiser," which was a variation on the popular 1918 World War I song "We're All Going Calling on the Kaiser." Together they created a set of musical bookends.

"Keep the Party Going"

No Other Girl, lyrics by Bert Kalmar, music by Harry Ruby, 1924

By the 1930s, live-theatre franchises were a thing of the past. Eventually, the concept of featuring the same characters in a series of shows with different plots was taken over by radio, television, and the movies. But stage musicals based on cartoons, comic strips, and comic books have continued to attract producers, librettists, songwriters, and audiences. Examples from the past sixty years include *Li'l Abner* (1958); *It's a Bird, It's a Plane, It's Superman* (1966); *You're a Good Man, Charlie Brown* (1967); *Annie* (1977); *The Addams Family* (2010); and *Spider-Man: Turn Off the Dark* (2011).

FIGURE 113. In addition to the comic strip generating stage plays, *Bringing Up Father* also spawned nine animated silent films; three live-action, two-reel shorts; six live-action feature films; and a radio program. Here is a graphic announcing that the *Bringing Up Father* tour had come to town. (*Coldwater Daily Reporter*, October 10, 1914.)

Appendix II

NOW APPEARING AT A THEATER NEAR YOU!

Stars of the Stage

From the time they first opened their doors for business, the managers of the three facilities featured in this work were successful in engaging those performers that were considered to be A-list celebrities. Although many of the actors who appeared on the opera house stages are not household names today, in their time they were considered to be major players that could attract audiences whenever and wherever they played. On the following pages are biographies of thirteen of the most popular stars that lit up the stages of rural community opera houses during the forty-year period that embraced the last two decades of the nineteenth century through the first two decades of the twentieth.

The Actors Know that Real Life Is on the Other Side of the Footlights

The House of Mirth, by Edith Wharton, 1905

Maude Adams (1872–1953) flew around the country in 1913 as Peter Pan eight years after she had appeared as that gravity-defying youth in James M. Barrie's classic play on Broadway. Adrian, Coldwater, and Red Jacket were among her stops as Peter Pan in Michigan.

Born Maude Ewing Kiskadden in Salt Lake City, Utah, Maude Adams was the daughter of Annie Adams Kiskadden, an actress with a traveling repertory company. Maude, who went on the road with her mother, made her first stage appearance when she was nine months old. In 1878, at the age of six, she appeared at San Francisco's California Theater

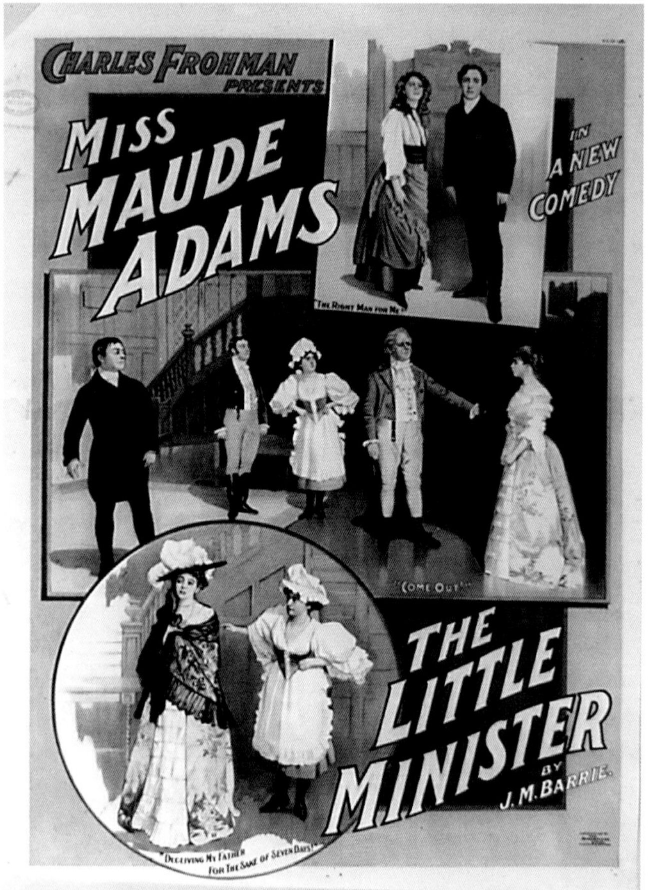

FIGURE 114. *The Little Minister* was the first production created by a theatre triumvirate that consisted of Charles Frohman, producer; James M. Barrie, playwright; and Maude Adams, actor. Together the three artists were responsible for five successful Broadway shows including *What Every Woman Knows* and *Peter Pan*. (Publisher: Strobridge Lith. Co. Cincinnati, New York, ca. 1897. Retrieved from the Library of Congress.)

in *Kit, the Arkansas Traveler* starring the original Kit, Frank Chanfrau. She played his young daughter, prekidnapping, and was billed as "Little Maude Adams."

While still a young woman, her work caught the attention of the prominent producer Charles Frohman, who put her under contract and, throughout her career produced most of the productions in which she appeared.

For some time, Frohman had tried to convince James M. Barrie to adapt his popular novel *The Little Minister* into a play. According to Maude Adams's biographers, Barrie resisted because he believed there was no actress who could play the major female character. However, when he attended a performance of *Rosemary* featuring Miss Adams, he apparently reconsidered his decision, since in 1897, with the young actress in the leading role, *The Little Minister* opened on Broadway where it played to standing-room-only audiences for three hundred performances. Maude Adams toured in the play on and off for twenty years; she brought it to the Calumet Theatre in June 1916.

After *The Little Minister* closed in 1897, she starred in a number of other works authored by Barrie, including *Peter Pan, or the Boy Who Wouldn't Grow Up*. For years, the story was that Barrie had written *Peter Pan* with Maude Adams in mind. He approached Charles Frohman about producing the play, but the producer was skeptical and dismissed it as a piece for children that did not belong on the Broadway stage. Supposedly, Barrie offered him some sort of sweet deal to produce one of his more traditional plays, *Alice-Sit-By-the-Fire*, in exchange for taking a chance on Peter, Captain Hook, and Tinker Bell. At least, that was the oft-told tale.

Both Adams's biographer, Armond Fields, and British author/screenwriter/director Andrew Birkin dispelled what may have been a theatrical urban legend. In his book *J. M. Barrie and the Lost Boys: The Real Story Behind Peter Pan*, Birkin claims that Charles Frohman was not resistant to the idea of producing the play. Conversely, he thought it would be a perfect vehicle for his professional darling, Maude Adams. It was Barrie who was resistant; he had envisioned "the boy who wouldn't grow up" being played by a boy, not by a thirty-three-year-old woman—but child labor laws prohibited a minor from performing on stage after 9:00 p.m.

Another story is recounted in Birkin's book and Armond Fields's biography *Maude Adams: Idol of American Theater, 1872–1953*. Included in both is a copy of a letter written in April 1904 by James Barrie to "My dear Maudie" in which he reveals that he has written a play, at the time titled *Peter and Wendy*, and that he wished she could play both those roles as well as that of Captain Hook. This might suggest not only that Barrie was open to the idea of a female Peter Pan but also that he was eager for that female to be Miss Adams. She read the script and told Mr. Frohman that she "was perfectly wrapped in a spell of desire to be Peter Pan himself."

But life intruded. Maude Adams had to have major surgery followed by a lengthy period of recuperation. Frohman and Barrie were eager to test adult theatergoers' reaction to a play that featured fairies, pirates, Indians, and a clock-ticking crocodile and decided to open the play in England without Maude Adams. *Peter Pan* premiered in London in December 1904.

However, in his Adams biography, author Armond Fields contends that having Peter Pan played by a woman was at the insistence of the London director, Dion Boucicault Jr., the son of *The Streets of New York* playwright, who cast his sister, Nina Boucicault, in the title role. Whoever thought of it, suggested it, insisted upon it, the tradition of Peter Pan being played by a woman was born.

The next year, Maude Adams played the role for over two hundred performances in New York and then took it on an extended tour traveling in a $30,000 railroad car. In addition to the American premiere, she also starred in three Broadway revivals of the play and took it on several more cross-country tours.

Prior to Adams's August 30, 1913, performance at the Croswell Opera House, the *Adrian Daily Telegram* pronounced:

> Maude Adams' portrayal of Peter . . . is credited with being one of the most strikingly beautiful impersonations of youth that is to be, or has been seen in the theater.

In addition to the character of Peter Pan created by Barrie, Adams played other characters created by other playwrights as well: Juliet in *Romeo and Juliet*, Portia in *The Merchant of Venice*, and Joan of Arc in *The Maid of Orleans*, to name a few. She became the most financially successful performer of her era with an estimated annual income of over a million dollars or the current equivalent of over twenty-two million dollars a year.

Her last performance on Broadway was in another play by James M. Barrie, *A Kiss for Cinderella* that opened on Christmas Day in 1916. Next, she spent three years at the General Electric Company in Schenectady, New York, where she assisted in the development of a new lighting system for the stage. From 1937 to 1943, she taught acting at Stephens College in Missouri.

At various periods in her life, she found it necessary to spend time at the Cenacle of St. Regis that provided a retreat for people in need of rest and spiritual renewal. She donated her estate at Lake Ronkonkoma, New York, to the Sisters of St. Regis and is buried on that property alongside Louise

FIGURE 115. Not only did Maude Adams play the leading role in *Peter Pan*, she also personally commissioned an artist with whom she allegedly co-designed her costume that consisted of tights and tunic cut from a camouflage-like patterned fabric adorned at the neck by what has become a fashion classic, the Peter Pan collar. (Photographer: Otto Sarony Co., ca. 1905. Photography Collection, the Miriam and Ira D. Wallach Division of Art, Prints, and Photographs, the New York Public Library, Astor, Lenox, and Tilden Foundations.)

FIGURE 116. During her long career, international star Sarah Bernhardt dominated the world stage; she was often referred to as "the world's greatest living actress." Over a thirty-six-year period, she toured America nine times; the last six were advertised as farewell tours. (Photographer unknown, ca. 1880. Retrieved from the Library of Congress.)

Boynton, who had been her companion for over forty-five years.

Sarah Bernhardt (1844–1923) was born in Paris as Henriette-Rosine Bernardt. She studied acting at the famous Comédie-Française where she first appeared on the stage in 1862 at the age of eighteen. She then left France for Belgium where she became the mistress of Henri, prince de Ligne, with whom she had a son.

She returned to the stage in 1866, acting first in France and then on stages throughout Europe. Her American debut in 1880 took place at the Booth Theatre in New York City followed by an extensive thirty-one-city tour. In addition to performing in North America and Europe, during her career Bernhardt also played in South America, Russia, Egypt, Australia, and Hawaii, which resulted in her being referred to as "the most famous actress the world has ever known."

Between 1880 and 1916, Bernhardt toured this country nine times performing roles from her vast repertoire of plays that included, among many others, *Phedre*, *La Tosca*, *Jeanne d'Arc*, and, of course, *La Dame aux Camelias* (aka *Camille*). She was also famous for assuming male characters, such as the son of Napoleon in *L'Aiglon*; the male lover, Pelleas, in Maeterlinck's *Pelleas et Melisande*; and Hamlet. The plays in which Bernhardt starred with her French company were performed in their native language, but audiences responded favorably whether or not they understood a word of the dialogue.

> Madame Bernhardt is the only French artist whoever made money in America, but the truth is that the American public did not go to see Sarah Bernhardt act, but to see Sarah Bernhardt. To see the woman who sleeps in a coffin and has pet snakes and does many other things that are not pleasant to mention in a Sunday newspaper. The truth is that in a sneaking way Americans admire Madame Bernhardt's personality. ("Between the Acts," *Nebraska State Journal*, April 8, 1894)

In 1911 "the Divine Sarah" ventured all the way to Michigan's Upper Peninsula on one of her many "Farewell, America" tours to perform *Camille* at the Calumet Theatre. She arrived in Red Jacket by private railroad car with many attendants.

As Bernhardt was in the country's most productive copper mining region, she requested to be taken down one of the mines. The story is that she met with some resistance, as a woman in a mine was believed to bring bad luck. She apparently insisted, and after all, she was "the most famous actress the world has ever known," so the descent of the divine was arranged. She arrived at the site shortly after 2:00 p.m. wearing a big-brimmed purple hat and a full-length seal skin coat. On June 1, 1911, the *Calumet Evening News* printed a full report of the adventure under the headline "Divine Sarah Goes Down Hancock Mine":

> The "greatest living actress" entered into the spirit of the lark. . . . A miner's "shiner" which is the official name for the lamp, was perched jauntily in her chapeau, and she announced herself in readiness. "But your furs, Madame." exclaimed Dr Scallon, who acted in the role of interpreter, "Your coat will be ruined." "Well," replied the madame, "so much the worse for the coat." A drop of

> fifteen hundred feet at dizzying speed brought the party to one of the main levels, and here Madame Bernhardt was treated to a journey of a mile on the underground electric tramway. When the return to the cage was made Madame Bernhardt insisted upon going to the bottom. "When I see the beginning of a thing I like to see the end," she declared with a girlish laugh. Another plum-met-like fall of 1,250 feet brought the cage to the bottom of the mine. This was the first time in her life however, that she has been down a mine and in commenting upon the trip she expressed herself as greatly delighted with the experience, which she declared to be one of the most enjoyable in her career.

Madame Bernhardt was a little less than truthful if she did say, as reported, that this was the first time she had been down a mine. In 1886, twenty-five years before coming to the Copper Country, she was on tour in South America. In a letter she wrote to her son from Chile she related an earlier mine experience:

> After lunch . . . we were transported to the mines in a freight car decorated with ribbons, flowers, and French flags. When we arrived, a motley crowd of miners, both women and men, were waiting for us. The two-hundred-foot descent into the underground is very dramatic.

The trip down the Hancock mine was not a maiden voyage for "the Divine Sarah," as she would have had it believed. Apparently, she was known for being as creative off stage as she was on stage when it came to dealing with reality.

FIGURE 117. Sarah Bernhardt in the last act of *Camille*. The actress played the role of the doomed young courtesan throughout her career—well into her sixties. (Photographer unknown, 1913. Retrieved from the Library of Congress.)

Her good friend, author Alexandre Dumas, *fils*, described her as an inveterate liar. When he was commenting on her extremely thin figure, he reportedly said, "You know, she's such a liar, she may even be fat!"

Ada Gray (1834–1902) enjoyed great popularity throughout the country, especially as Lady Isabel in the much produced melodrama *East Lynne*. She also performed many other roles both classical and contemporary; however, it was as Lady Isabel that she achieved her greatest success. She was first seen in Michigan playing that role at the Adrian Union Hall in 1867. During her career, she appeared at the Tibbits Opera House three times, twice in *East Lynne*.

In the review of *East Lynne*, a Coldwater journalist revealed his admiration for her performance:

FIGURE 118. Ada Gray began acting at an early age and played Juliet opposite John Wilkes Booth's Romeo in Rochester, New York, when she was fifteen. (Photographer and date unknown. Billy Rose Theatre Division, the New York Public Library for the Performing Arts, Astor, Lenox, and Tilden Foundations.)

> her strong portrayal of the rage and blindness of the jealous wife and the frenzy of the deserted and broken hearted mother . . . was most touching and drew tears from eyes that seldom weep. (*Courier*, January 23, 1884)

Two months prior to her 1884 appearance in Coldwater, a needlework rendering of her portrait was displayed in the window of a local store. The *Coldwater Republican* reported, "It is a remarkable piece of work and should be viewed by all."

Miss Gray was back in Coldwater as Lady Isabel two seasons later.

> the great emotional actress, Miss Ada Gray, returns to our city, and will appear . . . in the beautiful drama, "East Lynne." Miss Gray has been one of the most successful stars on the stage, crowded houses greeting her everywhere. (*Courier*, December 12, 1886)

It is estimated that during her career she played Lady Isabel over two thousand times throughout the United States. Of her New York appearance in *East Lynne* at Niblo's Garden Theatre the *Dramatic News* said, "No performance of so high an order has lately been given at Niblo's."

She was married twice, first to her manager and after his death to her leading man, British actor Charles F. Tingay. From her obituary published in the *New York Times*:

> Ada Gray, who won fame as Lady Isabel in "East Lynne" died on Wednesday . . . she was very popular with theatergoers, and became possessed of a considerable fortune. In various ways, all of her money was lost, and she became absolutely destitute. . . . Her marriage to Mr. Tingay estranged her from her family, and her later years were more or less unhappy.

FIGURE 119. Francesca Janauschek was born in Prague where, at the age of sixteen, she made her stage debut at the Royal Theatre. Two years later she was hired by the State Theatre in Frankfurt and was that company's leading actress for ten years. By the time she came to the United States she was an internationally acclaimed tragedienne. (Photographer and date unknown. Music Division, the New York Public Library. New York Public Library Digital Collections.)

Francesca "Fanny" Janauschek (1829–1904) was a formidable character actress whose initial appearance in this country was as Medea in 1867. In that production, she performed her role in German whereas the other cast members spoke in English. The following year she appeared opposite

Edwin Booth in *Macbeth*, and again, Janauschek spoke in German and Booth spoke in English. She took a yearlong hiatus from the stage to learn English, and by 1870 Madame Janauschek was back on the boards. For the next thirty years, she worked almost exclusively in America where she not only appeared in New York but also toured the country.

Janauschek was one of the last "grand tragediennes" that employed the acting style the sobriquet implies. Because of her physical stature, strong voice, and emotional power, she was well suited to play tragic characters such as Medea and Lady Macbeth. Toward the end of her career she all but abandoned Shakespeare and the classics to perform in melodramas. She added to her repertoire of strong characters Meg Merrilies, the wizened gypsy fortuneteller introduced by Sir Walter Scott in his 1815 novel, *Guy Mannering*. The stage adaptation was by Daniel Terry.

An item in the January 1, 1888, issue of the *Coldwater Republican* announced that "Manager Klock has closed an engagement with the renowned actress Janauscheck." At the time, it was believed that to attract an artist as celebrated as Francesca Janauschek to Coldwater was an incredible coup. According to the review of her Tibbits Opera House 1888 debut as Meg Merrilies, Janauschek delivered the goods: "she did not in the least disappoint expectation."

Two years later, on her farewell tour, she returned to Coldwater as Lady Macbeth. Prior to her arrival, the newspaper printed the review from the *Philadelphia Record* where she had recently appeared in the Scottish play.

> During the past week the greatest living of tragediennes has been playing an engagement in this city, which has been heralded as Janauschek's farewell to the stage. Mme. Janauschek has never manifested a fuller and more complete grasp of the resources of her art than during her engagement at the Opera House.

FIGURE 120. Late in her career, Janauschek added roles in contemporary plays to her repertoire of strong female characters. On this poster she is immortalized in the persona of mad Meg Merrilles in *Guy Mannering*. (Publisher: Courier Lith. Company, Buffalo, N.Y., 1880. Retrieved from the Library of Congress)

A stroke in 1900 left her paralyzed and partially blind. As she was bankrupt at the time of her death four years

FIGURE 121. When on tour, Thomas W. Keene was especially well received in small rural communities where he offered theatregoers a varied program; they could see him in *Macbeth* one night and in *Ten Nights in a Bar Room* the next. (Photographer unknown, ca. 1880. Billy Rose Theatre Division, the New York Public Library for the Performing Arts, Astor, Lenox, and Tilden Foundations.)

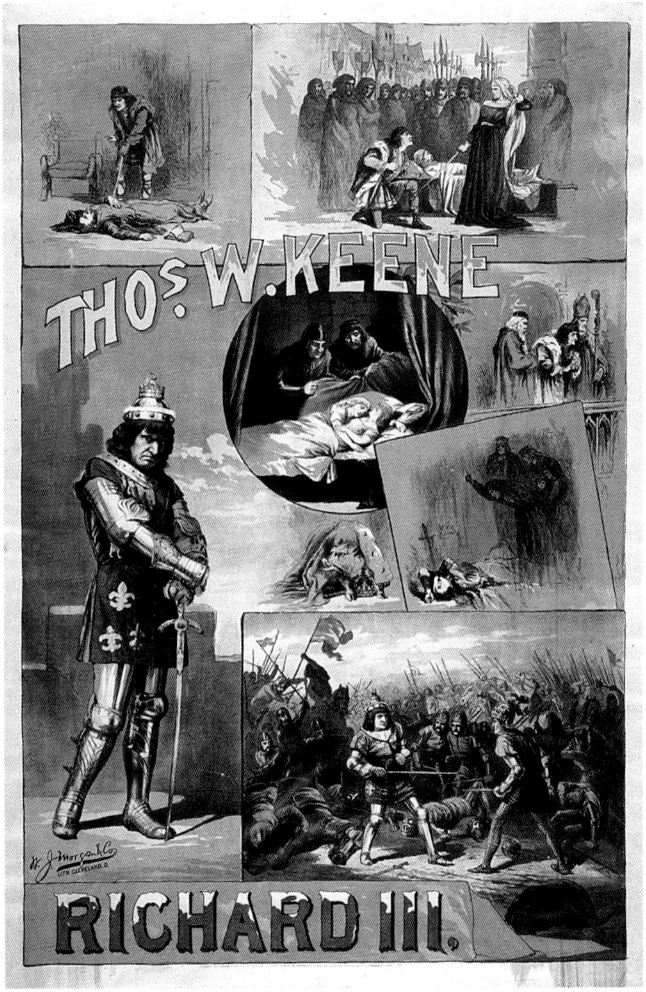

FIGURE 122. Reviewers were often critical of Thomas W. Keene's bombastic acting style but agreed that *Richard III* was his masterpiece. This poster, which promotes his performance as the manipulative despot, is one of a series that includes Keene as Othello and Keene as Macbeth. (Publisher: W. J. Morgan & Co., Cleveland, Ohio, ca. 1884. Retrieved from the Library of Congress.)

later, fellow actors raised the money to have her buried in a Brooklyn, New York, cemetery.

Thomas W. Keene (1840–98), born Thomas R. Eagleson in New York City, was cast as Brutus's servant, Lucius, in a professional production of *Julius Caesar* at the age of sixteen. For a short time, he was a member of an acting company where he primarily appeared in melodramas. There, he adopted a broad, bombastic performance style that he employed throughout his career—long after it had gone out of fashion. From 1865 to 1867, Keene worked at the Theatre Comique in Cincinnati, Ohio, where he appeared in both melodramas and classical plays. It was there that he first attempted the role of Richard III that was to become a staple in his repertoire.

Keene traveled to England in 1870 where he performed in London for four years. Soon after he returned to America, he decided that it might be to his advantage to play in smaller towns across the country where he could take on the major roles that had not been offered to him in Boston, Philadelphia, or New York City. The plan worked! He was successful in creating a favorable reputation and a loyal following outside of East Coast metropolitan venues.

Many critics considered his portrayal of Richard III to have been his greatest triumph. He played the ruthless king everywhere from Cincinnati to San Francisco, performing in anything from an opera house to a saloon. In 1883, he made his Tibbits debut in his most celebrated role.

> Manager Tibbits received a postal on Wednesday from Charley Starr in Three Rivers saying that a special car from that village . . . would arrive here on Monday loaded with people to hear Tom Keene in "Richard III" that evening. (*Courier*, April 7, 1883)

Both of the Coldwater newspapers had high praise for his performance. The *Courier* reported that "the manner in which he played the crafty, cunning, villainous . . . Richard III, won for him enthusiastic applause." The *Coldwater Republican* critic remarked that "Mr. Keene's performance was certainly a finished one and justly entitles him to the position which he occupies in the front rank."

Between 1885 and 1896, he made three stops in Coldwater where he appeared as a variety of Shakespearean characters; in May 1885, it was in a production of *Macbeth*. The *Courier* reviewer had a positive response: "Tom Keene made his second appearance in this city last evening . . . and gave a grand rendition of *Macbeth*." The *Coldwater Republican* critic was less impressed; his review was brief and to the point: "Thomas Keene played to a large audience in *Macbeth* . . . but failed to give as good satisfaction as on his previous visit."

Keene made his third and last appearance in Coldwater in December 1896, thirteen years after his first and two years before his death.

> Great anticipation had centered on Keene, who is an actor of the legitimate school of tragedy, but after witnessing his efforts in "Julius Caesar," it must be said; though in all kindness and with a feeling akin to pity, that age has withered the laurels he gathered twenty years ago. (*Courier*, December 12, 1896)

In his obituary, the *New York Times* included an analysis of his acting:

> his best work was not free from crudity and rawness, and some of the worst defects of an exaggerated style marred everything he did. But he was earnest and intelligent and strove for improvement. The loss of such an actor . . . is not to be passed over lightly.

Roselle Knott (1863–1948) was a Canada-born actress who had considerable success working in the United States. She starred on Broadway in the 1900 production of *Quo Vadis* playing Lygia, the Christian girl who is used as lion bait in the show's dramatic climax. During her career she became a major star on the road where she performed with Richard Mansfield in *A Parisian Romance* and with James O'Neill in *The Three Musketeers*. Eventually, she established her own touring company and, as an actor-manager, was known as an actress with the ability to create compelling characters and as a producer for her attention to detail. Between 1903 and 1907, she performed in Coldwater, Red Jacket, and Manistee several times in each city.

First, she toured with the play *When Knighthood Was in Flower* in the role that previously had been performed exclusively by one of America's most revered leading ladies, Julia Marlowe. Indeed, the press referred to Roselle Knott as "the Julia Marlowe of the West."

> Roselle Knott is an actress who is extremely well known throughout the country, better in fact than she is in New York City. She has been very successful in playing roles which Julia Marlowe has created . . . appearing in parts of the country where Miss Marlowe's tour did not take her. (*Burr McIntosh Monthly*, August 1905)

Miss Knott obviously took over the role with Miss Marlowe's blessing as the touring production of *When*

FIGURE 123. Roselle Knott toured the Midwest with great success. Reportedly, she was at the forefront of those who experimented with new cosmetic techniques. That may account for the presses' assessment that at the age of forty, the mother of a teenage daughter, she still appeared to be a "youthful beauty." (Photographer unknown, ca. 1903. Billy Rose Theatre Division, the New York Public Library for the Performing Arts, Astor, Lenox, and Tilden Foundations.)

FIGURE 124. "The Signal," a scene from a 1905 touring production of *When Knighthood Was in Flower* with Roselle Knott, as Mary Tudor. The Disney Studio produced a film adaptation of the play titled *The Sword and the Rose* starring Glynis Johns and Richard Todd in 1953. (Publisher: U.S. Lithograph Co., Cincinnati. N.Y. Retrieved from the Library of Congress.)

Knighthood Was in Flower was advertised as "Julia Marlowe's Original, Complete $20,000 New York Criterion Theatre Production . . . Gorgeous Costumes and Massive Scenic Effects."

In 1898, University of Michigan graduate Charles Major wrote the novel *When Knighthood Was in Flower* under the pseudonym Edwin Caskoden. It was adapted for the stage in 1901 by Paul Kester and tells the story of Mary Tudor, the young sister of Henry VIII, who is in love with a commoner, Charles Brandon. For political reasons, her brother, the king, demands that she marry the elderly French monarch, Louis XII. Henry uses as leverage the threat that if she refuses he will have Brandon, who has been framed for murder, beheaded. To save her lover, Mary acquiesces and marries King Louis who shortly thereafter dies. Mary, disguised as a boy, aids Brandon in his escape from imprisonment, and they elope; Henry accepts the marriage, and everyone lives happily ever after—except for one or two of Henry's wives.

Julia Marlowe starred in the original Broadway production in 1901, took the show on tour to large metropolitan areas, and brought it back to Broadway in 1904. Roselle Knott performed *When Knighthood Was in Flower* in the touring production that played in smaller towns in rural areas. When she appeared in the play at the Ramsdell Theatre in 1906, an article in the *Manistee Daily News* revealed that the playwright had not written the role of Mary Tudor for Julia Marlowe, but with Roselle Knott in mind.

Perhaps an equally apt sobriquet for Miss Knott would have been "the Ethel Barrymore of the West" as included in her touring repertory were two plays with leading characters that Miss Barrymore had originated in New York and Miss

Knott performed in Michigan: *Cousin Kate* and James M. Barrie's *Alice-Sit-By-the-Fire*.

By 1913, the end was in sight for star-propelled touring productions, and Roselle Knott disbanded her company.

Richard Mansfield (1854–1907) was considered to be "America's leading actor." He appeared in Red Jacket for one night only in his "direct from Broadway" success, Booth Tarkington's *Beaucaire*. It was quite a coup, as Mr. Mansfield seldom performed outside of New York, Boston, Chicago, and San Francisco. As good fortune would have it, he had three days open between his Chicago engagement and his scheduled appearance in California that made it possible for him to play in Duluth, Marquette, and Red Jacket before heading farther west.

His arrival in Red Jacket created great excitement, as reported in the newspaper on June 21, 1902:

> From now on until Tuesday, June 24, when Richard Mansfield appears at the Calumet theatre, things will be busy around there. . . . A dressing room will be built for the celebrated artist's use. Mansfield will arrive by special train. . . . The train consists of Mansfield's own private car; two sleepers for the sixty people in the company; and five baggage cars of scenery, baggage, crates of furniture, horses and other paraphernalia.

Born on an island in the North Sea to a Russian opera singer and a British merchant, Richard Mansfield attended school in Germany and then London where he studied art. In that his career as a painter afforded him little financial reward, he turned to something potentially more lucrative—acting! In 1879, he began performing with the D'Oyly Carte Opera Company in the comic works of Gilbert and Sullivan. He continued performing in comic operas until 1883 when he garnered attention performing his breakthrough role in *A Parisian Romance*.

He was recognized as a very versatile actor; his repertoire of characters included Cyrano de Bergerac, Beau Brummell, Richard III, and the dual personalities of Dr. Jekyll and Mr. Hyde. In 1894, Mansfield produced and starred in George Bernard Shaw's *Arms and the Man*, the first play by Shaw to be presented in America. As a producer, he was known for his lavish productions and his meticulous attention to detail.

Beginning in 1900, he had a string of Broadway hits including *The Scarlet Letter* and Moliere's *The Misanthrope*. His last Broadway appearance was in the title role of Ibsen's *Peer Gynt*.

According to an article printed in the *Manistee Daily News* at the time of his death in 1907, Mansfield had a reputation for being unapproachable and condescending:

> No monarch ever appeared more haughty than he in his attitude toward the ordinary people. Europe has half a dozen kings more easy to approach than was this King Richard of the stage.

His obituary in the *New York Times* pronounced: "He was the greatest actor of his hour, and one of the greatest of all times."

Robert Bruce Mantell (1854–1928) was born in Scotland, raised in Ireland, but spent most of his adult life in America. Drawn to the theatre at an early age, he declared

FIGURE 125. Storms's *Players Blue Book* of 1901 claimed that Richard Mansfield "ranks in America as does Sir Henry Irving in England." Mansfield was generally considered to be one of the greatest actors of his time. He was known for his versatility on stage and his arrogance off stage. (Photographer and date unknown. Billy Rose Theatre Division, the New York Public Library for the Performing Arts, Astor, Lenox, and Tilden Foundations)

his intention to pursue a career as an actor. His mother, opposed to the idea of her son on the stage, insisted that he not use the family name. Consequently, in 1876, he made his stage debut billed as Robert Hudson. Perhaps to further avoid creating any embarrassment for his family, he decided to pursue his career in America. At the age of twenty-four, using his true last name, Mantell, he joined Madame Helena Modjeska on a tour of the United States playing secondary roles. The following five years, he worked with a company in England and then decided to try America again where he received great recognition when performing in *Fedora*. His status was elevated from supporting player to leading man.

In her September 1907 article titled "The Alimony Poor" with the subtitle, "Noted Men with from One to Six Ex-Wives Who Have Found the Marrying Habit to be Debilitating to the Pocketbook," Mary C. Francis reported that one evening a process server forced his way into Mantell's dressing room with alimony demands and nonsupport arrest warrants on behalf of his wife, the mother of his two sons. At that point, the actor made the decision that he had sufficient drawing power to tour America with his own company and that evacuating the city would be prudent. He canceled his upcoming New York appearance, began a series of tours throughout the country, and in order to avoid arrest, did not appear in New York again for nearly a decade.

According to Ms. Francis, his personal life was no less fraught with drama on the road than it had been in New York. While Mantell was performing in Cincinnati with his leading lady, Charlotte Behrens, who was his current mistress, her irate husband threatened to shoot the actor on sight. That didn't happen, but immediately after she divorced her jealous spouse, Miss Behrens became the second of four Mrs. Mantells.

For a number of years, Mantell toured the country performing in a variety of plays including *Monbars*, an English adaptation of a French play that proved to be a profitable vehicle for him. It is another variation on the "Robin Hood" story of an outsider doing good by unconventional and unlawful means. In this version of the traditional scenario, the hero is a pirate. He and his crew plunder fortunes from British vessels in service to their country, France. Coldwater audiences had their first opportunity to see him in that play in 1889.

> Mantell is a strong actor and "Monbars" . . . gives admirable opportunity to bring out the full capacity of Mantell's powers as an actor. His support is in some respects quite good while in others it is not worth mentioning. (*Coldwater Republican*, April 19, 1889)

Five years later, he brought *Monbars* back to the Tibbits Opera House stage, and in 1899 he returned with a new vehicle, *Secret Warrant*.

> Those who had seen the gifted Robert Mantell in "Monbars" came with high expectations that were not disappointed, while those who had never seen him were given a treat they will hope to see repeated. (*Courier and Republican*, February 10, 1899)

Later the same year he appeared in *The Dagger and the Cross* that he performed again in 1903, his fifth and final appearance in Coldwater. On his tours, in addition to playing heroes in melodramas, he also portrayed Hamlet, Macbeth, Othello, and other Shakespearean characters.

Once his legal problems were settled, he returned to New York where he appeared in more than seventy-five productions between 1900 and 1923. He specialized in Shakespearean tragedies including *King Lear*, which was considered to be his greatest triumph. When he retired from the stage, he began a second career in films. Over a nine-year period, he made seven feature films and one short that consisted of scenes from *Monbars*.

Helena Modjeska (1840–1909) was the first lady of the Polish National Theater before she immigrated to the United States. Born Helena Opid in Krakow, Poland, she began her stage career in 1861, and by 1865 she was performing in Warsaw where she became established as a star.

Primarily for political reasons, in 1876 she and her second husband, Count Bozenta, along with several other dissident artists, fled Poland. They bought a ranch near Anaheim, California, with the intention of creating an ideal agricultural colony or commune. Modjeska's original idea was to forsake her "life upon the wicked stage" in order to be "home, home on the range." But because of the drought and depression of 1877 and because none of the group had any previous farming or ranching experience, they were forced to abandon the plan.

Modjeska made the decision to return to the stage in this country, and to that end, she quickly achieved a command of English. Her American debut took place in San Francisco in 1877; she then played New York.

The actress spent most of her career touring America

FIGURE 126. Until late in his career, Robert B. Mantell performed more often on tour than in major theatre centers. This poster advertising his 1904 tour indicates the range of his repertoire, "classic and romantic productions." He was the great-uncle of actress Angela Lansbury. (Publisher: J. Ottmann Lith. Co., N.Y. Retrieved from the Library of Congress Prints and Photographs Division.)

FIGURE 127. "Among the greatest celebrities of the stage, few if any have made greater artistic success than Helena Modjeska." So stated Storms, the author of *The Players Blue Book* in 1901. Despite her Polish accent, Madame Modjeska was considered the premier interpreter of Shakespeare's female characters. (Photographer and date unknown. Billy Rose Theatre Division, the New York Public Library for the Performing Arts, Astor, Lenox, and Tilden Foundations.)

where every performance was a major event. Critics and fellow thespians praised her refinement, graceful figure, sympathetic voice, and handsome dress.

In addition to the women who inhabited the plays by the Bard, her repertoire of characters included Camille, Mary Stuart, Marie Antoinette, and Lady Isabel in *East Lynne*. Audiences in Louisville, Kentucky, were the first in the country to be introduced to Nora in Henrik Ibsen's *A Doll's House* when, in 1883, Modjeska produced and starred in the drama there.

It was not unusual for a popular, well-known performer to orchestrate a number of farewell tours. In 1894, Modjeska announced her intention to retire, which elicited the following comment from the *Nebraska State Journal*:

> It has been announced that Madame Modjeska will retire from the stage next year . . . we can ill afford to lose that great artist who has done more to raise the standard of [the] American stage than any other actress who ever lived.

Indeed, Modjeska did not retire in 1895 as announced. She was still going strong in 1900 when she first toured Michigan. The *Detroit News* reported, "Modjeska is no longer young, but she is still great."

In 1905, at the age of sixty-five, she embarked on another national tour that took her back to Red Jacket to perform the title role in *Mary Stuart*. Five years earlier, she had played the same role as well as Lady Macbeth at the Calumet Theatre. The press releases informed readers that this was her "Farewell America Tour." The farewell turned out to be a long goodbye, as she was still touring two years later.

When she was not on tour, she resided in California—she was an adopted daughter of the Golden West. After her death, the North Peak of Saddleback Mountain was named Modjeska Peak, and the area in which she lived in now called Modjeska Canyon. She is buried in Krakow where the city theater is named in her honor.

Hortense Rhea (1843–99) first performed at the Tibbits Opera House in *Yvonne* in 1884 where the local press expressed its enthusiasm for the actress and the play.

> The great event of the season at Tibbits Opera House . . . is the engagement of the great French society star Rhea in a new powerful five-act drama, "Yvonne." (*Coldwater Republican*, September 16, 1884)

Her appeal was so great that special passenger trains transported residents from communities east of Coldwater back and forth so that they could attend her performance. Additional arrangements were made so that patrons could be brought from the west on a freight train. The result was that the house was sold out for Mlle. Rhea's appearance.

Born in Brussels to French parents, Hortense Barbe Loret, stage name Rhea, was orphaned early in her life and was sent to a convent school in France. After she completed her education, at the suggestion of a mentor, she decided to pursue an acting career. To that end, she studied at the Conservatoire de Paris and in 1871 was seen in Brussels on the stage for the first time. She then toured throughout Europe until she was invited to join the company at the French Imperial Theatre in Paris. Later, by special invitation from Tsar Alexander II, she appeared at the Russian Theatre in St. Petersburg. Five months into the residency, it ended abruptly when the tsar was assassinated.

She next went to London, and after attaining a command of English, she opened there in *Much Ado About Nothing* in 1881. The *London Times* critic wrote: "There was much that was clever in Mlle. Rhea's Beatrice, very much that was pretty and charming. Mlle. Rhea is French to the fingertips." Other reviewers were less enthusiastic stating that "as an impersonation of Beatrice, her performance . . . leaves something to desire." After her London debut, she came to America where she performed for the next eight years.

Rhea was more successful playing in towns outside of New York City where, with her charm and beauty, her French accent, and her exquisite costumes, she was a very attractive novelty to American regional audiences. At some theaters where she performed, ticket buyers were rewarded with her photograph, her autograph, her biography, and a collection of her poems.

In 1888, Rhea brought her production of *Much Ado About Nothing* to Coldwater. For the Shakespearean comedy, she had her gowns created by the House of Worth in Paris. There were those critics who complained about her thick French accent, especially when she was performing Shakespeare, but they always gave her couture costumes a rave review. When she performed in Indiana, the *Lafayette Times* exclaimed, "Her costumes were the most magnificent ever seen upon our stage."

In addition to *Much Ado About Nothing*, other plays she performed on tour were *The School for Scandal*; *Camille*; *The Queen of Sheba*; and *Josephine, Empress of France* in which her French accent was not a liability. The critics wrote of her beauty and grace and stated that her acting ability was "rarely equaled."

Rhea had planned to tour America in 1898 in a series of Shakespearean plays. Unfortunately, the tour never materialized as her health began to fail; she returned to France where she resided until her death.

FIGURE 128. The French actress Hortense Rhea, who was a major attraction when she toured the Midwest, was known for wearing couture gowns that were made for her in Paris. (Publisher: Courier Litho. Co., Buffalo, N.Y., ca. 1881. Retrieved from the Library of Congress.)

FIGURE 129. Versatile actor Otis Skinner played everything from the introspective prince Hamlet to the extroverted poet Hajj in *Kismet*. This poster promotes one of his many national tours. (Publisher: Courier Litho. Co., Buffalo, N.Y., ca. 1899. Retrieved from the Library of Congress.)

Otis Skinner (1858–1942) starred in twenty-five Broadway productions including *Francesca da Rimini*, which he brought to the Calumet Theatre in 1901.

Skinner, the son of a minister, was born in Cambridge, Massachusetts. When he decided to pursue an acting career, his father not only approved of his son's choice but also arranged for him to meet a theatre producer. That meeting launched his career, and in 1877 he made his stage debut at the Philadelphia Museum wearing blackface and playing an elderly servant in a play titled *Woodleigh*.

By the time he was thirty, he was performing significant secondary roles on tour with Edwin Booth and Helena Modjeska. After the death of Booth, Skinner assumed the leading roles opposite Modjeska. He attained star status by the mid-1890s, when he played Hamlet to great acclaim in Chicago.

He was considered to be one of the most versatile actors of his time and successfully played a wide range of characters in a wide range of plays from contemporary comedies to Shakespearean tragedies. During his fifty-year career in New York and on tour, he performed over three hundred roles including Richard III, Romeo, Falstaff in *Henry IV, Part I* and *The Merry Wives of Windsor*, as well as Shylock opposite Maude Adams as Portia in *The Merchant of Venice*.

His signature role was not from Shakespeare but something more exotic—Hajj, the beggar-poet, in *Kismet*. He first played that character on Broadway in 1911, then on tour for twenty years as well as in two film versions made in 1920 and 1930.

After his first performance at the Calumet Theatre,

he returned three times but never in *Kismet*. Instead, he performed in other less well-remembered plays. His last New York appearance in a major role was as Uncle Tom in the 1933 revival of *Uncle Tom's Cabin*. Coming full circle, he began and ended his career wearing blackface makeup.

Eva Tanguay (1878–1947) made her first Broadway appearance in 1898 at the age of twenty. Soon, she was performing as a headliner in vaudeville, and although she took an occasional hiatus to appear in the *Ziegfeld Follies* or a musical comedy, she always returned to the two-a-day variety show.

As a performer, she was known for her wildly imaginative, one-of-a-kind costumes. One of her more scandalous outfits was fashioned after women's undergarments of the period—corset and pantaloons—fabricated in theatrical materials and covered with spangles.

Her rowdy, energetic performance style was described as "cyclonic." Prior to her appearance at the Ramsdell Theatre in 1907, the *Manistee Daily News* prepared its readers for the whirlwind that was about to descend upon them: "She is the essence of nerves and action, ceaseless and tireless."

Because of the popularity of her signature song, "I Don't Care" (lyrics by Jean Lenox, music by Harry O. Sutton), that she introduced in 1905, she was known as the "I Don't Care Girl," which was a particularly appropriate moniker for her.

I don't care, I don't care,
What they may think of me.
I'm happy go lucky,
Men say I am plucky,
So jolly and care free.

In addition to "I Don't Care," which she often sang as an encore at the end of her performance, she was also famous for singing songs filled with double entendres: "I Want Someone to Go Wild with Me," "It's All Been Done Before, but Not the Way I Do It," and "Go as Far as You Like." Her voice ranged from a squeaky giggle to a brassy belt and was compared to the wail of a prehistoric creature.

Her offstage antics were as outrageous as those she performed on stage. She paid for numerous advertisements promoting herself and released stories recounting her alleged adventures including an attempted kidnapping. She had several well-publicized affairs and was married three times; one was real, two were bogus. The first marriage was legitimate; the next was a mock wedding to famous female impersonator Julian Ellinge—he dressed as the bride and, in the role of the groom, she wore men's formal attire—and the last was to her piano accompanist, twenty-six years her junior, which was done as a publicity stunt and was quickly annulled.

Eva Tanguay appeared at the Calumet Theatre three times, the first in the year the playhouse opened in a play with songs titled *Who Is Who*. She brought that play back to Red Jacket the following season. In 1907, she appeared at both the Calumet and Ramsdell Theatres in *A Good Fellow*. Chances are that at the end of each performance she regaled the audience with her squeaky-voiced rendition of "I Don't Care."

It was reported that she lost two million dollars in the 1929 stock market crash. By the end of her career, she suffered from arthritis and diminishing eyesight and was nearly destitute.

FIGURE 130. Eva Tanguay was the highest paid vaudeville performer of her time and "was famous not only for the sums she made but for those she spent. Her bill for gloves and hose alone was one thousand dollars a month. She dressed and lived in a grand manner, giving away her money freely." Sophie Tucker, *Some of These Days*, 1945. (Photographer unknown, ca. 1900. Billy Rose Theatre Division, the New York Public Library for the Performing Arts, Astor, Lenox, and Tilden Foundations.)

Walker Whiteside (1869–1942) had great success performing on Broadway, in London, and throughout the United States. He was particularly popular in the Midwest where audiences considered him "one of their own." He was born in Indiana, raised in Illinois, and launched his career by touring the Midwest for nine years with various Shakespearean companies.

When the Whiteside family moved to the Chicago area, Walker, still in his teens, began to study acting at the Dramatic Conservatory of Chicago. There he played many of Shakespeare's tragic characters who were well beyond his age with great success: Othello, Shylock, and King Lear.

In 1884, at the age of fifteen, he entered the world of professional theatre at Chicago's Grand Opera House in a production of *Richard III*. In 1893 Whiteside first appeared in New York City at the Union Square Theatre playing Richelieu and Hamlet. Eventually, he traded in his Shakespearean costumes for more contemporary clothes. As ticket buyers became less interested in the classics and, instead, flocked to contemporary comedies, period romances, and tales of the exotic, Whiteside followed the trend by directing and acting in more commercial fare.

His first contemporary hit was the 1909 drama *The Melting Pot* in which he played a Russian Jew whose family had been killed in a pogrom. The young immigrant composes a successful "American Symphony," a work that necessitates a mix of instruments working together in harmony that is his metaphor for America, the melting pot. Whiteside performed the role on Broadway, on tour, in London, and, subsequently, on film. It was followed by several other major stage successes including a period romance, *The Royal Box*, that in addition to playing the leading role, he produced and directed.

We Are King, which he also produced and directed, was a personal triumph for him, as he assumed two very different characters, a roving journalist and the tyrannical King of Mahnburg. The plot was not new: a commoner happens to resemble a royal personage, which leads to many complications and mistaken identities.

For most of his career, he alternated appearances on Broadway with extended tours across the country. While he performed in other Michigan venues, he did more productions at the Calumet Theatre than in all of the others combined. All told, he was seen at the playhouse twelve times between 1900 and 1916, ten times live and two times in the film version of his Broadway success *The Melting Pot*.

> In the time that Mr. Whiteside has played before the people of this city he has put on quite a variety of productions from tragedy to comedy and has shown himself capable of handling any part with an aptness that is truly becoming a star. (*Copper Country Evening News*, January 19, 1904)

In several shows with plots involving foreign intrigue, he played exotic characters of various ethnicities. He was particularly successful as a Chinese villain with poison fingernails in the 1914 Broadway production of *Mr. Wu*. Following that he played an Indian prince in *The Hindu* in 1922, the titular character in *The Arabian* in 1927, and a Japanese prince in *Sakura* in 1928. However, in 1932, his last Broadway appearance was in a contemporary comedy, *Three Men and a Woman*.

FIGURE 131. Walker Whiteside made the transition from a greatly admired interpreter of Shakespearean protagonists to becoming a popular film star appearing in contemporary dramas and comedies. (Photographer: White Studio, ca. 1900. Billy Rose Theatre Division, the New York Public Library Digital Collections.)

The End

"Always Leave Them Laughing When You Say Good-Bye"

Little Johnny Jones, lyrics and music by George M. Cohan, 1904

Acknowledgments

"Take a Bow"

Take a Bow, lyrics by Benny Davis, music by Ted Murry and Benny Davis, 1944

This is my standing ovation for all the people without whose support and assistance this project would never have taken flight. Please, take a bow!

At Michigan State University Press

- Gabriel Dotto, *Director*
- Kristine M. Blakeslee, *Managing Editor*
- Annette Tanner, *Digital Production Supervisor*
- Editorial and Marketing Staffs

In Coldwater

- Christine Delaney
- Bonnie Sherman
- Judy Groholske
- Matt Biolchini

In Calumet

- Laura Miller
- Jeremiah Mason
- Gloria Kivela
- Joanne Thomas
- Elaine Buchbinder
- Jackie Trancik
- Gerald Antcliff
- Art Limback

In Manistee

- Mark Fedder
- Xavier Verna
- Steve Harold
- Mark Niesen
- Beverly Wilkens
- JoAnn Muma

In General

- Katharine Strand-Evans
- Melanie Goulish
- Thomas Vranich
- Erik Nordberg
- Pam Westover
- Ruth and Frank Zinn

Thanks also to Stephanie Burdick, Carolyn L. Gillespie, Stephen Francis Kiersy, Mabel Winetta Oas, and Patricia Lin Ridge, whose research and scholarly works made an invaluable contribution to this tome.

FINAL CREDITS

Books and Sources

"A Trip to the Library"

She Loves Me, lyrics by Sheldon Harnick, music by Jerry Bock, 1964

Aiken, George. *Uncle Tom's Cabin*. London: Dodo Press, 2008.

Bald, F. Clever. *Michigan in Four Centuries*. New York: Harper & Row, 1954.

Barras, Charles M. *The Black Crook*. In *Nineteenth Century American Plays*, ed. Myron Matlaw. New York: Applause Theatre Books, 2001.

Baum, L. Frank. *The Wizard of Oz*. N.p.: Theatre Arts Press, 2013.

Birkin, Andrew. *J. M. Barrie and the Lost Boys: The Real Story Behind Peter Pan*. New Haven: Yale University Press, 2003.

Bordman, Gerald. *American Musical Theatre: A Chronicle*. 2nd ed. New York: Oxford University Press, 1992.

Bordman, Gerald, and Thomas S. Hischak, eds. *The Oxford Companion to the American Theatre*. 3rd ed. New York: Oxford University Press, 2004.

Boucicault, Dion. *The Streets of New York: A Drama in Five Acts*. London: Forgotten Books, 2012.

Chesley, Gene, comp. *National List of Historic Theatre Buildings*. Forest Hill, MD: League of Historic American Theatres, 1979.

Collins, David. "George M. Cohan in America's Theater." Davecol8.tripod.com.

Cooke, Washington. "A History of the Croswell Opera House." Unpublished manuscript, Croswell Opera House Archives, 1932.

Doty, Mrs. Duane. *The Town of Pullman*. Chicago: T. P. Struhsacker, 1893.

Dumont, Frank. "The Younger Generation in Minstrelsy and Reminiscences of the Past." *New York Clipper*, March 27, 1915.

Eckert, Kathryn Bishop. *The Sandstone Architecture of the Lake Superior Region*. Detroit: Wayne State University Press, 2000.

Fields, Armond. *Maude Adams: Idol of American Theater, 1872–1953*. Jefferson, NC: McFarland, 2004.

Francis, Mary C. "The Alimony Poor." In *The Scrap Book*, vol. 4, no. 3. New York: Frank A. Munsey, 1907.

Goethe, Johann Wolfgang von. *Faust, Parts I & II*. Translated by A. S. Kline. N.p.: Poetry in Translation, 2003.

Goldman, Emma. *The Social Significance of the Modern Drama*. Boston: Richard Badger, Gorham Press, 1914.

Harbach, Otto. *Madame Sherry*. San Bernardino: Theatre Arts Press, 2015.

Harrington, Kevin, comp. *Red Jacket Theater and Town Hall, Elm & Sixth Streets, Calumet, Houghton County, MI*. Historic American Buildings Survey. Washington, DC: U.S. Department of the Interior, 1975.

Hoyt, Charles H. *A Trip to Chinatown*. New York: Feedback Theatrebooks and Prospero Press, 1996.

Irving, Washington, Dion Boucicault, and Joseph Jefferson. *Rip Van Winkle, as Played by Joseph Jefferson*. Whitefish, MT: Kessinger Publishing, 2005.

Julius Cahn's Official Theatrical Guide. New York: Publication Office, Julius Cahn, 1896–1920.

Kerwin, James L. "A Cultural Landmark: Calumet's Goal—Coppertown USA." *Detroit News*, March 14, 1976.

League of Historic American Theatres. http://www.lhat.org.

MacKaye, Steele. *Hazel Kirke: A Domestic Comedy Drama in Four Acts*. Whitefish, MT: Kessinger Publishing, 2010.

Mates, Julian. *American Musical Stage: Two Hundred Years of Musical Theatre*. Westport, CT: Praeger, 1987.

Mayo, Margaret, and Salisbury Field. *Twin Beds*. New York: Samuel French, 1931.

Pistick, Kevin. *Michigan's Historic Theatres and Opera Houses*. 2017. http://michiganoperahouses.com.

Polk's Michigan State Gazetteer and Business Directory (1927–28). Detroit: R. L. Polk, 1927.

Pratt, William W. *Ten Nights in a Bar Room*. New York: Samuel French, n.d.

Seilhamer, George O. *History of the American Theatre during the Revolution and After*. Honolulu: University Press of the Pacific, 2005.

Smith, Cecil. *Musical Comedy in America*. New York: Theatre Arts Books, 1950.

Splake, T. Kilgore. "The Calumet Opera House and Theater." *Above the Bridge*, Winter 1996.

Storms, A. D. *The Players Blue Book*. Worcester, MA: Sutherland and Storms, 1901.

Tucker, Sophie. *Some of These Days*. New York: Garden City Publishing, 1945.

Water Winter Wonderland. http://waterwinterwonderland.com.

Wheeler, Mrs. Edward D. "History of Manistee." *Manistee Daily News*, May 1899.

Wood, Mrs. Henry. *East Lynne: A Drama in Five Acts*. Agawam, MA: Silver Street Media, 2011.

Listed below are those sources that provided the majority of research for this book and the years consulted.

- *Adrian Daily Telegram*, 1898–1921
- *Adrian Daily Times and Expositor*, 1873–1904
- *Calumet (Evening) News*, 1907–1928
- *Coldwater Daily Reporter*, 1898–1921
- *Coldwater Republican*, 1868–1897
- *Copper Country Evening News*, 1896–1907
- *Courier*, 1882–1897/1906–1912
- *Courier and Republican*, 1897–1906
- *Daily Mining Gazette*, 1899–1928
- *Manistee Daily Advocate*, 1903–1914
- *Manistee Daily News*, 1901–1914
- *Manistee News Advocate*, 1914–1921
- Red Jacket Common Council Minutes, 1896–1903

All quotations from newspaper articles and advertisements as well as from letters and journals were retrieved from the following archives and collections:

- Adrian District Library
- Calumet Theatre Archives
- Calumet Village Records
- Cheboygan Opera House Files
- Coldwater Branch District Library, Holbrook Heritage Room
- Croswell Opera House Archives
- Houghton County Historical Society Archives
- Keweenaw National Historical Park Archives
- Lenawee County Historical Museum Archives
- Manistee County Historical Museum Archives
- Manistee County Library
- Michigan Technological University Archives and Copper Country Historical Collections

Index

A Trip to Chinatown, 193–194; *A Trip to Coontown*, 179; *The Wizard of Oz*, 27, 111, 194–197
Adams, Maude, 87, 185, 211–214, 226
Adrian Union Hall, xiv, xxviii, 140, 215. *See also* Croswell Opera House
Agassiz, Alexander, 57, 77
American Company, xx–xxi, xxii
animal acts, 38–39, 132
architects: Beman, Solon Spencer, 99, 107–108, 109, 111; Charles K. Shand, 65, 67–68, 70, 71, 74; Mortimer L. Smith, 7–8; J. B. Sweatt, 64
athletic events, 39–41, 92, 131

Bara, Theda, 150, 159
Barrymore, Ethel, 33, 220–221
Barrymore, Georgiana "Georgie" Drew, 33
Bernhardt, Sarah, xxiv–xxv, 214–215
Birth of a Nation, The, 148–150

calcium lights, xxvii
Calumet and Hecla Mining Company, 57, 60–61, 63, 64, 73, 82
Calumet Theatre, xvii, 95; architectural style, 70, 99; construction/interior design, 69, 70–71, 72–75; financing, xiv, 68–69; lighting, 75; remodeling/renovation/restoration, 71, 77–78; scenery, 76, 77
Calumet, Michigan. *See* Red Jacket, Michigan
Campanari, Giuseppe, 43
casting, interracial, 179, 181–182
censorship, xviii–xxii, 17
Chanfrau, Francis "Frank," 30–31, 211–212
Cheboygan Opera House, xiv
circuits, xxiv–xxv, 87, 146–147. *See also* Klaw and Erlanger
Cohan, George M., 33, 89–90, 127–128, 172, 201–202
Coldwater Players, 22

Coldwater, Michigan, 3–5
Cole, Bob, 179–181
composers: Berlin, Irving, 202; Reginald De Koven, 44, 81–83, 201; Victor Herbert, 200, 201; J. Rosamond Johnson, 180–181; Jerome Kern, 202
concerts, lectures, and entertainment series, 27, 41–43, 45–47, 92–93, 132–133
copper miners' strike, 61–63
Copper Range Hotel, 76
Croswell Opera House, 213. *See also* Adrian Union Hall

Daniels, Frank, 200
Davis, Jesse Bartlett, 44–45
Dickinson, Anna, 45–46

Finnish entertainment, 93
fires: Iroquois Theatre, xxvii–xxviii, 15; Coldwater, 4; Calumet Theatre, 77–78; Manistee, 103; Scandinavian Opera House, 106
Fitzsimmons, Robert, 40

ghosts and paranormal activity, 86, 105–106
Gilbert and Sullivan, 27, 33, 91, 121, 221
Gray, Ada, 28, 159, 215–216

Hallam, Lewis, the Younger, xx–xxii
Harrigan and Hart, 172, 181–182
Hendricks, Ben, 174–175
Houghton, Douglass, 56

immigrant work force, 58–59, 101
Italian Hall tragedy, 62–63

Janauschek, Francesca "Fanny," 216–218
Jefferson, Joseph, 128–129, 159–161
Jefferson, Thomas, 129–130, 161

Keene, Laura, xxv
Keene, Thomas, 218–219
Kellerman, Annette, 149–150
Keweenaw Playhouse, 167, 188
Kilties, The, 92, 132
Klaw and Erlanger, 142, 147. *See also* circuits
Klock, George W., 13, 41
Knott, Roselle, 127, 219–221

lectures. *See* concerts, lectures, and entertainment series
Lewis, Henry Clay, 5

MacKaye, Steele, xxiii
Maffitt, James S./Lone Fisherman, The, 34–35
magicians, mystics, and hypnotists, 38, 92, 131–132
management: Calumet Theatre Company, 78–79; John D. Cuddihy, 71–72, 81, 84, 85; Charles Frohman, 212–213; Huldah Henning, 13–14, 20; Joseph Henning, 12–14, 20; John T. Jackson, 14–20, 31–32, 47, 48, 49, 51, 146, 198–199; Charles M. Southwell, 109, 116, 119; John Stronach Jr., 135, 136
Manistee Civic Players, 116, 136
Manistee, Michigan, 100–104
Mansfield, Richard, 219, 221
Mantell, Robert, 221–223
Marlowe, Julia, 219–220
meetings and community events, 47–49, 94, 133–134
minstrelsy, 48, 134, 139–145; Al G. Field Greater Minstrels, 141–142;

Bryant's Minstrels, 140; Christy's Minstrels, 139, 140; Duncan Clark's Lady Minstrels and New Arabian Nights, 144–145; Georgia Minstrels, 144; Haverly's United Mastodon Minstrels, 140; "Jim Crow," 129, 139; John W. Vogel's Big City Minstrels, 141, 143; Virginia Minstrels, 139, 140
Mitchell, Julian P., 195
Modjeska, Helena, 85–86, 223–224
Montgomery and Stone, 197, 200
Morrison, Lewis, 165
moving pictures, 50–51, 78, 94–95, 122, 135, 148–150; Edison Manufacturing Company, xxix, xxx, 162; Lyman H., Howe's Travel Festival, xxix–xxx, 135, 147–148; movie theatre chains, 20–22, 116; projectors and stereopticons, xxix–xxx, 94
Murray and Mack, 84–85, 172–173, 178–179
musicals, comic operas, operettas: *Black Crook, The*, 27, 189–193; *A Chinese Honeymoon*, 119–120, 121; *Evangeline, or The Belle of Acadia*, 32, 34–35; *Finnigan's Ball*, 84–85, 172–173; *The Highwayman*, 81–82, 83; *Hoity-Toity*, 123–124; *Humpty Dumpty*, 29–30, 128; *Irene*, 90; *Madame Sherry*, 18–19, 197–198; *The Maid of Arran*, 25, 26; *The Shoo-fly Regiment*, 180–181; *The Tattooed Man*, 200;

National Theater Owner's Association, xxv, 87
Niblo's Garden Theatre, 34, 35, 189, 216

O'Neill, James, 87–88, 219
Olcott, Chauncey, 170–172
Old American Company. *See* American Company
olios/specialties, xxi
opera houses: designation xxii; name derivation, xiii–xxii; number, xiv, xv
Orchard Beach Theatre, 136

Pickford, Mary, 50–51
plays and musicals by genre: cartoon musicals, 202–207; "girl" plays and musicals, 184–185; island musicals, 198–199; social issue dramas, 130, 185–187; Western sagas, 182–184
plays: *Abie's Irish Rose*, 188; *Captured by Wireless*, 35–36; *East Lynne*, 28, 158–159, 215–216; *Faust*, 28–29, 83, 85, 164–165; *Hazel Kirke*, xxiii; 161–162; *Kit, the Arkansas Traveler*, 30–31, 211–212; *The Melting Pot*, 228; *Monbars*, 222, 223; *Peck's Bad Boy*, 127–128; *Peg O' My Heart*, 173–174; *Peter Pan*, 211–213; *Quincy Adams Sawyer*, 122; *Rip Van Winkle*, 28, 128, 129, 130, 159–161; *Seven Keys to Baldpate*, 89–90; *The Span of Life*, 125, 177–178; *The Streets of New York*, 166–167; *Ten Nights in a Bar Room*, 162–164; *Twin Beds*, 187–188; *Uncle Tom's Cabin*, 28, 29, 87, 155–158, 227; *Up in Mabel's Room*, 90; *When Knighthood Was in Flower*, 127, 219–220; *Wildfire*, 88
playwrights, librettists, and lyricists: Barrie, James M., 211–213; L. Frank Baum, 26–27, 194–197; Dion Boucicault, 160, 166; Clyde Fitch, 184–185; Charles H. Hoyt, 124–125, 183–184, 193–194; James Weldon Johnson, 180; Glen McDonough, 195; Harry B. Smith, 44, 81, 83; Augustus Thomas, 182
political speeches and rallies, 46, 94
prohibition. *See* temperance and prohibition

race: *See* casting, interracial
Ramsdell Assembly Hall/Rotary Hall, 106–107, 109, 114–116, 121
Ramsdell Theatre, xvii–xviii, 116–117, 134; architectural style, 99, 108; construction/interior design, 108–113; financing, xv, 107; lighting, 113–114; remodeling/renovation/restoration, 77, 113; scenery, 110–111, 121

Ramsdell, Frederic, 110
Ramsdell, Thomas Jefferson "T. J.," 99, 104–109, 116, 120–121, 132
Red Jacket Common Council, xvii, xix, 64–65, 66–69, 71, 72, 75, 76, 77, 94
Red Jacket Fire Engine House, 65, 67, 78, 81
Red Jacket Opera House, xxvii, 64–67, 77
Red Jacket Town Hall, 63–67
Red Jacket, Michigan, 55–60
Remenyi, Eduard, 43–44
Rhea, Hortense, 224–225
Russell, Lillian, 88–89

Scandinavian Opera House, 106, 128
Scanlan, William J., 169–170
scene technology and transformation scenes, xxv–xxvii, 156–157,166–167, 192, 195
scenic artists and set designers: Burridge, Walter Wilcox, 111, 121, 182, 197; L. B. Chevalier, 9–10; Howard Tuttle, 76. *See also* Ramsdell, Frederic
seating capacity and stage dimensions: Calumet Theatre, 75; Ramsdell Theatre, 113; Tibbits Opera House, 8
Shakespeare productions, 31–32, 84, 85–86, 125–126, 216–217, 218–219, 225, 226, 228
Shute's Saloon, 76
Skinner, Otis, 226–227
songs: "After the Ball," 194–195; "Come Home, Father," 163; "Every Little Movement (Has a Meaning All Its Own)," 197–198; "I Don't Care," 227; "In Michigan," 196; "Oh, Promise Me," 44; "Under the Bamboo Tree," 180; "You Naughty, Naughty Men," 192
Sousa, John Philip, 41–42, 92, 201
Southwark Theatre/Opera House in Southwark, xx–xxi
stock companies, xxiii–xxiv, 27, 36–38, 91, 131
Sullivan, John L., 39–40

Tanguay, Eva, 127, 227–228
Taylor, Laurette, 174
temperance and prohibition, 46–47, 103–104
Templeton, Fay, 32–33, 34
Tibbits Opera House, 20–23; architectural style, 7–8; construction/interior design, 8, 9, 10–12; financing, xiv–xv, 5–6, 13–14; lighting, 9, 11; remodeling/renovation/restoration, xxx–xxxi, 10, 12–13, 15, 20–23; scenery, 9–10
Tibbits, Barton, 3, 5, 6–9, 11–12, 20, 25, 26, 27, 41
touring productions, xxii–xxvi, 177, 188

Van Courtland, Ida, 36
Vanes, Dennis, 20, 147
vaudeville, xxi, 38, 50, 91, 94, 95, 131, 135, 145–147

Weber and Fields, 32, 123–124
White, Porter J., 29, 125, 165
Whiteside, Walker, 83–84, 228–229
Wilson, Al H. "Metz," 175–176